ART *and* SUBURBIA

ART

and

SUBURBIA

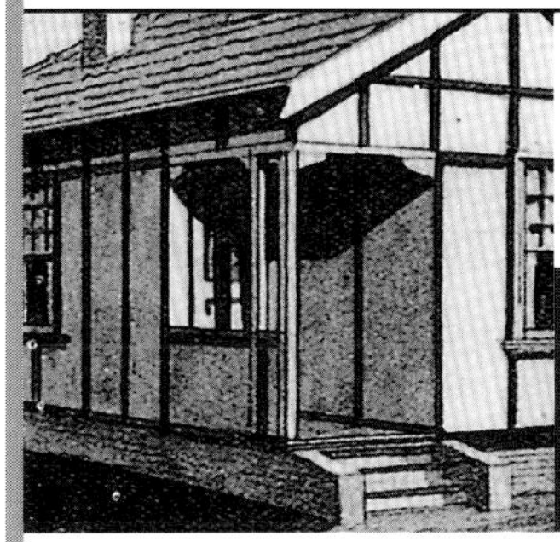

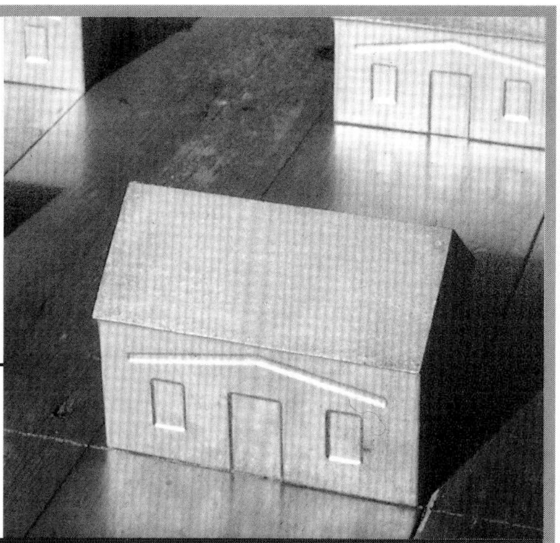

A World Art book by Chris McAuliffe

CRAFTSMAN
HOUSE

Distributed in Australia by Craftsman House,
20 Barcoo Street, Roseville East, NSW 2069,
in association with G+B Arts International: Australia,
Canada, China, France, Germany, Hong Kong, India,
Japan, Luxembourg, Malaysia, Russia, Singapore,
Switzerland, The Netherlands, United Kingdom,
United States of America.

ISBN 976 6410 29 1

Design: Terminal Design
Printer: Toppan, Singapore

Contents

7 ACKNOWLEDGEMENTS

8 LIST OF ILLUSTRATIONS

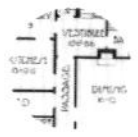
10 INTRODUCTION: suburbs, suburban, suburbia

17 COLOUR PLATES

CHAPTER 1 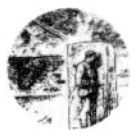 42 THE NINETEENTH CENTURY: rural myths and urban dreams

CHAPTER 2 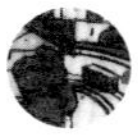 50 FROM THE 1920s TO THE 1940s: suburb to suburbia

CHAPTER 3 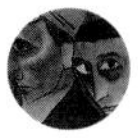 64 THE 1950s: the siren song of suburbia

CHAPTER 4 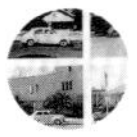 76 THE 1960s: truce & tolerance

CHAPTER 5 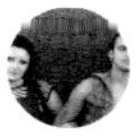 88 THE 1970s: local colour

CHAPTER 6 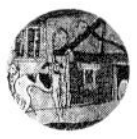 102 THE 1980s AND BEYOND: the postmodern suburb

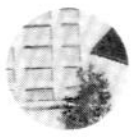
122 CONCLUSION

129 FURTHER READING

133 INDEX

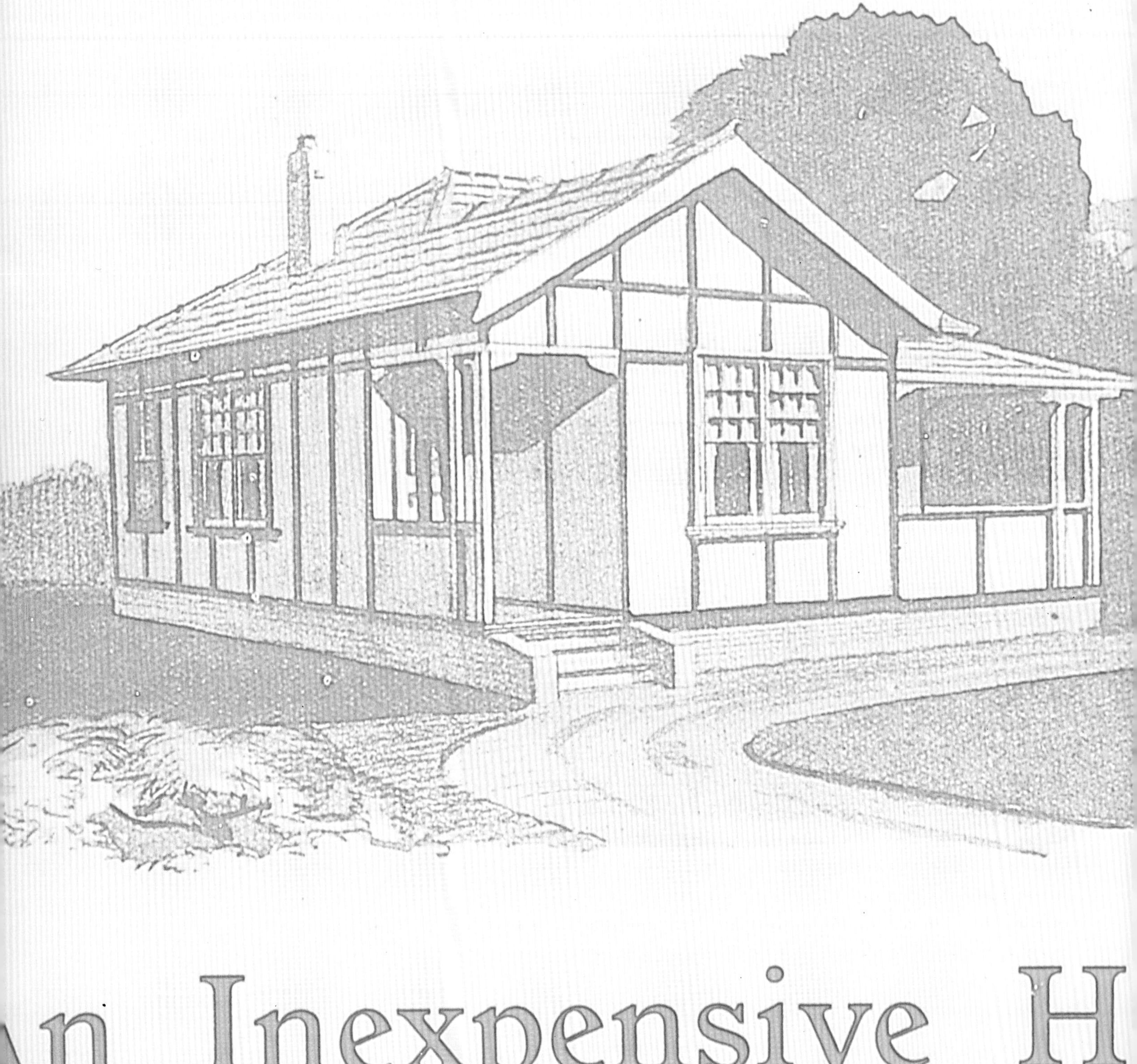

An Inexpensive H

with DURABESTOS, the tough, rigid, build

ACKNOWLEDGEMENTS

The origins of this book lie in an attitude rather than a specific moment. Much as I dislike generational labels, I am of that post-Pop generation that abandoned strict measures of cultural value, or even reversed them. I began my involvement with contemporary art in the 1980s, a time when a trip to the suburbs meant not boredom but flashes of intensity (The Cure at the Prospect Hill Hotel, Kew), and a new Birthday Party album was more important than any art exhibition. This attitude gelled into a more specific project as I began to meld art historical method with Cultural Studies, and bore its first fruit when, with Chris Healy and Sarah Ferber, I edited *The Beasts of Suburbia*, a collection of essays on the Australian suburbs. It was Sarah and Chris who first encouraged me to put my thoughts about art and suburbia on paper, and I thank them for their prompting. The third chapter of this book is a variant of that project, while the book as a whole builds on our many discussions of suburban themes. More broadly, I received support and encouragement from all those people who were prepared to take my gradually focusing thoughts seriously: colleagues in the department of fine arts at the University of Melbourne, and in the Faculty of Arts in general; editors at journals such as *Polis, Art + Text* and *Art and Australia*; convenors and audiences at forums at the National Gallery of Victoria, the Adelaide Festival and the Museum of Modern Art at Heide; and, finally, the many students whose enthusiasm for the subject convinced me of both its appeal and merit.

It is one thing to convince oneself that a book ought to be written: it is something else entirely to produce it. This book is the product of many people's labour. The team at *World Art* — Ashley Crawford, Ray Edgar, Terence Hogan, Stephanie Holt and Christopher Waller — gave me advice and support, both practical and moral, throughout the project. This book is a measure of their skill, professionalism and commitment to contemporary art publishing. I also thank Max Marks of Terminal Design for design of the book, John Simkins for indexing and Lyndell Brown for proofreading. Research assistance was provided by Tim Sowden and Melinda Martin, who conquered my misgivings regarding delegation by persistently demonstrating a genuine understanding of, and sympathy for, the project. Discussions with Tim while supervising his MA on '50s art and suburbia brought many ideas into focus. Melinda consistently second-guessed me, transforming vague fishing expeditions into bumper catches. Finally, Stephanie Holt coordinated the project and edited the text, while converting me to the still somewhat questionable pleasures of the breakfast meeting.

I am grateful to all those artists, dealers, museums and libraries who provided me with reproductions. In particular, the staff of the libraries of the department of architecture at the University of Melbourne and the Department of Planning, Victoria assisted with documentary images. Dr Phillip Goad of the department of architecture at the University of Melbourne generously assisted me in sifting through documentary photographs. Wherever possible, photographers and lenders have been credited. I apologise for any omissions in both respects.

LIST OF ILLUSTRATIONS

INTRODUCTION

PLATES

Plate 1: Anonymous, *The Land of Promise*, undated (1880s), coloured lithograph. Collection: Vale Collection, La Trobe Collection, State Library of Victoria, Melbourne.

Plate 2: Frederick McCubbin, *Winter Evening, Hawthorn*, 1886, oil on canvas, 51 x 76 cm. Collection: Castlemaine Art Gallery and Historical Museum, gift of J. T. Tweddle, 1926.

Plate 3: John D. Moore, *Chaos*, 1923, oil on canvas, 61 x 76 cm. On loan to the Art Gallery of New South Wales from Robin Moore. Photograph courtesy of the Art Gallery of New South Wales.

Plate 4: Danila Vassilieff, *Children Playing, Fitzroy*, c.1937, oil and pencil on canvas, 49.1 x 60.9 cm. Collection of Geelong Art Gallery, purchased with the assistance of the Caltex-Victoria Government Art Fund, 1979.

Plate 5: Clarice Beckett, *Bay Road, Foggy Morning*, c.1926, oil on hardboard, 29 x 37 cm. Courtesy of Rosalind Hollinrake.

Plate 6: Harald Vike, *Untitled (The Saint)*, 1947, oil on canvas.

Plate 7: John Brack, *The New House*, 1953, oil on canvas on board, 127 x 55.8 cm. Collection: Private collection. Photograph courtesy Deutscher Fine Art, Malvern.

Plate 8: Dale Hickey, *Untitled 67–68*, 1967–68, oil on canvas, 173 x 173 cm. Collection: National Gallery of Victoria, Felton Bequest 1968.

Plate 9: Robert Rooney, *Cereal Bird Beaks II*, 1969, synthetic polymer paint on canvas, 250 x 132 cm. Courtesy Monash University Gallery.

Plate 10: Peter Kennedy, *Introductions*, 1974–76, watercolour, 43.7 x 45 cm. Collection: Darnell Collection, University of Queensland. Photograph courtesy of the artist.

Plate 11: Jenny Watson, *House Painting: Kallista* (Large and Small Versions), 1976, oil on canvas, 178 x 214 cm and 91.5 x 106.7cm. Courtesy National Gallery of Victoria.

Plate 12: Mandy Martin, *Picket Fences*, 1980, photo-silkscreen on paper, 45 x 65 cm. Courtesy the artist and Christine Abrahams Gallery.

Plate 13: Howard Arkley, *Nubrick*, 1986, acrylic on canvas, 160 x 120 cm. Courtesy of the artist and Tolarno Galleries.

Plate 14: Howard Arkley, *Ultra Kleen*, 1992, acrylic on canvas, 135 x 173 cm. Courtesy of the artist and Tolarno Galleries.

Plate 15: Ken Searle, *West #6*, 1990, oil on canvas, 122 x 259 cm. Courtesy the artist and Watters Gallery.

Plate 16: Constanze Zikos, *Death Double*, 1992, enamel on laminex, 150 x 106 cm. Courtesy the artist and Irene Sutton Gallery.

Plate 17: Lin Onus, *Fruit Bats*, 1990, self-skinning foam, fibreglass matt, resin, acrylic, enamel paint and Hill's hoist, 250 x 250 x 250 cm. Courtesy the artist ad Gallery Gabrielle Pizzi.

Plate 18: Jon Campbell, *31 Myrtle Street*, 1987, acrylic enamel on cotton duck, 150 x 115 cm. Collection: Private collection, Melbourne.

Plate 19: Nicholas Mau (RedPlanet Graphics), *Death of the Suburban Dream*, 1993, screenprint, 51 x 64 cm.Courtesy RedPlanet Graphics.

Plate 20: Jon Cattapan, *Woden Valley Insect No. 3*, 1994, gouache, ink on paper, 35.5 x 26cm. Private collection. Courtesy the artist and Irene Sutton Gallery, Fitzroy. Photographer: Kenneth Pleban.

Plate 21: Sarah Curtis, *Neighbours Arcadia* (detail), 1994, oil on canvas and acrylic on wall, 439 x 772 cm. Courtesy the artist.

Plate 22: Tracey Moffatt, from "Scarred for Life" series, 1994, offset print, 80 x 60 cm. Courtesy the artist and Karyn Lovegrove Gallery.

Plate 23: Reg Mombassa, *Insectile Space-monsters Approach Sleeping Family*, 1995, house enamel and oil paint on paper, 33 x 24 cm. Courtesy the artist and Watters Gallery.

Plate 24: Bill Henson, *Untitled 1985–86*, 1985–86, Type C colour photograph, 106.5 x 60.5 cm. Photograph courtesy Roslyn Oxley 9 Gallery.

CHAPTER 1

p. 45: William Tibbits, *Why Pay High Rents? Inspect the pretty villas and family mansions of Moreland Park*, c.1886, coloured lithograph, 63.2 x 99.8 cm. Collection: Haughton Collection, La Trobe Collection, State Library of Victoria.

p. 46: Robert J. Haddon, "Small Suburban Villa", c. 1908, from his *Australian Architecture*, George Robertson & Co., Melbourne, c.1908.

p. 47: Arthur Streeton, *Near Heidelberg*, 1890, oil on canvas, 53.5 x 43 cm. Collection: National Gallery of Victoria, Felton Bequest 1943.

p. 48: "A Walk from Kew to Heidelberg", *The Illustrated Australian News*, Feburary 1st, 1890. Courtesy State Library of Victoria.

p. 49: "A Picturesque Suburb" (Heidelberg), *The Australasian*, February 6th, 1987. Courtesy State Library of Victoria.

CHAPTER 2

p. 52: Concrete home, from *Everyman's Home*, A. McCubbin, Melbourne, 1922.

p. 53: "An Inexpensive Home", advertisement for Wunderlich Limited, from *Book of Australian Bungalows: Homes designed along distinct lines to suit Australian conditions*, Bookstall Co., Sydney, c.1925.

p. 54: Percy Leason, *Getting On*, 1927, cartoon from *Table Talk*, April 25th, 1927. Courtesy State Library of Victoria.

p. 55: Noel Counihan, *At the Corner of Nightingale Street*, 1944, oil on canvas, 58.5 x 50.5 cm. Collection: Bank of Melbourne. Courtesy Mrs Pat Counihan.

p. 56: David Moore, *Surry Hills Street*, 1948, gelatin silver print.

p. 57: Sali Herman, *Suburbia*, 1947, oil on canvas, 55 x 75 cm. Collection: Private collection. Courtesy Holdsworth Gallery.

p. 58: Clarice Beckett, *Wet Day, Brighton*, 1921, oil on board, 17 x 22 cm. Courtesy Rosalind Hollinrake.

p. 59: Eveline Syme, *Sydney Tram Line*, 1936, colour linocut on buff oriental tissue, 24.4 x 17.9 cm. Collection: Ballarat Fine Art Gallery.

p. 61: Margaret Preston, *Implement Blue*, 1927, oil on canvas on paperboard, 42.5 x 43 cm. Collection: Art Gallery of New South Wales, gift of the artist, 1960.

p. 63: David Strachan, *The Gossips*, c.1937, black conte on paper, 23.7 x 29.9 cm. Collection: Newcastle Region Art Gallery.

CHAPTER 3

p. 66: "The Old, The New", Housing Commission of Victoria Annual Report 1957–58. Courtesy Department of Planning, Victoria.

p. 67: South Australian Housing Trust villas. Courtesy Department of Planning, Victoria.

p. 67: Adelaide Flats, South Terrace. Courtesy Department of Architecture, University of Melbourne.

p. 68: Plan of "Stow Court" development, South Australian Housing Trust, 1957. Courtesy Department of Architecture, University of Melbourne.

p. 69: John Brack, *The Unmade Road*, 1954, oil on canvas, 73.5 x 50.5 cm. Photograph courtesy of Sotheby's Australia.

p. 70: John Brack, *New Houses*, 1954, pencil on paper, 39.2 x 50.2 cm. Collection: National Gallery of Australia.

p. 70: "Four Decorative Pieces" from *The Australian Womens Weekly*, July 22nd, 1953. Courtesy State Library of Victoria.

p. 71: Record covers, "Wildlife in suburbia" by Barry Humphries, 1958-59. Courtesy of Barry Humphries and Currency Press.

p.72: Robert Dickerson, *Wynyard Station*, 1959, oil on hardboard, 122.5 x 184 cm. Collection: Ballarat Fine Art Gallery. Courtesy of Jennifer Dickerson.

p. 73: Mark Strizic, *Riversdale Road, Camberwell* c.1960. Courtesy the artist and Christine Abrahams Gallery.

p. 74: Charles Blackman, *The Shadow*, 1953, tempera on cardboard, 59.2 x 75.4 cm. Collection: Museum of Modern Art at Heide. Photographer: John Brash.

CHAPTER 4

p. 78: Chadstone Shopping Centre, Melbourne and Chadstone Shopping Centre carpark. Both courtesy Department of Architecture, University of Melbourne.

p. 79: Mark Strizic, "The City from Prospect Hill Road, Canterbury, 1967". Courtesy the artist and Christine Abrahams Gallery.

p. 80: Dale Hickey, *Untitled*, c.1968, synthetic polymer on canvas, 194.5 x 334 cm, diptych. Collection: Art Gallery of Western Australia. Photograph courtesy of Robert Lindsay Gallery, Melbourne.

p. 81: "Dale Hickey watches Jim Emmins construct a fence inside the Pinacotheca gallery, St Kilda", October 1969. Photograph courtesy of *The Age*.

p. 82: Paddington Street, 1960s. Courtesy Department of Architecture, University of Melbourne.

p. 83: Robert Rooney, *Holden Park 1 & 2, May 1970*, 1970, sixteen colour photographs each 8.9 x 8.9 cm, sheet 76 x 102 cm. Collection: Monash University Art Collection. Photographer: Richard Crompton.

p. 84: "Edna in Humoresque Street, Moonee Ponds". Courtesy of Barry Humphries and Currency Press.

p. 84: Victor Majzner, *Green Vent*, 1970, oil on canvas, 122 x 244 cm. Courtesy of the artist.

p. 86: Ian Burn, *Systematically Altered Photograph: The Suburbs*, 1968, black & white photograph and photocopy on paper, 150 x 120 cm. Collection: National Gallery of Australia. Photograph courtesy of the estate of the artist.

p. 87: Suburban subdivision, Broadbeach, Gold Coast. Courtesy Department of Architecture, University of Melbourne.

CHAPTER 5

p. 90: Prototype Radburn housing, Fisher, Canberra, 1971. Courtesy Department of Planning, Victoria.

p. 91: Radburn housing estate, Curtin, Canberra, 1971. Courtesy Department of Planning, Victoria.

p. 91: "Proposed re-development project illustrating integration of new with old," from *Housing is People*, Housing Commission Victoria, Melbourne, 1972.

p. 92: Geoffrey Hogg with Turana residents painting mural, Turana Youth Training Centre, Brunswick, 1980. Photograph courtesy of Geoffrey Hogg.

p. 93: Geoffrey Hogg, assisted by Jan Duncan, Gwenda Wiseman and Mark Wotherspoon, Turana Youth Training Centre – First Mural, 1980. Photograph courtesy of the artist.

p. 94: Peter Kennedy, *Introductions* (installation view, National Gallery of Victoria, October 1976), video cassette and monitor, 11 watercolour paintings, documentation.

p. 95: Carol Jerrems, *Sharpies*, 1976, gelatin silver photograph, 17.8 x 25.2 cm. Collection: National Gallery of Victoria. Gift of Christine Godden, 1991.

p. 96: Michael Shannon, *Suburban Landscape, Melbourne*, 1978, oil on linen 121.5 x 197.5 cm. Collection: Mallesons Stephen Jaques, Melbourne. Courtesy estate of the artist and Charles Nodrum Gallery.

p. 97: Merchant Builders, Conservation cluster housing, Doncaster, Melbourne, 1972.

p. 98: Micky Allan, "Live In Show" (installation views), 1978, photography, drawings, household items and performance, George Paton Gallery, University of Melbourne.

p.99: Kerrie Lester, *Red Brick House*, 1981, synthetic polymer paint stencilled onto stitched and padded canvas, 104.2 x 167.6 cm. Collection: Newcastle Region Art Gallery.

p. 100: Ronald Hawke, *Hill's Hoist*, 1973, acrylic on canvas, 106 x 122 cm. Collection: Newcastle Region Art Gallery.

CHAPTER 6

p. 104: Tim Hurburgh, "Ellesmere Court, Princess St, Kew, Melbourne". Courtesy Department of Architecture, University of Melbourne.

p. 105: Howard Arkley, *Secession* (detail), acrylic on canvas, 1979. Courtesy of the artist and Tolarno Galleries.

pp. 106 & 107: Aleks Danko, *Day In, Day Out (Second Version)*, 1991. Collection: Queensland Art Gallery, Brisbane. Photographer: Warwick Page.

p. 109: Victor Mazjner, *Creature Comforts*, 1989, oil on canvas, 106.5 x 122 cm. Collection: Artist's Collection. Photograph courtesy of the artist.

p. 110: Nicholas Nedelkopoulos, *The Great Australian Dream*, 1987, etching, aquatint with plate tone on woven paper. 10 x 50.3 cm. From the series "For Every Thinking Person". Collection of Christos and Donna Nedelkopoulos. Photo courtesy of the artist. Photographer: Paul Mathews.

p. 113: Ron McBurnie, *Dogs Bottles*, etching and aquatint, 20 x 31 cm, 1988.

p. 115: Andrew Sibley, *The Madonna of the Rotary Clothes Hoist*, 1994, lithograph, image size 70 x 49 cm, paper size 76.5 x 56.5 cm. Edition of 25. Courtesy the artist and Lyall Burton Gallery, Melbourne.

p. 117: Gordon Bennett, *Murder/Suicide* from the series "Home Sweet Home", 1993, watercolour and pencil on paper, two sheets, each sheet 27.5 x 19 cm. Collection: Michael Aleksander, Surfers Paradise, Queensland. Courtesy Irene Sutton Gallery.

p. 118: Sarah Curtis, *Neighbours Arcadia* (installation view, Temple Gallery, Melbourne), 1994.

p. 119: Glen D. Clarke, *Reductio ad Absurdum* (details) installation at Plimsoll Gallery, Hobart, 1994.

p. 121: Mikala Dwyer, *Star* (details), installation at Plimsoll Gallery, Hobart, 1994.

CONCLUSION

p. 125: Bill Lane, *Shades Type 8A*, *Shades Type 8B* and *Shades Type 8C*. All 1994–95, black & white photographs. Also computer-generated pie chart. All courtesy of the artist.

p. 126: Kate Daw, *Voice, Homes & Gardens, 1959*, 1995, ink on linen, 22 x 30.5 cm. and *House, 1959*, 1995, oil on linen, 51 x 66 cm. Both courtesy of the artist and William Mora Gallery.

p. 126: Darren Wardle, *Dust Control (Yallambie)*, 1995, oil on canvas, 134 x 110 cm. Courtesy of the artist.

suburbs

suburban

suburbia

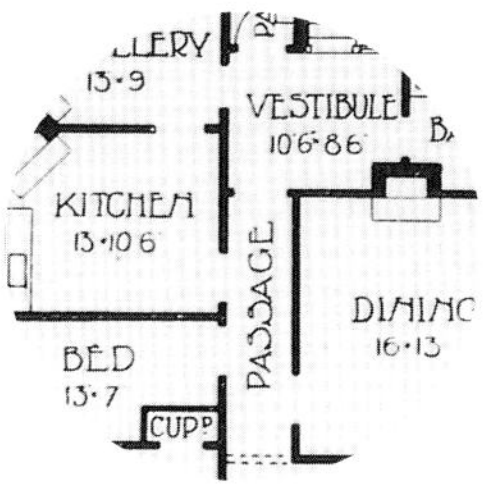

Writing on nineteenth century morality in his *History of Sexuality,* Michel Foucault noted a significant paradox: for all their supposed prudishness, the Victorians spoke constantly about sex. Far from keeping sex hidden, the processes of repression made it all the more prominent. For sex to be forcefully banished to the shadows, it first had to be continually brought to light.

The same paradox can be found in the relationship of Australian artists to the suburbs. For more than a century Australian artists, writers, musicians and film-makers have grappled with suburban geography, architecture, lifestyles and values. They have addressed the physical nature of the suburbs (particularly their landscape and architecture), and the behaviour, values and ideologies associated with them (which I will term 'suburbia'). Suburbs and suburbia have often been condemned by artists, who have found them confusing and threatening. Yet as a result, the suburbs have become a leitmotif of Australian art and writing, one whose meaning is assumed to be self-evident but is, paradoxically, always up for grabs.

Such is the puzzling status of the suburbs: they are continually displayed, only to be declared a subject beneath the dignity of art; they are a subject of endless fascination, yet are repeatedly characterised as banal; they are condemned as uniform and monotonous, yet seem to provide an endless variety of imagery. Only in recent years have artists found ways to move beyond this pattern of attraction and repulsion, pointing the way towards a new appreciation of the suburbs and their acceptance as a legitimate subject for the arts.

The assumption that Australian artists don't picture the suburbs — or at least haven't until recent decades — has been almost a cliché of Australian art history. In fact there is an intriguing and diverse history of suburban images from the nineteenth century and throughout the first half of the twentieth, although often in media (such as print or watercolor), style (including decorative modernisms), or genre (such as architectural studies, still lifes or streetscapes) that traditionally held little prestige. Images of the suburbs were central to the vision of some of the most significant artists to come to prominence in the 1950s and 1960s. During the 1970s the diversity of understandings of, and approaches to, the suburbs multiplied. It is now the norm, rather than the exception, for artists to address the suburbs in the course of their work. Art history is also, now, more inclined to consider the suburbs and a history of suburban imagery. This stems from a realisation that the task of analysis goes beyond establishing the meaning of a motif within art, and must encompass its meaning within society as a whole. The final chapters of this book, therefore, will provide a more detailed examination, and greater number of examples, from the art of the most recent decades.

This book, therefore, traces the suburbs and suburbia in the visual arts, commencing with the origins of the suburbs in the mid-nineteenth century and working towards the predominantly suburban culture that is the distinguishing feature of contemporary Australia. Each chapter offers an overview of the historical conditions of the suburb, outlines the dominant cultural attitudes to the suburbs of that period, and considers the ways in which artists sustained or challenged such attitudes. It will be useful, first, to define some key terms and indicate the conceptual foundations used throughout the book.

DEFINING THE SUBURB

There are no straightforward definitions of the suburb, even within the vocabularies of geography, urban planning or public administration. Various measures have been put forward — size of population, density of settlement, physical relationship to the city centre, legal or administrative status — but the suburb remains an elusive entity. This uncertainty about how to define the suburb threads through discussions of it, and ultimately leads to the complexity of the suburb's cultural meanings.

Frequently the suburb is spoken of as something marginal ('out there' on the fringes of the metropolis) or as something in between known sites (neither rural nor urban but somewhere 'inbetween'). This tendency to define the suburb by a process of differentiation — by saying what it *is not* (not city, not country, not centre) rather than what it *is* — has given the term its flexibility, allowing us to speak of the suburbs in metaphorical, as well as material, terms.

We can understand and define the suburb by its *location* (separate, but not necessarily distant from, the city centre); by its *history* (related to the housing demands of the growing cities produced by industrialisation); by its *function* (providing residential housing and related services); by its specific forms of *organisation* (local government, zoning regulations, service infrastructure, transport systems); and by its *population* (originally, conventional 'nuclear' or extended families; now, more diverse types of household). Although these may seem straightforward ways of defining or describing the suburbs, such attempts at objective description are almost immediately coloured by value judgements. One generation or social group, for example, might value proximity to the central city: another might value distance from it. Terms such as 'inner', 'outer' and 'middle' make implicit value judgements, which may define the suburb as either positive or negative, dependent on the social and ideological position of the person who uses them. Such designations, of course, also change over time, as a metropolis grows and suburban development extends into new areas.

It is very difficult to define the suburbs without addressing the way of life they produce. As discussion turns to lifestyle and attitudes, the noun 'suburb' quickly becomes an adjective: 'suburban'. What concerns most commentators is not the physical nature of the suburbs, but what the suburbs stand for. Through commentary on the suburban way of life, the suburb becomes a site at which a whole range of ideologies can be articulated.

The suburb and the suburban way of life are caught up in debates on issues such as the relative merits of city and country living, the positive and negative effects of industrialisation, the status of the individual within society, the nature of the family, the idea of community, and the values of consumer society. Such issues can all be invoked by the word 'suburbia'. Used to refer to the way of life, values and ideologies of suburban culture, 'suburbia' is a term whose meaning constantly shifts. What lies at the heart of these shifting definitions of the suburb and suburbia is the issue of representation. Definitions of the suburb have, in effect, evolved into reflections on suburbia, which in turn have amounted to efforts to make suburbia stand for something else, such as national character or the 'Australian way of life'. It is no wonder that the motif has attracted artists.

THE DEVELOPMENT OF THE SUBURB

Several key periods in the development of the Australian suburb can be identified, each of them relating to economic and ideological factors. In the nineteenth century the aspirations of colonists to a new and better life, the prosperity of the 1880s, and technological innovations such as the railway generated a boom in suburban growth. This consolidated a peculiarly Australian faith in home ownership as the key to the good life. With the suburb established as the dominant model for urban growth in Australia, the early decades of the twentieth century saw efforts to control it (through the new field of 'town planning'), to perfect it (through the 'garden city' movement), and to exploit it (through the emergence of consumer society).

Economic and social reconstruction after World War 2, particularly through planned housing estates, coupled with Australia's embrace of the automobile, sent the suburbs sprawling and accelerated the separation of suburb from city centre. Initially, in the 1950s, this produced so-called 'dormitory suburbs', from which workers — predominantly men and unmarried women — commuted to work, often into the city centre or 'CBD' (Central Business District). This separation of work and home life maintained a connection between the new outer suburbs and the older industrial and commercial areas of the centre. Suburb-dwellers, then, oscillated back and forth: between suburb and centre; between leisure and labour.

In the 1960s and 1970s, as employment was decentralised — with industry moving to the outer suburbs or new industrial estates on the suburban fringe, and service industries moving into the suburbs — this distinction broke down. Suburbs became more self-contained and the centre less important. If commuting was necessary at all, it often took place between different suburbs rather than from suburb to centre.

Since the 1970s, suburban change has involved both the continuing expansion of the suburbs — with new estates encroaching into surrounding areas, often absorbing what were formerly country towns — and the remaking of inner and middle suburbs. Inner suburbs, which may have formerly housed predominantly working-class or itinerent populations, are being redeveloped: nineteenth century mansions, since subdivided into flats or boarding houses, are being restored to spacious family homes; blocks of flats are being redesigned as fashionable 'inner city apartments'; disused warehouses are turned into 'lofts'; old workers cottages are renovated by 'first-home buyers'. Such changes have raised concerns about the nature of these suburbs, prompting calls for conservation of existing buildings, and efforts, often through innovative public housing projects, to house long-term residents in danger of being squeezed out in the course of gentrification.

THE MEANING OF SUBURBIA

The meanings attached to suburban life are generated at a number of different levels. Locally these meanings might be produced through participation in the daily life of a community, such as shopping, gardening or commuting. Residents may also self-consciously engage in activities that generate such meanings. Community groups and activities — sporting clubs, conservation groups, schools, churches, even Neighbourhood Watch — send very clear messages about residents' ambitions for their suburbs.

On a broader scale, such meanings might be generated in the mass media, in soap operas, dramas or sitcoms set in suburban neighbourhoods, or in lifestyle and 'infotainment' programmes. These different levels are drawn together when people living in the suburbs watch and reflect on such programmes, or when public debates focus on whether programmes such as *Neighbours*, *Home and Away* and *Burke's Backyard* provide accurate or appropriate images of Australian identity. The meanings of the suburbs, then, are produced in the interplay of lived experience (what people do) and symbolic exchange (what people are seen to be doing, and how they want to appear).

While suburb-dwellers make meaning as they live their lives, the benchmarks against which they measure their experiences, their hopes and disappointments, are often established elsewhere. It is too crude to suggest that more-dominant sources of meaning, such as the media, advertising, popular culture, or more-respectable ones, such as art, impose meanings on the suburbs. However, when the authority of the media or art is accepted, they provide the values and framework within which people understand their experience.

This hegemony (the process whereby ideologies are accepted and emulated rather than imposed) can help to explain why people might accept an image of the suburbs in the media or art as real, even if it does not tally with their own experience. It can also help explain why art images — which are often exaggerated or inaccurate — are accepted as revealing the 'truth' about the suburbs.

ARTISTS AND SUBURBIA

Like Foucault's Victorians, Australian artists reveal a good deal about themselves and their culture in their simultaneous embrace and rejection of the suburbs. Their works have more than just descriptive or documentary interest — although these records of the physical appearance of the suburbs and the behaviour of suburb-dwellers, past and present, *are* a useful part of the general cross-referencing of historical research. Their artworks also reveal complex struggles for meaning within Australian culture as a whole. The attitudes to the suburbs and suburbia that are embedded in, or triggered by, artworks are far more important than their 'documentary' function, for suburban images are filtered through aesthetic and social ideologies that shape the meanings and status attributed to their subject.

Artists' approaches to the suburbs raise larger issues. What kinds of culture does Australia possess or desire? What kinds of identity are available to people in Australia? How are these cultures and identities enacted and displayed? How are they ranked, relative to each other? What ideologies underlie the surfaces and behaviours of everyday life? Images of the suburbs might be interpreted as symptoms of broader cultural attitudes to Australian identity and the role of urban living within it.

These sorts of questions are particularly important, because art has a privileged status in the production of symbols of national identity. It is not just that art has produced powerful icons of certain versions of Australianness — Sidney Nolan's Ned Kelly, Russell Drysdale's outback cricketers, Brett Whiteley's Sydney sunbathers. Art routinely circulates through institutions, such as museums and public architecture, that are devoted to enshrining nationhood, and it routinely provides the mass media — TV, newspapers, films, advertising — with a symbolic vocabulary of landscape and national character.

Images of the suburbs do not simply *reflect* social opinion: these artworks also *shape* opinion, reinforcing or subtly modifying existing ideas. Images of the suburbs and suburbia, therefore, can never have a single, unchanging meaning. Born out of existing visions of Australian life and identity, they always fuel further debate on the nature of this identity, and contribute to the development of new images and understandings.

What is at issue when an artist makes an image of the suburbs or suburbia is the significance she or he attributes to them, and the broader cultural significance that is then attributed to the artwork. This is the problem that threads through this book. Do artists simply reflect suburban life, or do they participate in the construction of the meaning of the suburbs by offering society images that reduce the complexities of suburbia to familiar symbols? When suburb-dwellers see and understand the realities of their lives through symbols that artists have created in order to reflect on (and judge) those lives, we have arrived at a point where reality and ideology are increasingly difficult to separate.

In addressing this question we might have to reassess the truth of artists' images of the suburbs. It may be that their truth is not literal but ideological; that is, these images are true to the extent that they reflect dominant attitudes to the suburbs at a given time, not because they accurately depict the suburbs or suburban life. At the same time, artists have frequently challenged received wisdoms and questioned conventional symbols. It may be that artists have used images of the suburbs and suburbia to argue against prevailing opinion and to reappraise the nature and value of suburban life. Put very simply, the aim of this book is to explore the ways in which artists have accepted and perpetuated dominant attitudes towards the suburbs, and the ways in which they have attacked such beliefs.

Artists' reactions to the suburbs over the past hundred years have, speaking broadly, moved from avoidance to condemnation to acceptance. Only in recent decades has Australian culture come to an acceptance, however uneasy, of the pros and cons of suburbia: its amenity and the price demanded for it; its awkward fusion of uniformity and diversity; its often ambivalent status as the heartland of Australian life. Artists have responded by re-evaluating the suburbs, replacing anti-suburbanism with positive explorations of suburbia.

To understand adequately the status of the suburbs within the visual arts, we must explore artists' complicity with dominant systems of belief. And when we seek artworks that challenge such structures, we must not assume that an artist's challenge to authority is straightforward or wholly successful. As a result, a sceptical undercurrent flows through this book. Many artists have questioned negative interpretations of the suburbs — especially their supposed uniformity — and have contributed to the growing recognition of suburbia as a complex and substantial way of life. Yet we must also acknowledge that, for many years, it was symbols developed by artists that sustained the image of the suburbs as a cultural and existential wasteland.

Artists' attitudes to the suburbs have in many ways matched those of cultural commentators in general. Artworks have tended to follow distinctions — made in sociology, political science, literature and other disciplines — between city and country, uniformity and individuality. However, issues peculiar to the visual arts cast a distinctive slant on some of these conventions. For while artists have turned to suburbia as an emblem of the Australian way of life, they have simultaneously struggled to understand the position of art within that way of life.

A complex anti-suburban rhetoric has often suggested that suburbia was the antithesis of Australianness; the conformity of the city dweller being contrasted unfavourably with the rugged independence of the bush pioneer. Artists have frequently elaborated on this rhetoric, opposing the supposed shallowness and uniformity of suburbia to the adventurous vitality of art. In making suburbia the symbolic enemy of art, artists made each image of the suburbs a microcosm of art's very struggle for existence in a hostile environment.

Yet this easy contrast of suburbia and art is shot through with contradictions. For every clichéd image of suburban uniformity, for every depiction of the suburbs as the very antithesis of genuine culture, there is another that takes pleasure in the comforts of community or finds a richness of experience in everyday activities. For every artist who offers the suburb as the epitome of the Australian way of life, there is another who rejects the notion of a singular 'Australianness' or an official version of the Australian character.

PLATE 1

Anonymous,
The Land of Promise, undated (1880s)

The prosperity of the 1880s cemented the status of the suburb as the preferred mode of urban living. New housing estates promised a new life, fresh air and open spaces, consolidating the association of the suburb with health, comfort, security and family life, and the contrast of these with the woes of the inner city.

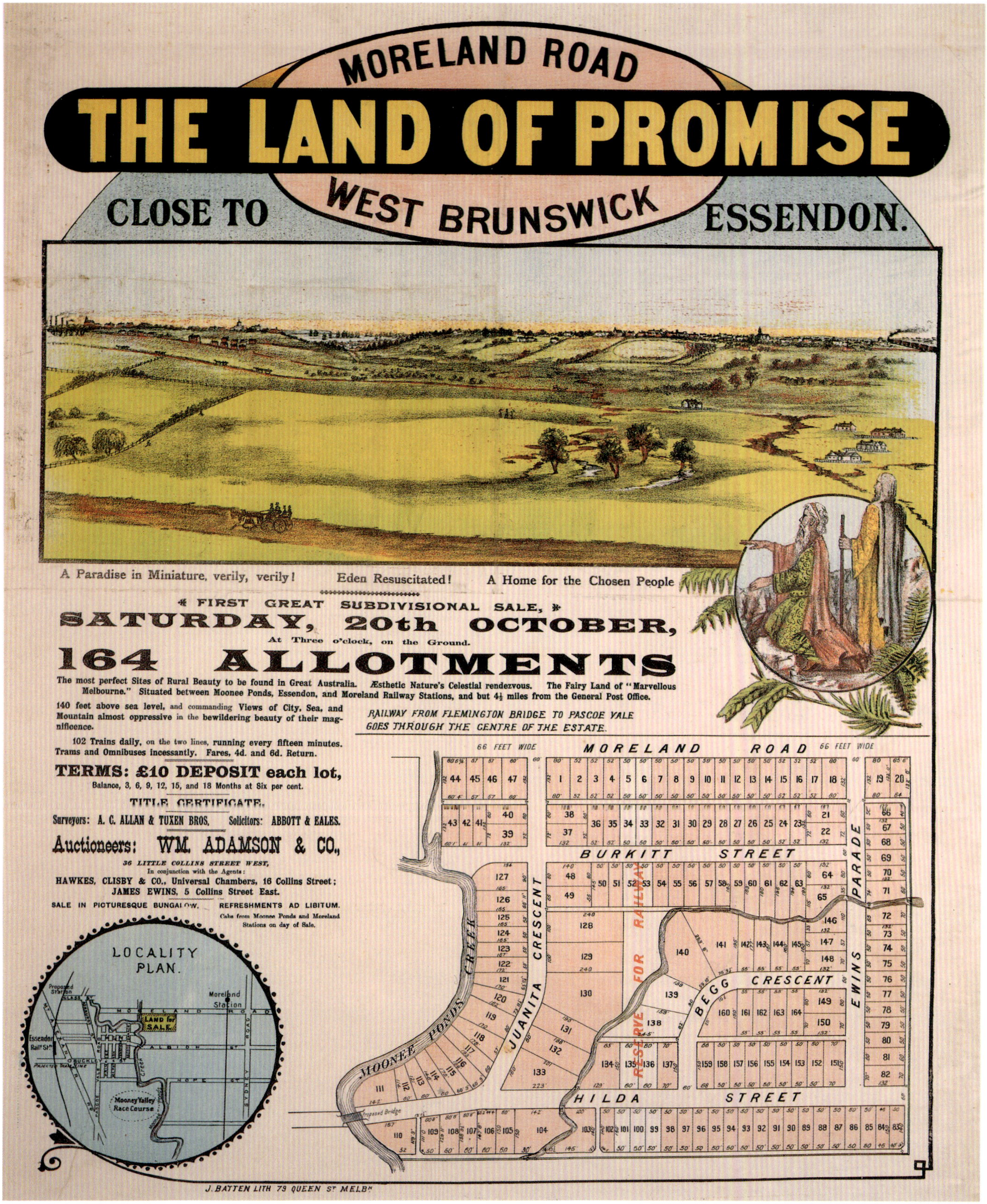
MORELAND ROAD
THE LAND OF PROMISE
WEST BRUNSWICK
CLOSE TO
ESSENDON.
A Paradise in Miniature, verily, verily!
Eden Resuscitated!
A Home for the Chosen People
FIRST GREAT SUBDIVISIONAL SALE,
SATURDAY, 20th OCTOBER,
At Three o'clock, on the Ground.
164 ALLOTMENTS
The most perfect Sites of Rural Beauty to be found in Great Australia. Æsthetic Nature's Celestial rendezvous. The Fairy Land of "Marvellous Melbourne." Situated between Moonee Ponds, Essendon, and Moreland Railway Stations, and but 4½ miles from the General Post Office.
140 feet above sea level, and commanding Views of City, Sea, and Mountain almost oppressive in the bewildering beauty of their magnificence.
102 Trains daily, on the two lines, running every fifteen minutes. Trams and Omnibuses incessantly. Fares, 4d. and 6d. Return.
TERMS: £10 DEPOSIT each lot,
Balance, 3, 6, 9, 12, 15, and 18 Months at Six per cent.
TITLE CERTIFICATE.
Surveyors: A. C. ALLAN & TUXEN BROS. Solicitors: ABBOTT & EALES.
Auctioneers: WM. ADAMSON & CO.,
36 LITTLE COLLINS STREET WEST,
In conjunction with the Agents:
HAWKES, CLISBY & CO., Universal Chambers, 16 Collins Street;
JAMES EWINS, 5 Collins Street East.
SALE IN PICTURESQUE BUNGALOW.
REFRESHMENTS AD LIBITUM.
Cabs from Moonee Ponds and Moreland Stations on day of Sale.
RAILWAY FROM FLEMINGTON BRIDGE TO PASCOE VALE GOES THROUGH THE CENTRE OF THE ESTATE.
66 FEET WIDE
MORELAND ROAD
BURKITT STREET
JUANITA CRESCENT
MOONEE PONDS CREEK
RESERVE FOR RAILWAY
BEGG CRESCENT
EWINS PARADE
HILDA STREET
LOCALITY PLAN.
Moreland Station
LAND for SALE
Essendon Railʷ Stⁿ
Mooney Valley Race Course
J. BATTEN LITH 73 QUEEN Sᵀ MELBᴺ

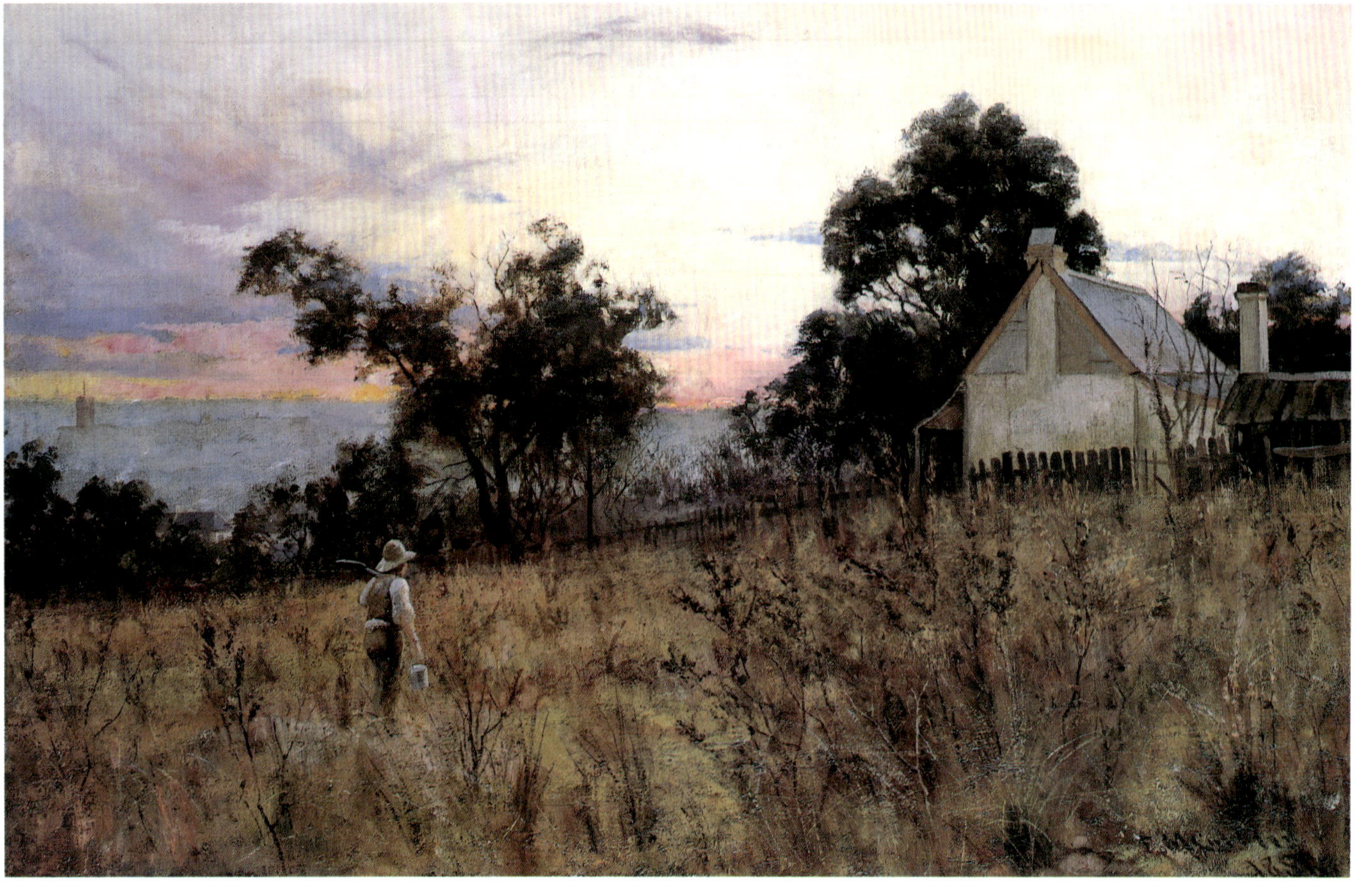

PLATE 2

Frederick McCubbin,
Winter Evening, Hawthorn, 1886

In Frederick McCubbin's *Winter Evening, Hawthorn* the sun sets behind the distant spires of Melbourne as a workman walks home to his slab hut. The artist implicitly acknowledges the reality of the suburb — the expanse of the city is evident in the background — but attempts to conceal its existence beneath the nostalgic metaphor of the bush pioneer.

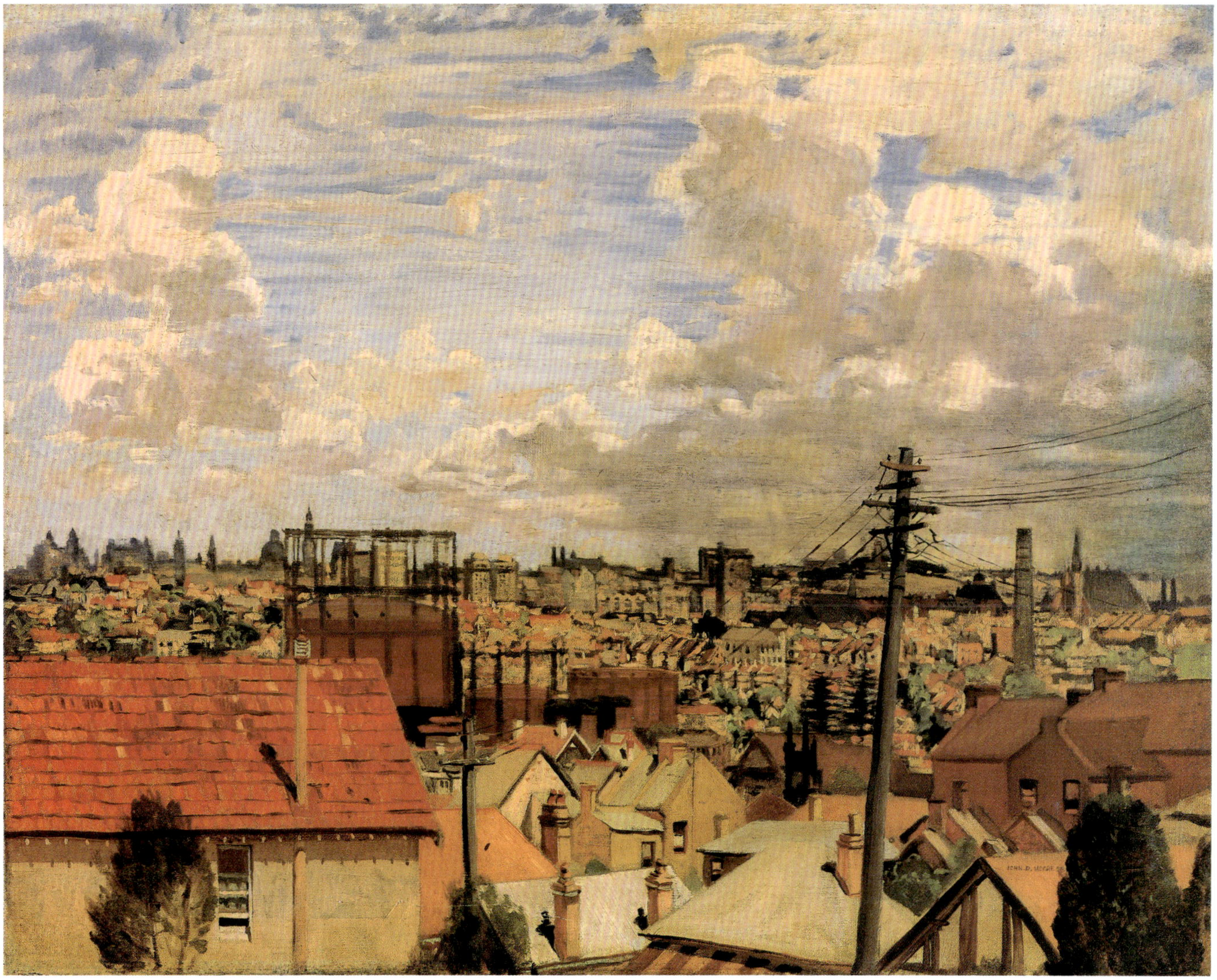

PLATE 3

John D. Moore,

Chaos, 1923

An architect as well as an artist, John D. Moore focuses on the roofs of suburbia, one of the few architectural elements offering variety in a geography of restricted plots and shrinking houses. *Chaos* is an unusual image for the 1920s, for it depicts Australian cities as chaotic and over-democratic, rather than predictable and conformist.

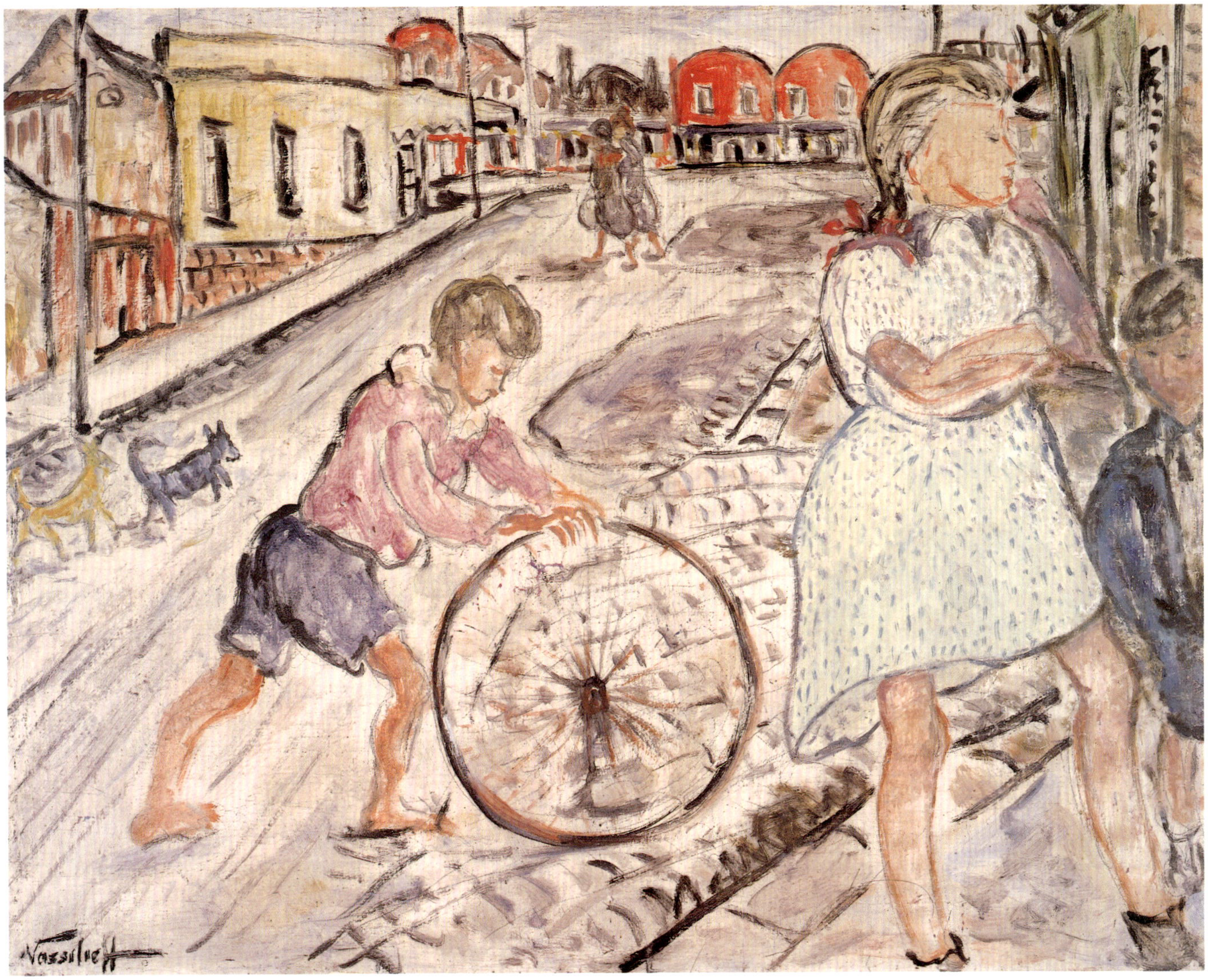

PLATE 4

Danila Vassilieff,

Children Playing, Fitzroy, c.1937

Even as moral crusaders decried the corrupting conditions of slum life, Danila Vassilieff found childlike innocence, mutual respect and support in the inner city, depicting these with a light line and decorative colour without concealing the real struggles of the population.

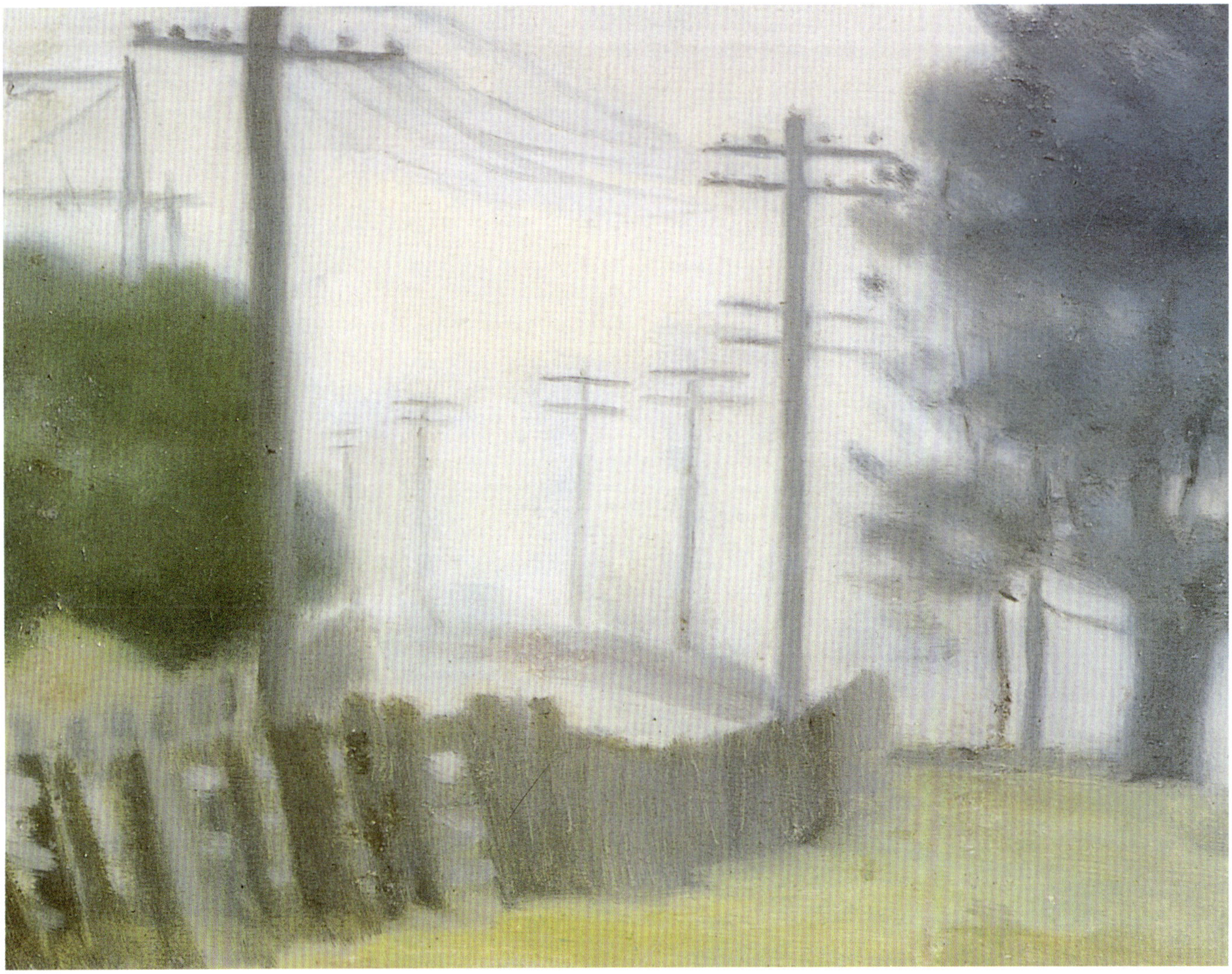

PLATE 5

Clarice Beckett,

Bay Road, Foggy Morning, c.1926

Clarice Beckett's views of bayside Melbourne trace the appearance of the garden suburb, but roads, fences and telegraph poles are everywhere in evidence. Their geometry straightens out the curves of the garden city, and signals a demand for technological amenity that would eventually take priority over the picturesque.

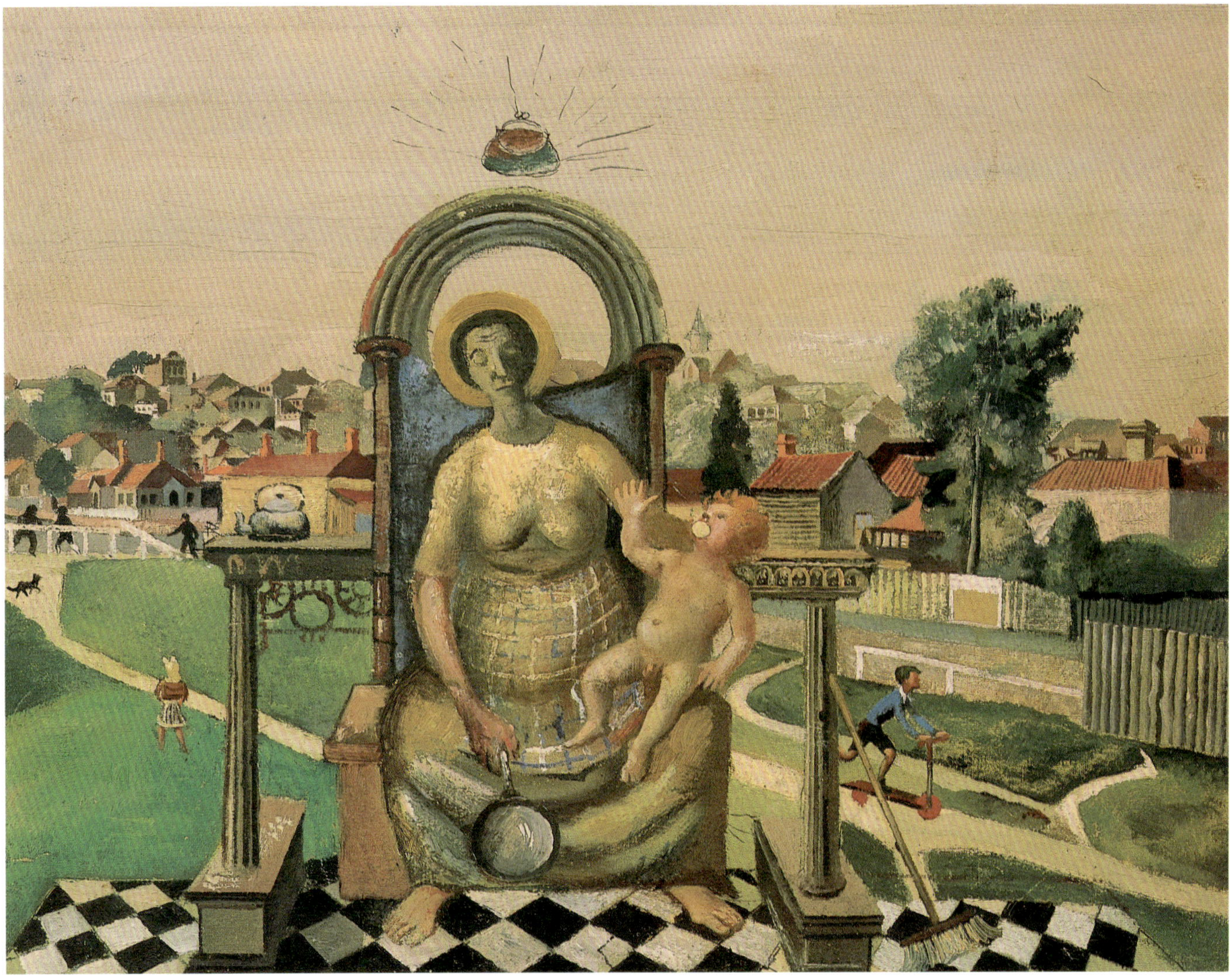

PLATE 6

Harald Vike,

Untitled (The Saint), 1947

Harald Vike's elaborate suburban imagery preserves the suburb's contradictions. The child evokes both the power of maternity and the 'barefoot and pregnant' housewife. The tools of housework evoke domestic drudgery but are counterbalanced by the amenity of the park and the majesty of the woman herself.

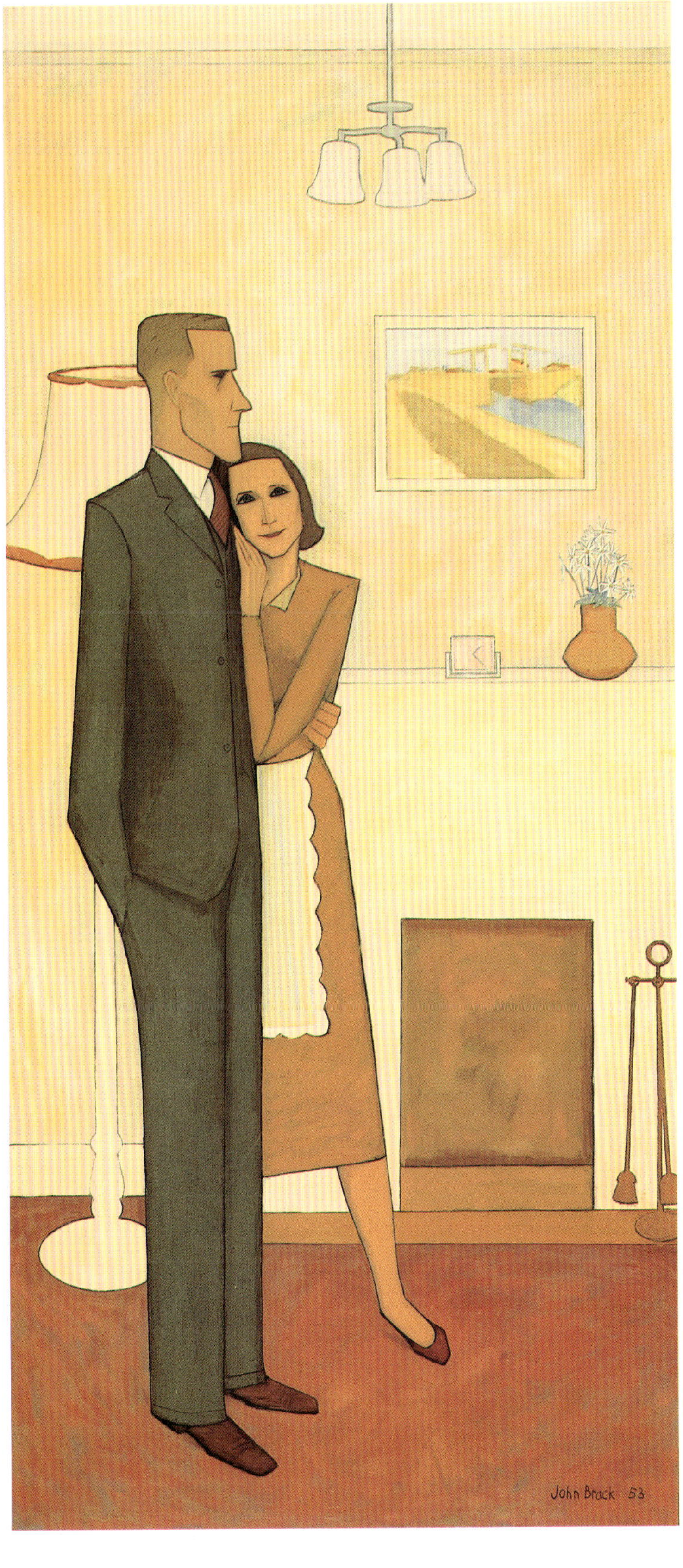

PLATE 7

John Brack,

The New House, 1953

The relationship of the new post-war suburbs to national identity was a complex one. John Brack's *The New House* shows cultural aspiration reduced from heroic nationalism to mere acquisitiveness. The happy couple can see no further than a world of subdivisions and hire-purchase.

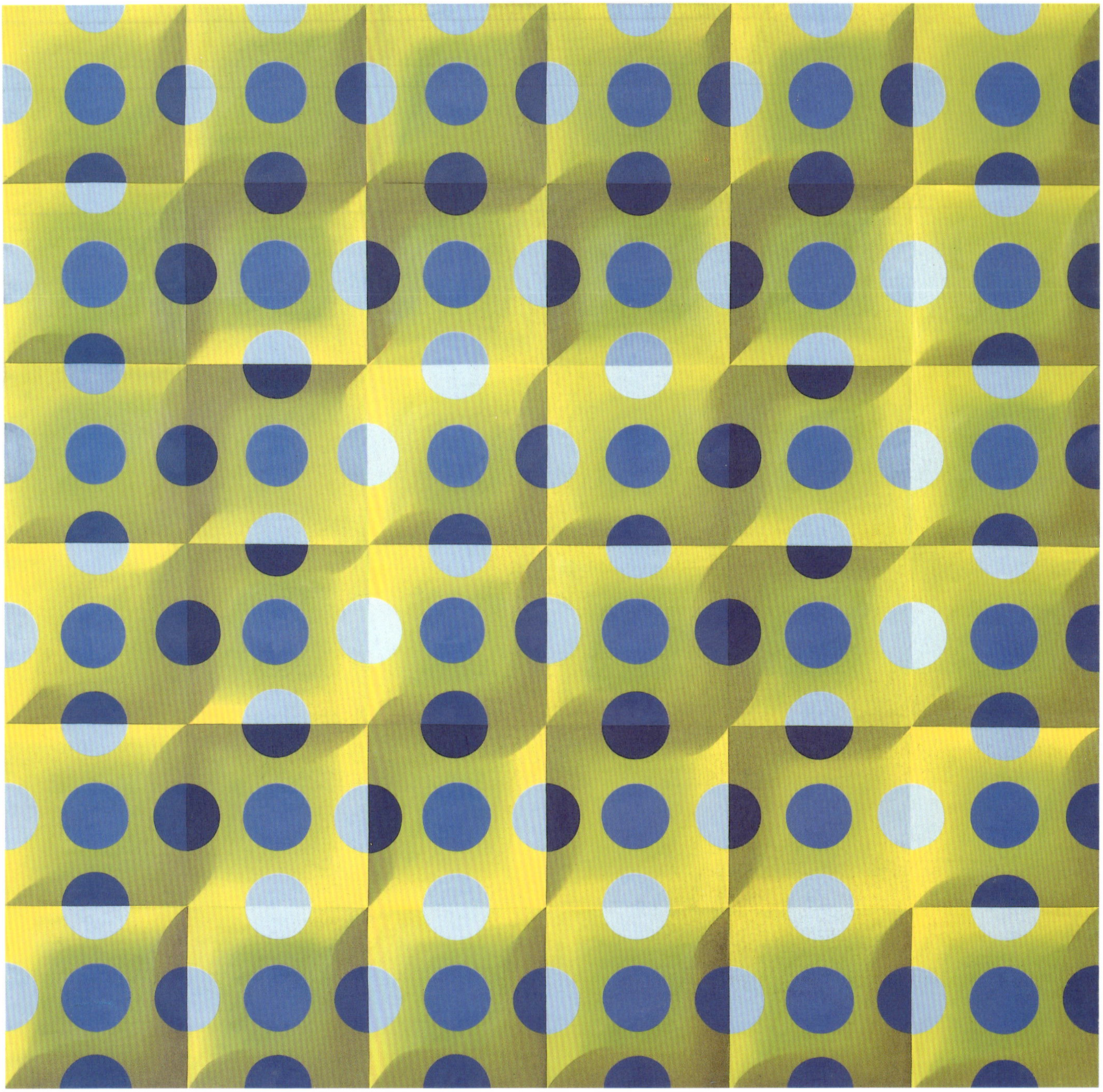

PLATE 8

Dale Hickey,

Untitled 67–68, 1967–68

Dale Hickey used the suburbs ironically to engage in a debate with international art styles. *Untitled 67–68* is derived from a suburban artefact — a mass-produced quilt — and the work is a deliberate hybrid, combining art and the suburbs; realism and abstraction; a unique painting and the mass-produced goods of consumerism.

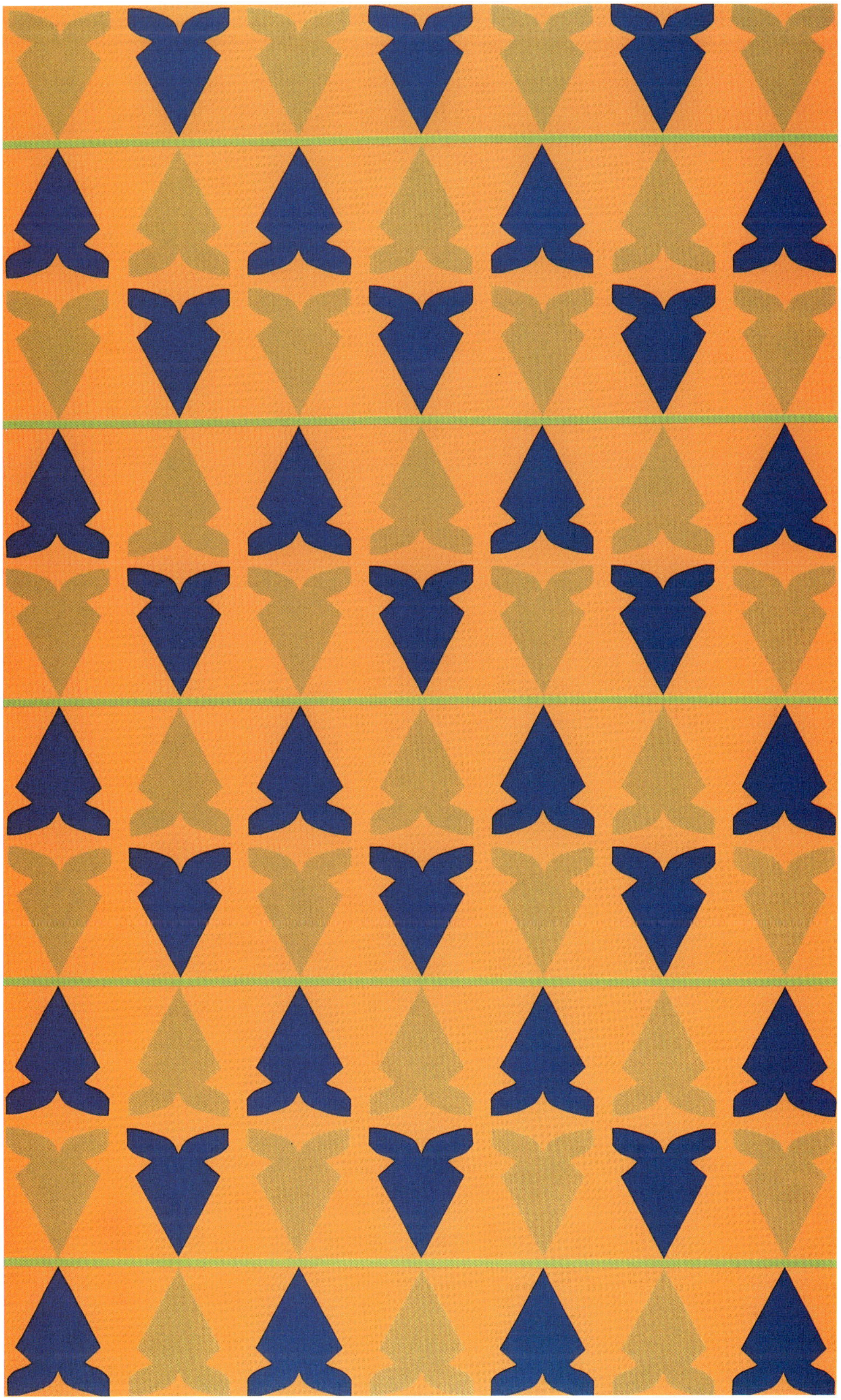

PLATE 9

Robert Rooney,

Cereal Bird Beaks II, 1969

Robert Rooney, in his 'hard-edged' paintings of the late 1960s, used domestic motifs to corrupt the principles of Colour Field Abstraction. In *Cereal Bird Beaks II* — an abstract painting based on a cereal box — the tainted status of suburbia acts as a virus eating away at 'high' art and good taste.

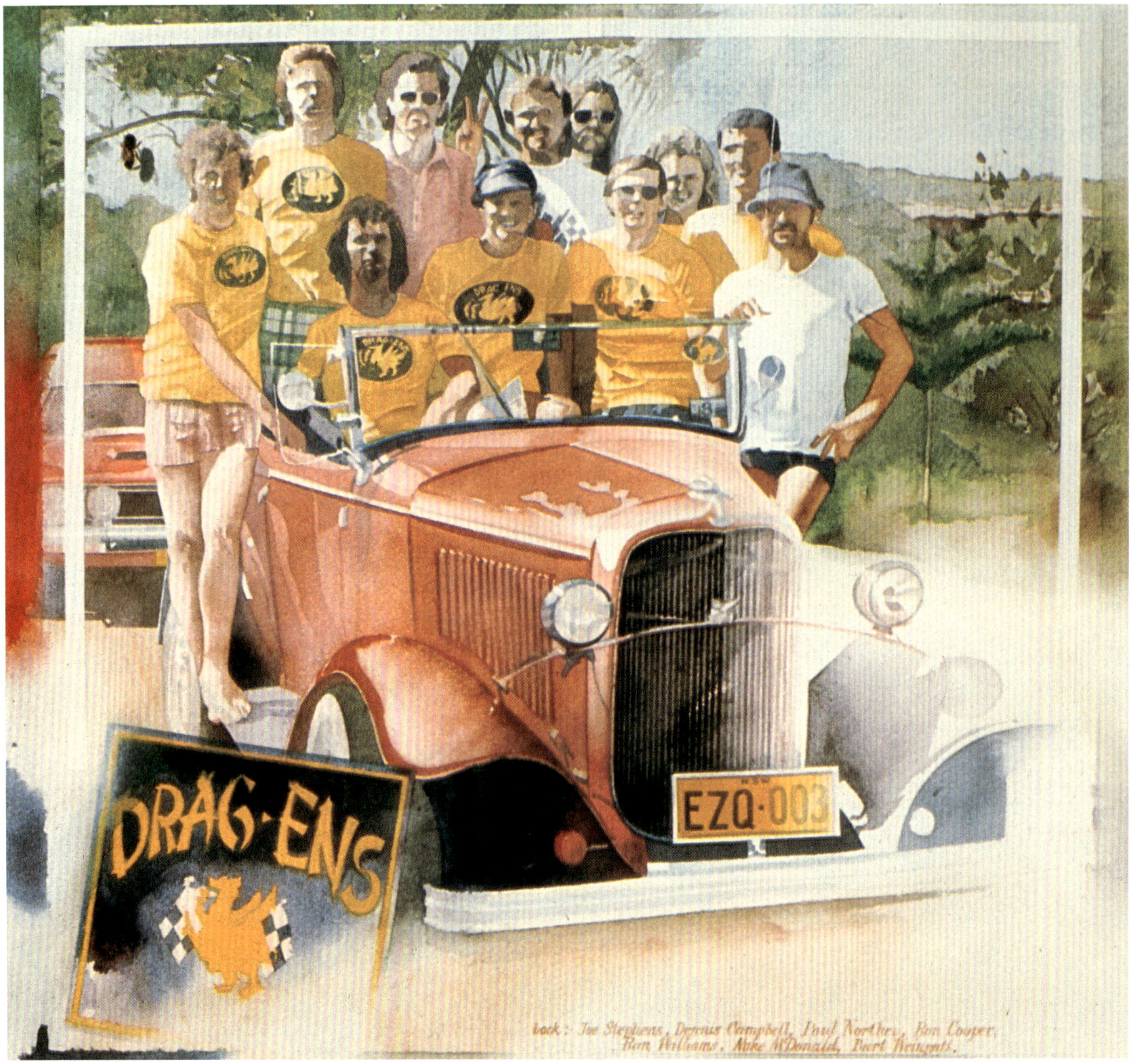

PLATE 10

Peter Kennedy,
Introductions, 1974–76

The Conceptual artists of the 1970s viewed artworks as analytical propositions about the nature of art and the operation of culture. In *Introductions*, Peter Kennedy's aim is neither to condemn the suburbs nor to document them, but rather to actively participate in, and contribute to, their culture.

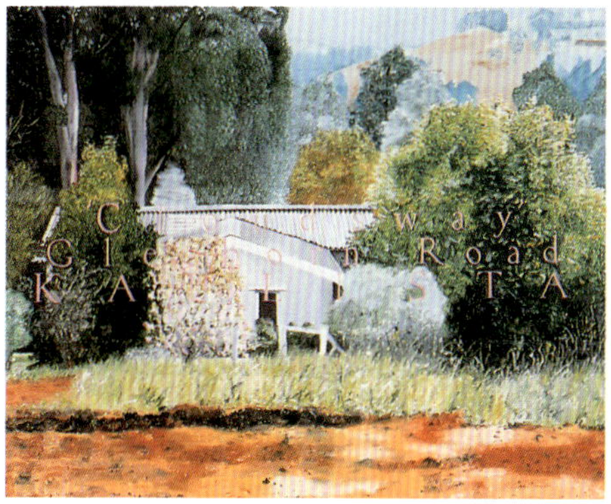

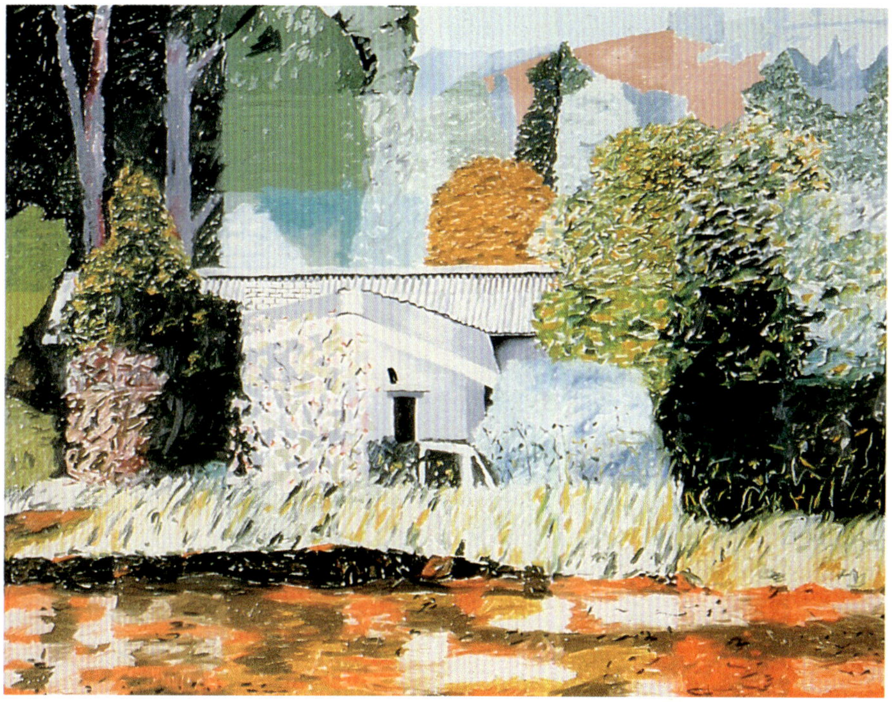

PLATE 11

Jenny Watson,

House Painting: Kallista

(Large and Small Versions), 1976

In Jenny Watson's "House" series, meaning is elusive. The paintings are as much about what cannot be seen as what can. The public faces of the houses — their facades — reveal something of the social status of their inhabitants, but the private life of their interiors remains hidden.

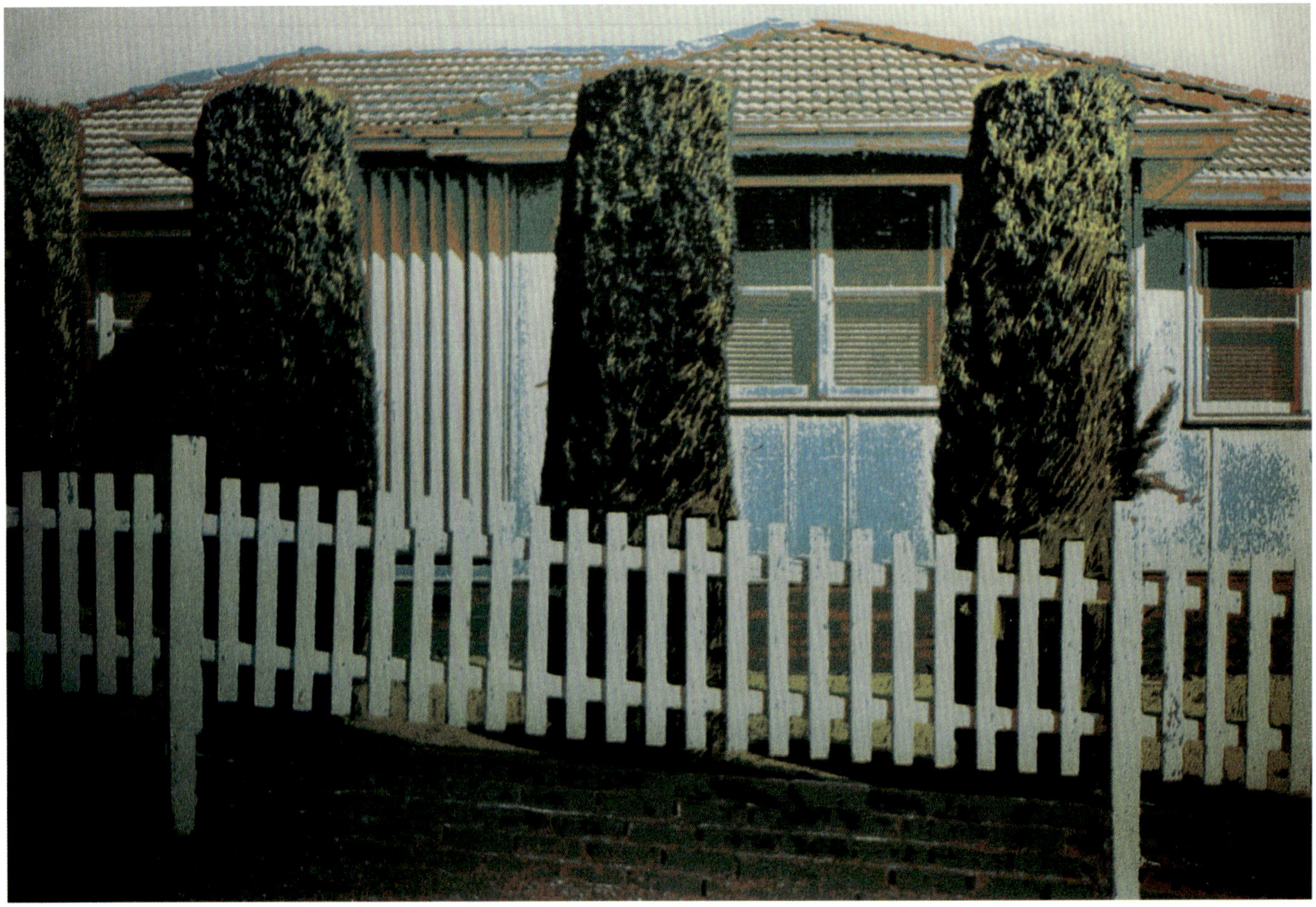

PLATE 12

Mandy Martin,
Picket Fences, 1980

Mandy Martin's series of photo-silkscreen images of Queanbeyan, Canberra reflects a feminist vision of the house as prison; the suburban woman its presumed captive. In *Picket Fences*, the very demeanour of the house seems to hint at the psychological state of its inhabitant: withdrawn, defensive and agoraphobic.

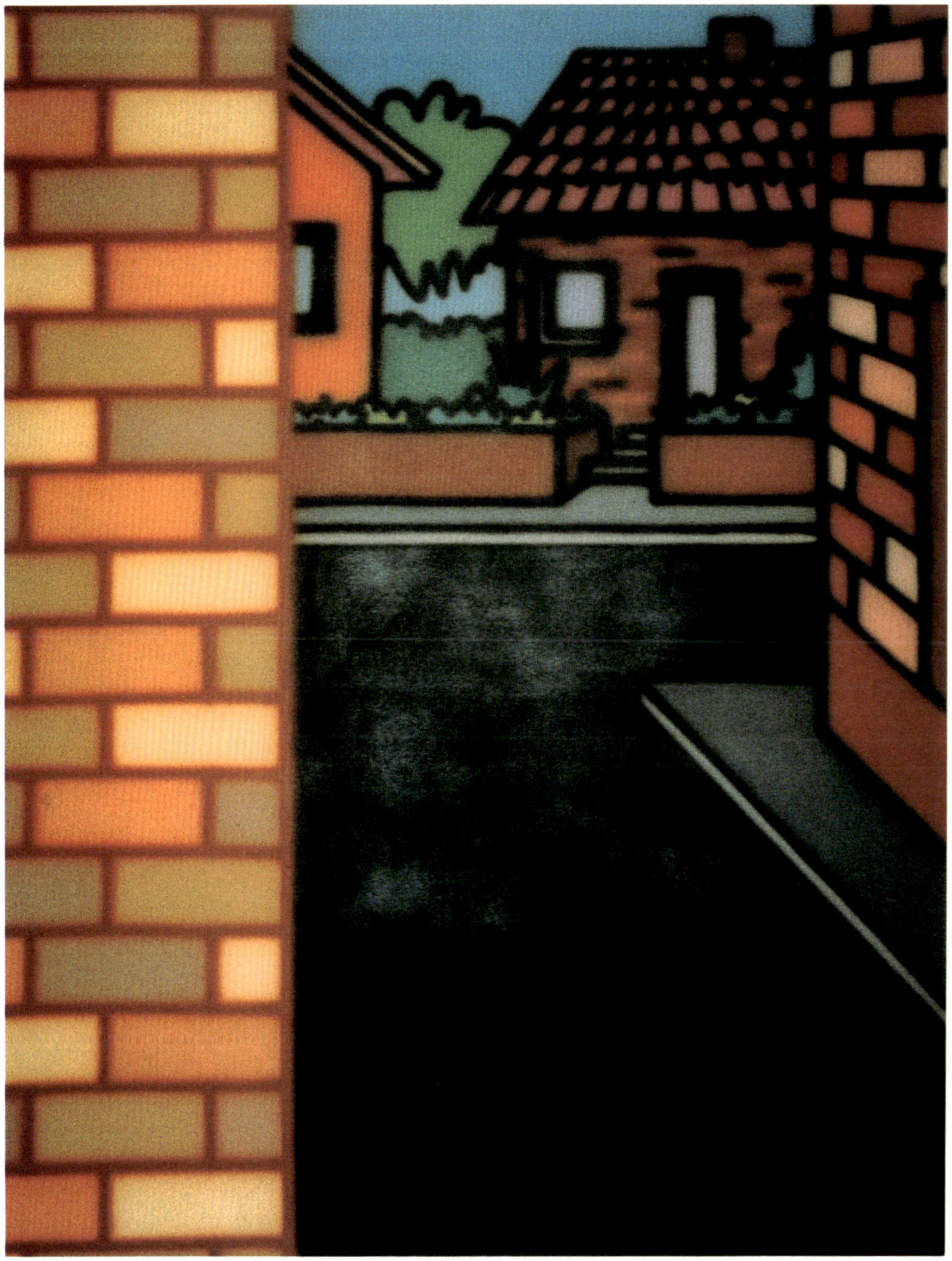

PLATE 13

Howard Arkley,
Nubrick, 1986

Since the late 1970s Howard Arkley has been cataloguing the styles of suburbia. His air-brush paintings and drawings trace a bewildering variety of facades, driveways, fences, gardens, screen doors and rooflines. Rather than epitome of sameness, Arkley finds the suburb a source of difference.

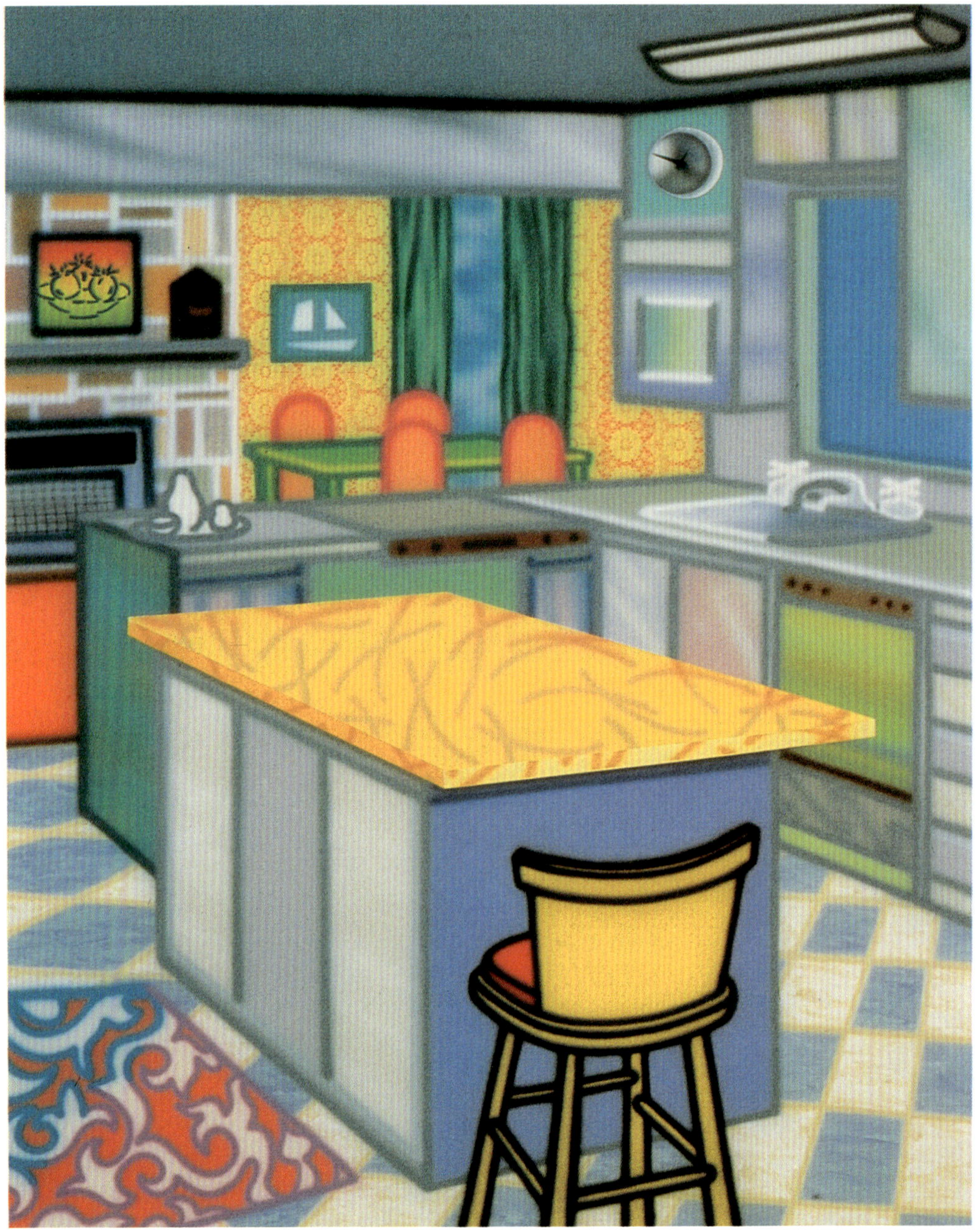

PLATE 14

Howard Arkley,

Ultra Kleen, 1992

The flaring and flickering effects of line and colour have a metaphorical resonance; it is as if the suburbs escape our gaze. They can be painted, drawn and viewed, but not pinned down. After decades of art condemning the suburbs, Arkley implies that the suburbs defeat art.

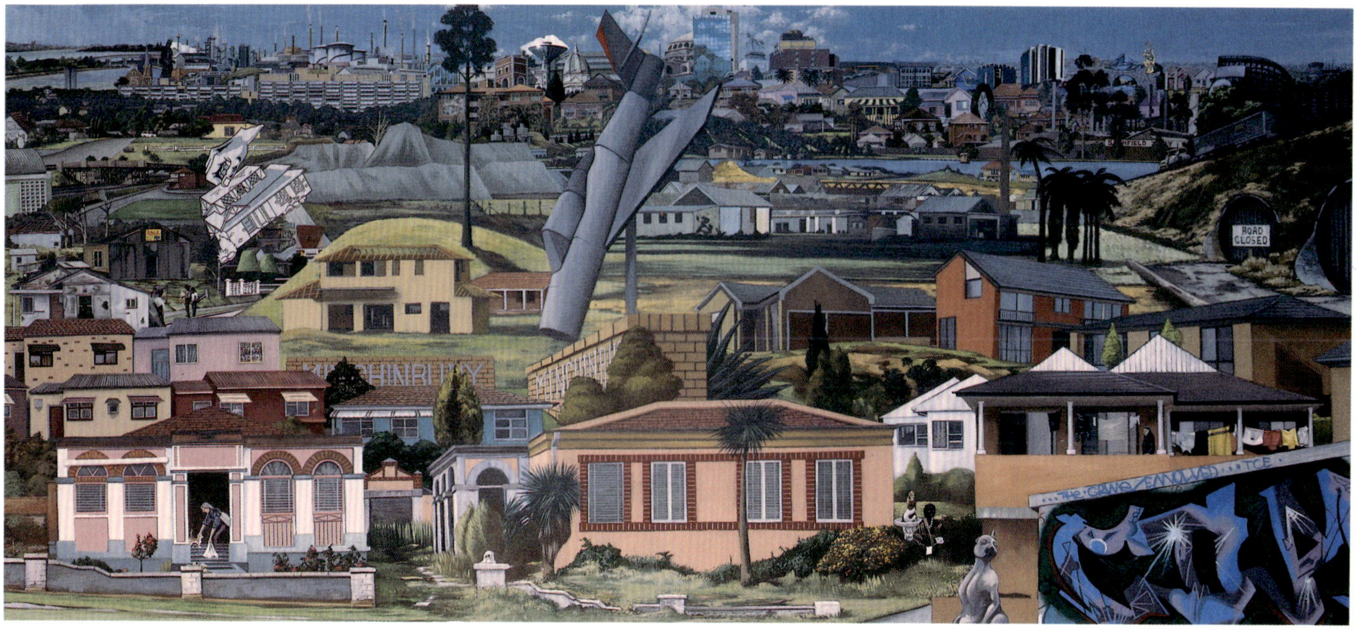

PLATE 15

Ken Searle,
West #6, 1990

Ken Searle's is a profoundly humanist vision of the western suburbs. Refusing to accept the clichés about 'Westies', he depicts an intricate suburban infrastructure, an elaborate set of spatial and social relations. Parks and factories, homes and shops, work and play: all fuse together.

PLATE 16

Constanze Zikos,
Death Double, 1992

The migrant home often combines elements of Anglo-Australian culture with a decor that evokes the migrant's country of origin. Constanze Zikos transfers this hybridity to art, using household materials — Laminex and enamel paint — and combining the geometric abstract style of many Anglo-Australian artists, with decorative motifs from classical Greece.

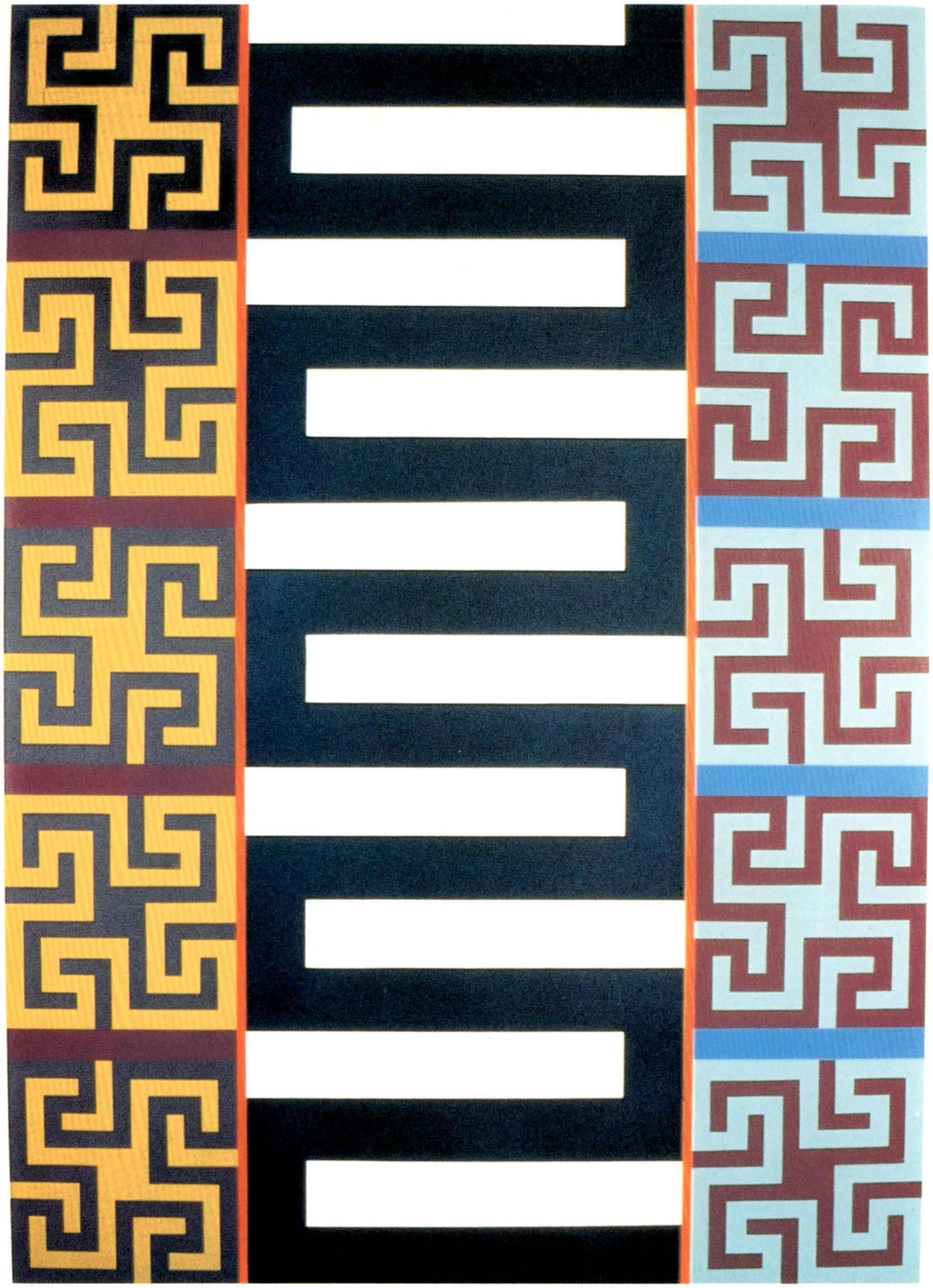

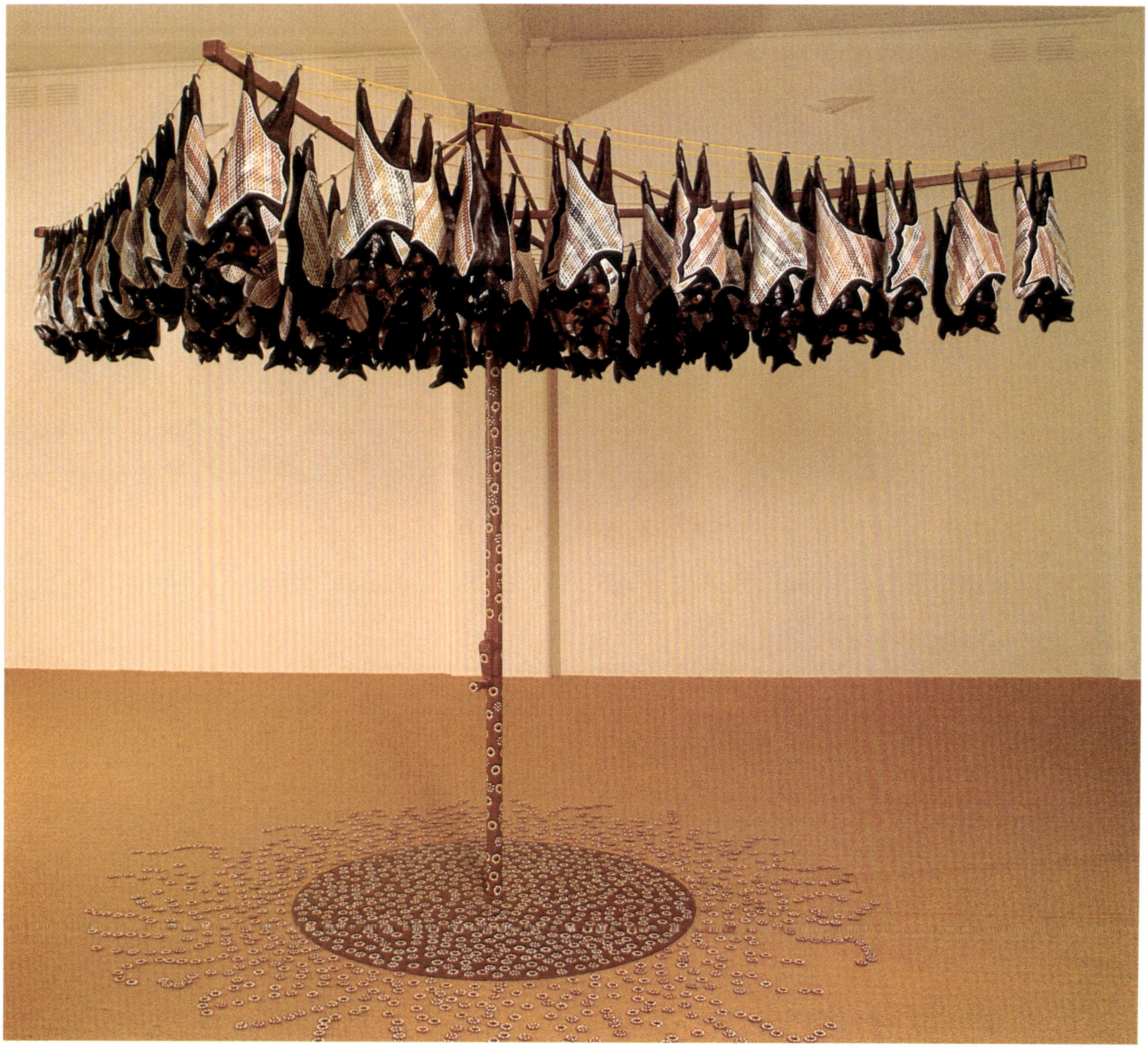

PLATE 17

Lin Onus,

Fruit Bats, 1990

Lin Onus also plays with contrasting categories to emphasise the persistence of difference. *Fruit Bats* combines a found object — the Hill's Hoist — and sculpted forms; Western representational illusionism and the abstraction of an Aboriginal cross-hatching technique. The work is humorous, but there is an undercurrent of anger.

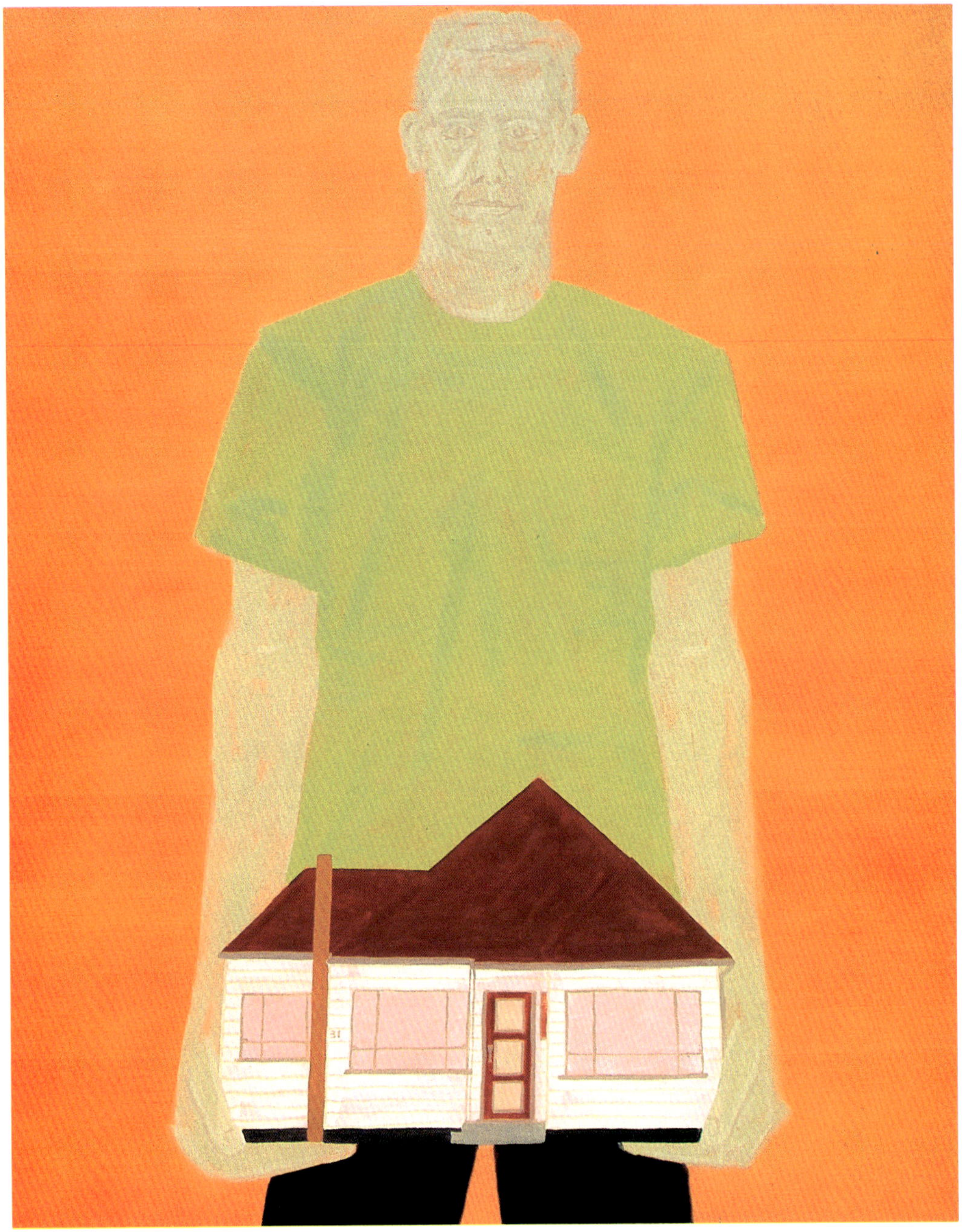

PLATE 18

Jon Campbell,

31 Myrtle Street, 1987

Jon Campbell's image of his family home in Altona, a semi-industrial western suburb of Melbourne, is a deliberate contrast to his images of youth rituals and street culture. The artist paints himself holding the suburban house in which he grew up, emphasising its personal significance to him.

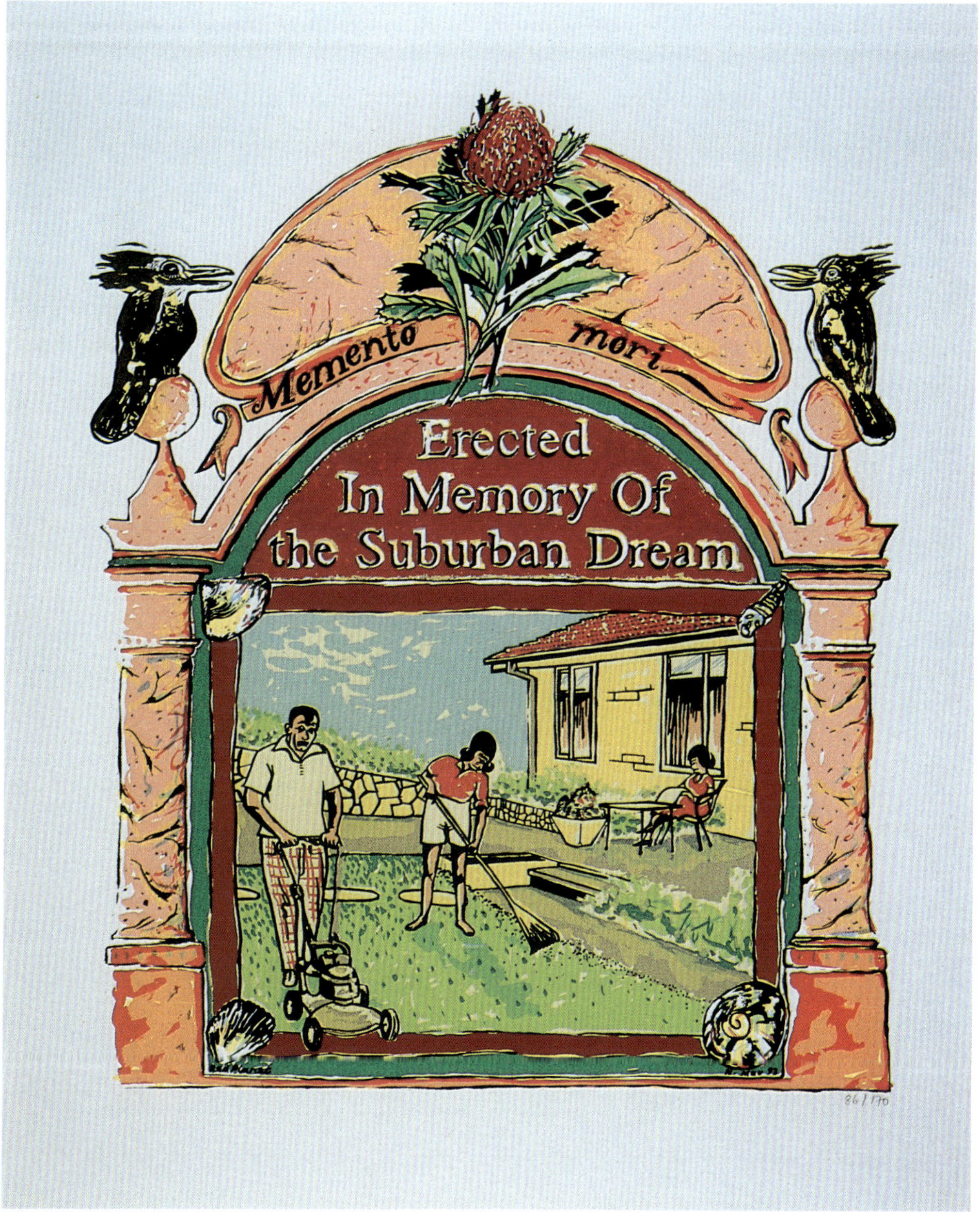

PLATE 19

Nicholas Mau (RedPlanet Graphics),

Death of the Suburban Dream, 1993

Nicholas Mau's poster *Death of the Suburban Dream* diagrams the gender roles perpetuated in education, books and children's play: domestic chores are the role of the mother; the public face of the home — the garden — is the father's job; and the children follow their appointed models dutifully.

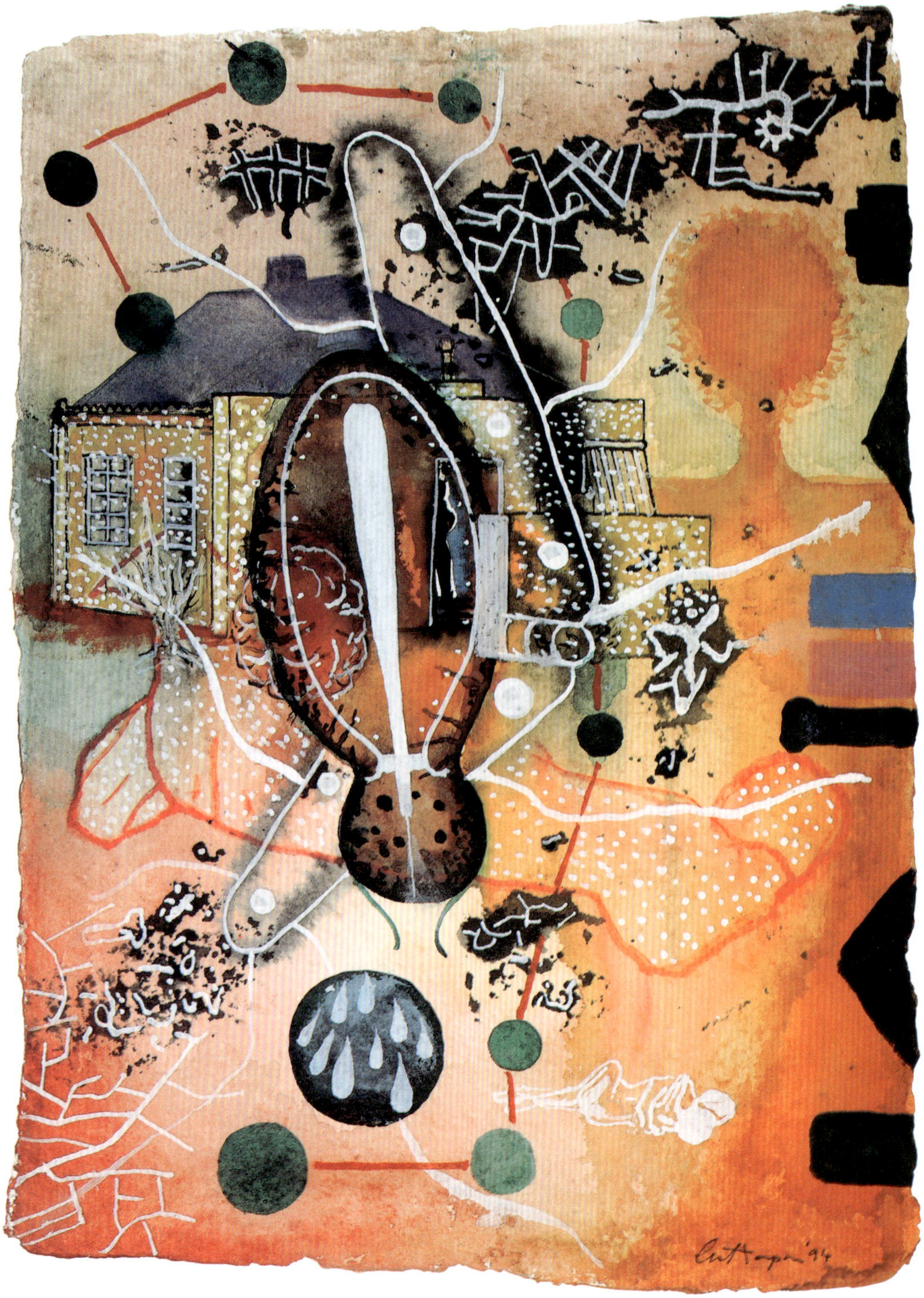

PLATE 20

Jon Cattapan,

Woden Valley Insect No. 3, 1994

An ant colony seems an apt metaphor for suburban life, with its incessant labour, constant motion to and fro, and rigidly defined social system. But Jon Cattapan's *Woden Valley Insect No.3* peels away the restrained facade of suburban streets to reveal a passionate, even sexual landscape.

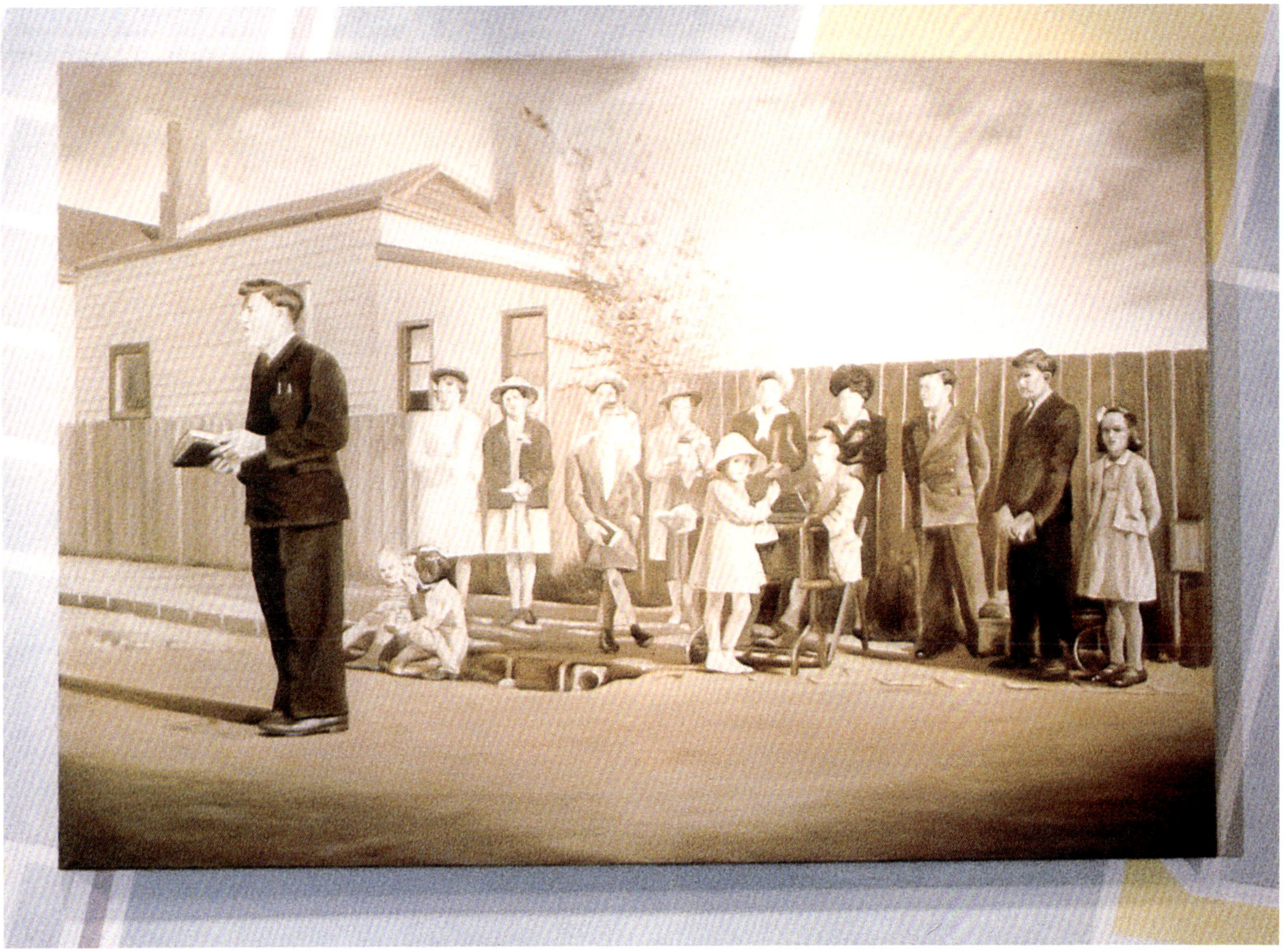

PLATE 21

Sarah Curtis,
Neighbours Arcadia (detail), 1994

Sarah Curtis's installation reflects upon the artist's strict religious upbringing. On a more abstract level, the work also hints that the very conservatism of suburbia may exceed the bounds of propriety. As the site of a religious crusade, Curtis's suburb has all the fervour of Cattapan's sexualised landscape.

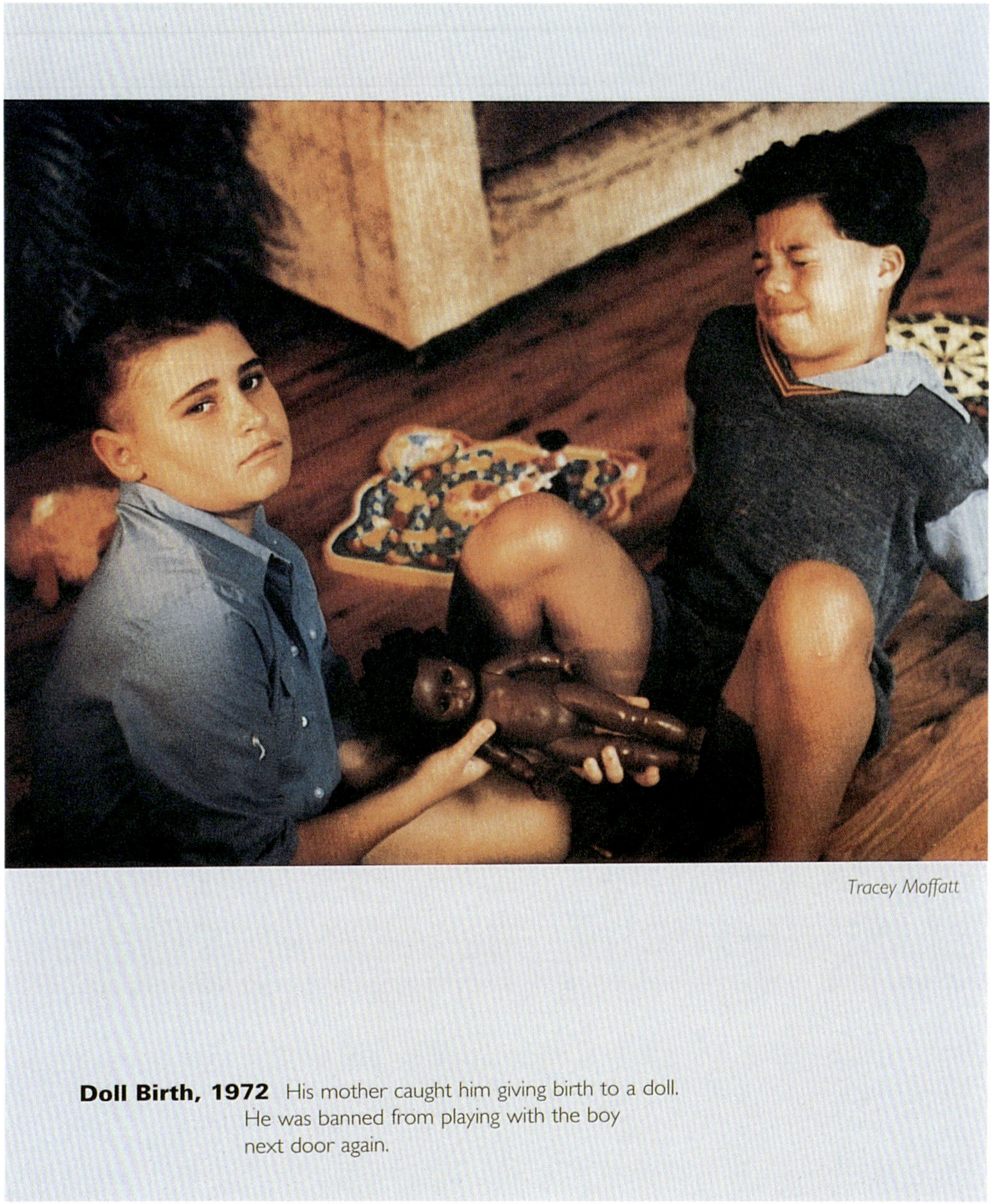

PLATE 22

Tracey Moffatt,
from "Scarred for Life" series, 1994

In Tracey Moffatt's 1994 series "Scarred for Life", the customs of the suburbs are documented as if for the armchair traveller. The family home is a battleground: psychological warfare is its chief weapon. Rules governing behaviour, gender roles and appearances are strictly enforced.

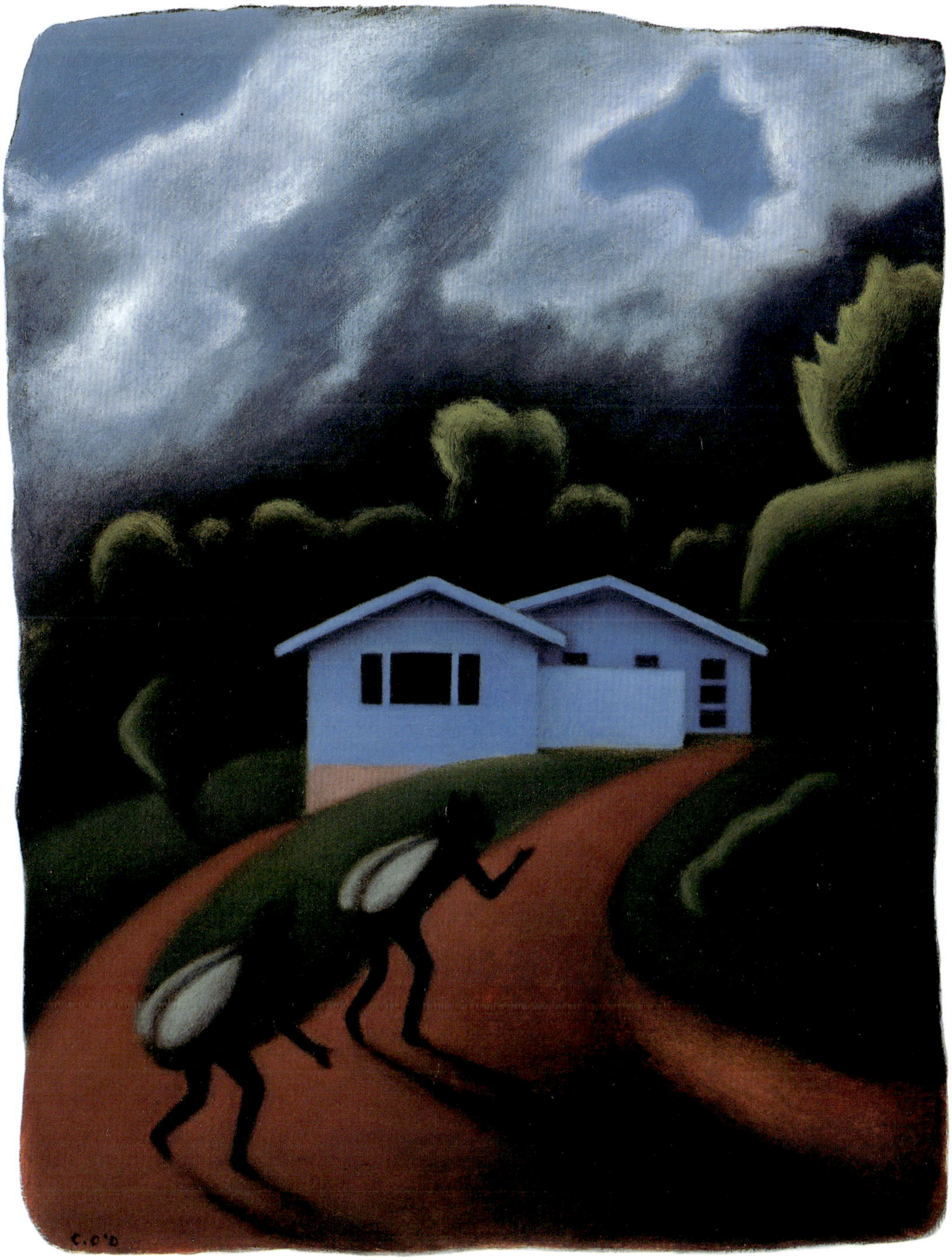

PLATE 23

Reg Mombassa,

Insectile Space-monsters Approach Sleeping Family, 1995

Reg Mombassa's suburbs are brimming over with life. In *Insectile Space-monsters Approach Sleeping Family* he presents a hitherto invisible life of hallucinogenic vision and paranoid nightmares. His eccentric vision parodies earlier treatments of the suburbs as alien, and argues for psychic realities beyond the reach of rational knowledge.

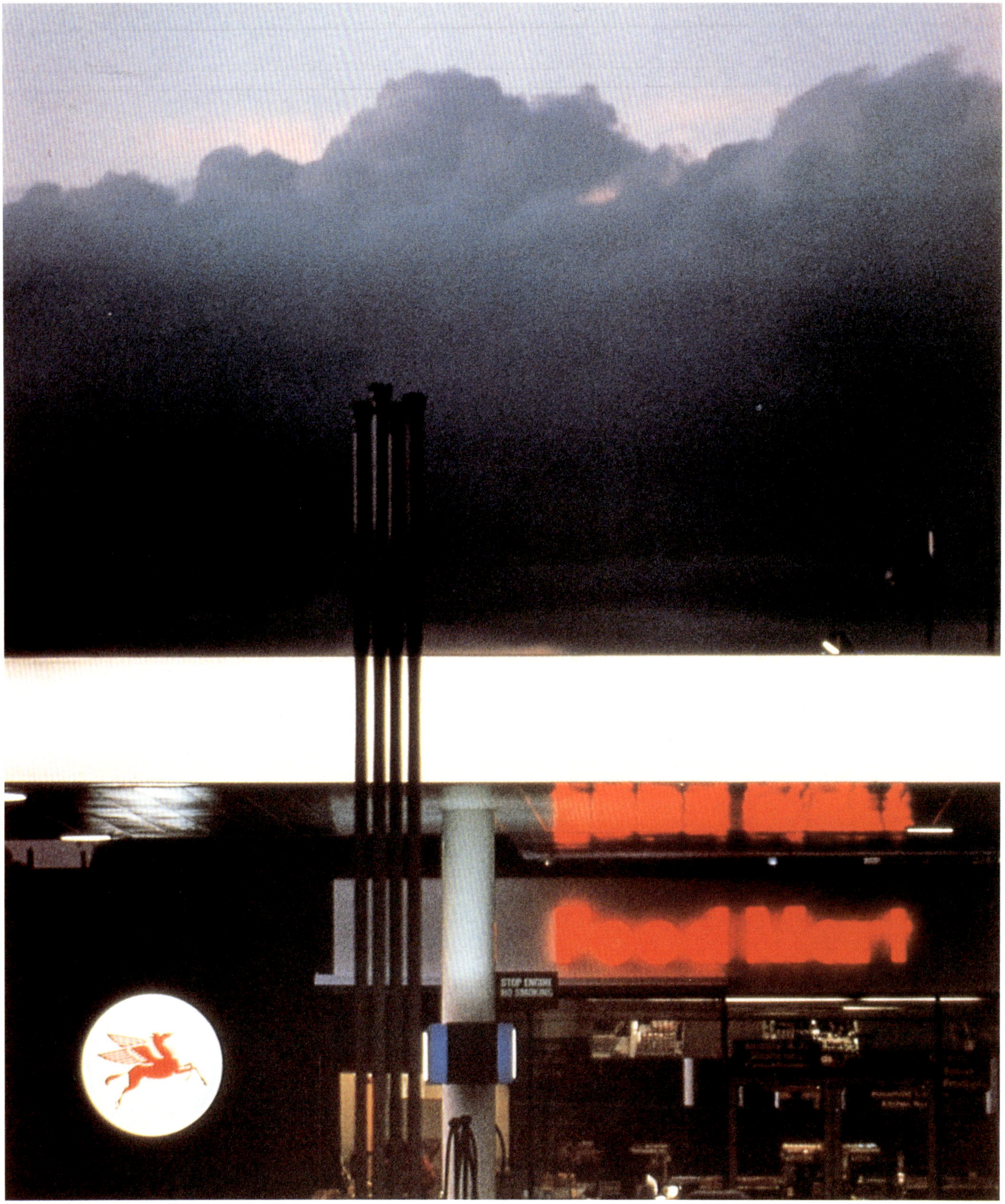

PLATE 24

Bill Henson,
Untitled 1985–86, 1985–86

Attempts to express pessimistic attitudes to Australian culture through images of suburban banality or ugliness seem increasingly forced. It is not just the pessimistic romanticism of Bill Henson's photograph that makes it seem dated; it is the apparent belief that it is sufficient to say that the suburbs are materialistic, without reflecting on the ways in which they have changed so dramatically in recent years.

rural myths & urban dreams

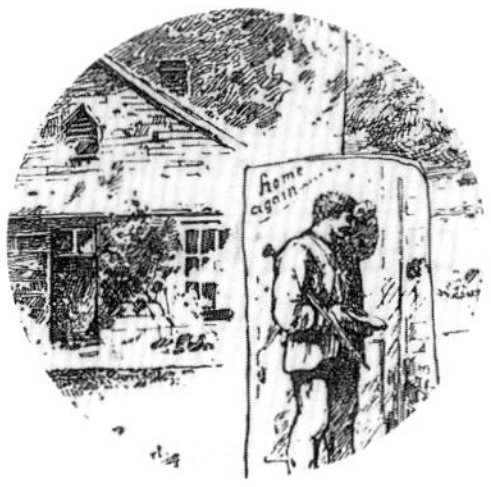

Although popular conceptions of Australian identity have always been constructed around outback and bush life, since the late nineteenth century Australia has been among the most urbanised nations in the world. Urban living has always been the lot, indeed the preference, of the majority. By 1881, less than 100 years after white settlement, over half of the population lived in urban settlements. By 1921, this figure had climbed to 62%, and by 1954 it had reached 79%. Recent census figures show that 85% of Australians live in urban areas. Since urban is defined as a settlement with a population greater than 1,000, these figures include towns too small to incorporate suburbs, but not so small as to preclude suburban attitudes on the part of their inhabitants. Predominantly suburban metropolises such as capital cities contained 35% of the population in 1907, 50% in 1947, and just under 60% in 1981.

The establishment of the suburbs in the late nineteenth century provided opportunities to illustrators who produced advertising images [Plate 1] and to artists such as William Tibbits, who painted 'portraits' of new homes or subdivisions. One of these suburbs, Heidelberg, also gave its name to the 'Heidelberg School' of fine artists, which included Arthur Streeton and Frederick McCubbin. Their work, however, defined a nationalist iconography that obscured, rather than celebrated, suburban expansion.

It is strange that the Australian townsman should have so thoroughly inherited the English love of living as far as possible away from the scene of his business and work during the day ... Nearly everybody who can lives in the suburbs ... The colonist is very fond of living in his own house and on his own bit of ground, and building societies and the extensive mortgage system which prevails enable him easily to gratify this desire.

Richard Twopenny, from *Town Life in Australia*, 1883

THE LAND BOOM AND BEYOND

Graeme Davison, the foremost historian of the Australian suburb, has described how the suburban ideal was promoted by government from the onset of white settlement and appealed strongly to the migrant population seeking a new start. Suburban development was consolidated, by the 1880s, by economic factors including high wages, low unemployment and cheap land. Nineteenth century ideologies such as Evangelicalism, Romanticism, Sanitarianism and Capitalism — each for its own reasons — presented suburban life in a positive light. The suburb, Davison argues, had set the pattern for non-Aboriginal settlement, answering fundamental needs and aspirations.

In the late 1880s, buoyed by the prosperity generated by gold rushes and the pastoral industry, Australian cities experienced a building boom. Property speculators developed suburbs on the fringes of large cities, especially in Melbourne and Sydney. Coupled with existing aspirations to a better life, and a faith that the rural fringe of the city offered the physical environment in which to live it, the prosperity of the 1880s cemented the status of the suburb as the preferred mode of urban living. Following or anticipating the extension of tram and train lines, suburbs like Moreland, in Melbourne, were built on land previously used for farming.

Advertisements for new housing estates promised a new life, fresh air and open spaces, consolidating the association of the suburb with health, comfort, security and family life, and the contrast of these with the woes of inner-city slums. In contrast to the high density of settlement in the original suburbs surrounding metropolitan centres, the new suburbs featured large lots, detached houses, and amenities such as gas and water.

At the same time, efforts were made to preserve a rural tone, albeit a rather English one, in the name of the suburb. In *The Rise and Fall of Marvellous Melbourne*, Davison notes Hawthorn, Burwood and Glen Iris among such names. From the outset, then, fringe suburbs were presented as a hybrid of the urban and the rural, modern convenience and rustic charm, combining the best of both worlds in images shot through with utopian dreams, commercial hyperbole and nationalistic aspirations.

SELLING THE SUBURBS: WILLIAM TIBBITS

One artist who reflected the centrality of urban development in Australian consciousness at this time was William Tibbits. Tibbits plied a trade as a topographical watercolourist, painting 'portraits' of houses for proud owners or giving pictorial form to housing estates that existed only on the drawing board of the developer or in the dreams of prospective purchasers. Here the realities, or at least the potentials, of the suburb were foremost.

The house and urban infrastructure dominated these images to the exclusion of all else. The appearance of the home, the provision of utilities (gas, water, public transport), a sense of amenity (roads, yards, parks, fresh air), and of course price were paramount. Then as now, the catchphrase of the real-estate marketeer was 'Location, Location, Location'. Tibbits was at pains to throw the best possible light on these outer reaches of 'Marvellous Melbourne'.

What Tibbits portrayed was the urban, domestic future of Australia. This was a future at odds with the rural imagery and values of the bush legend prevalent in literature, poetry, song and the popular media. Yet Tibbits's suburban imagery, while embodying the suburban dreams of the populace, did not challenge these nationalist symbols.

The heavy responsibility of constructing an 'official' imagery of national identity fell to oil painting, a fine art medium of high status and authority demanding

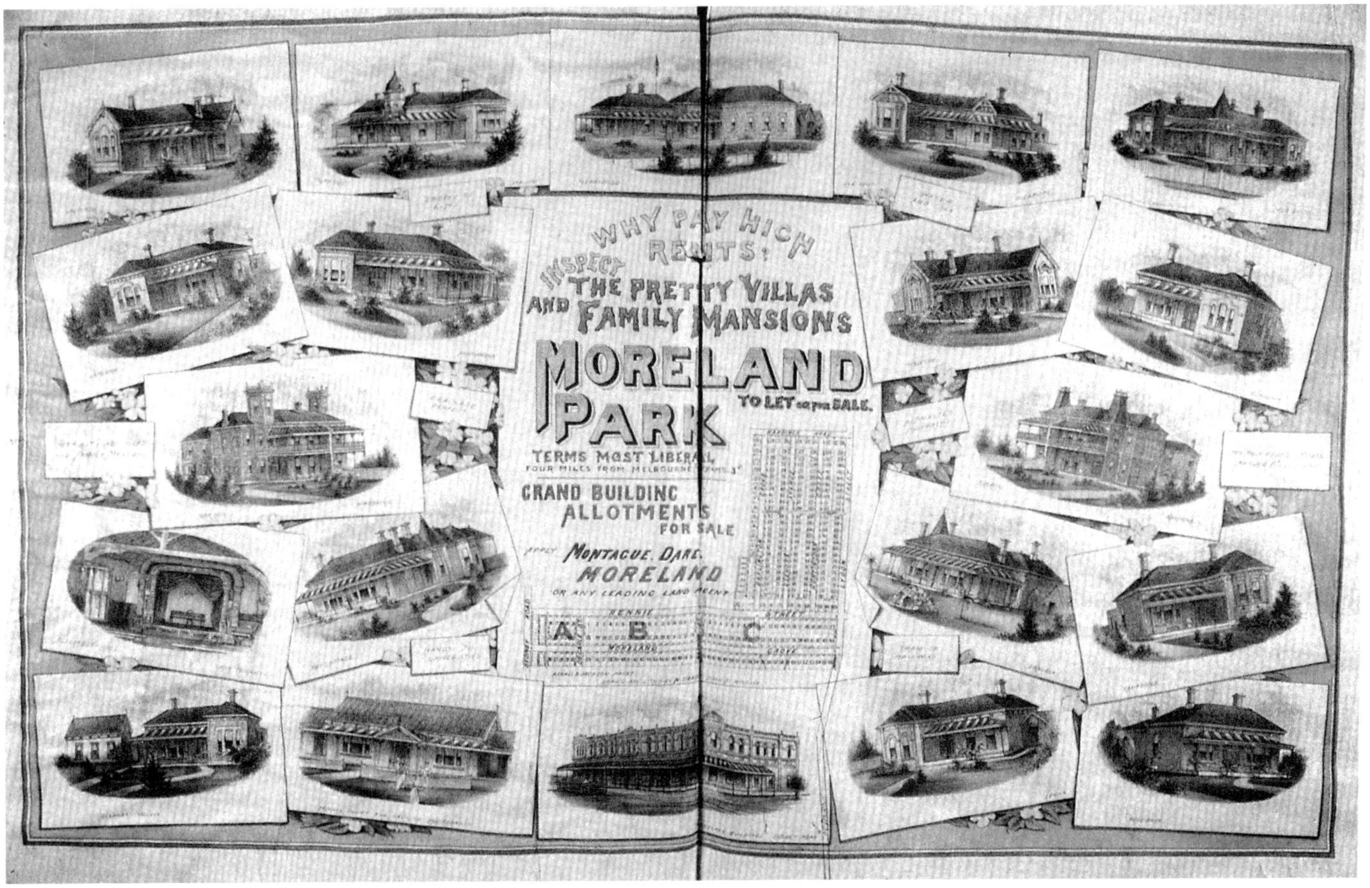

William Tibbits,

Why Pay High Rents? Inspect the pretty villas and family mansions of Moreland Park, c.1886 elevated subjects. Tibbits's topographical views, in contrast, were regarded as 'commercial' rather than 'fine' art, an assumption reinforced by their association with the real-estate industry. Consequently, it was not expected that this work aspire to a national imagery or embody nationalist values. Skilled as he was, Tibbits did not have the status of a fine artist, and as a result the suburbs were regarded as an acceptable subject for his work.

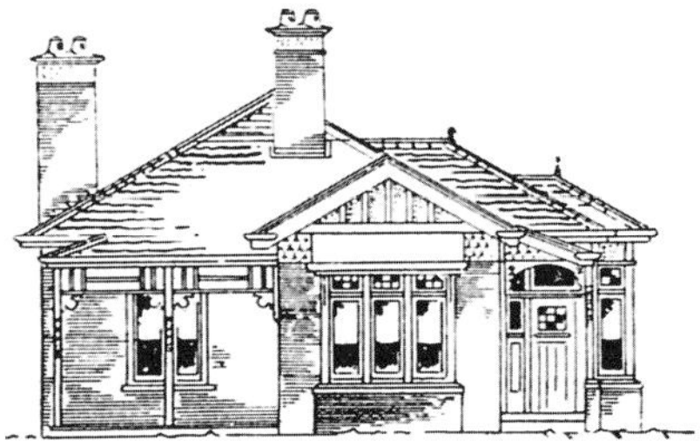

MYTHICAL HEIDELBERG: ARTHUR STREETON

Although the suburbs were becoming the bedrock of the Australian dream, fine artists were literally turning their backs on them. Working in the shadow of the new suburban subdivisions, the Heidelberg School painters chose to represent Australian culture through pastoral and bush myths. Like their contemporaries in poetry and literature (especially the nationalistic writers of the *Bulletin*, such as Henry Lawson and 'Banjo' Paterson), Arthur Streeton, Tom Roberts, Frederick McCubbin and Charles Conder

After lunch today I went to Heidelberg with my brother Pills ... we crawled up the hill to Eaglemont and lay watching the sky and the beautiful beautiful line of distance and the ranges, dim hills charmed as it were with Bushfire smoke. A perfect hour of pastoral dreamy loveliness – yes I lay there one hour enjoying as only the few are privileged to enjoy and I wanted for nothing.

Arthur Streeton, from a letter to Tom Roberts, April 1892

associated the city with materialism, conformity and the debilitating side effects of industrialisation. In doing so, they laid the foundations for the ambivalent contrasting of country and city, nature and culture, that was to complicate artists' visions of Australian identity for years to come.

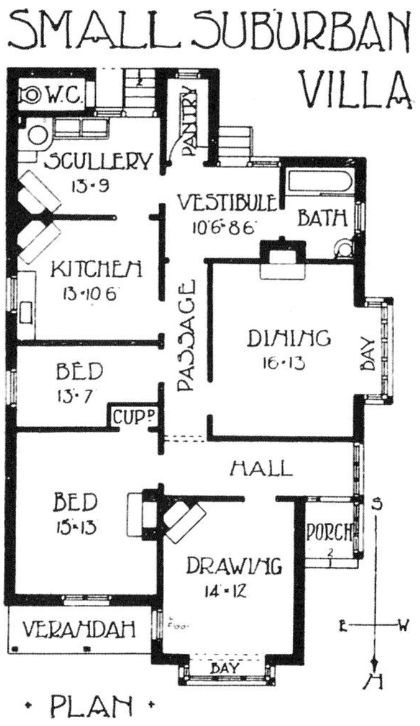

Robert J. Haddon,
"Small Suburban Villa", c. 1908

Artists and suburb-dwellers alike sought to escape the city centre. But if the latter were happy simply to leave behind the material discomforts of the centre for the gardens and villas of the suburbs, the artists went one step further. Artists argued that Australian identity could only be found beyond the city, in the exploits of pastoral workers and bushmen. And yet the Heidelberg School artists were no bushmen; they painted for an urban audience, conforming to urban ideologies. Their pictorial myth-making allowed 'city bushmen' to imagine an affiliation with bush life, even if their only contact with it was through illustrated newspapers or sedate picnics at designated beauty spots.

Arthur Streeton's *Near Heidelberg* (1890) is typical of this phenomenon. Painted in high tones of blue and gold, it answered the demand for a style that captured the distinctive qualities of the Australian landscape. The intense glare of the Australian sun, and the sparse vegetation and broad expanse of the bush are all there, but an odd note is sounded by the figures in the foreground, strolling casually in their finery. These are day-trippers, not bushmen; they follow well-beaten paths in a tamed landscape. Even the scraggly limbs of the gum trees take on a decorative role in Streeton's composition, rendering the bush amenable by conferring a picturesque ambience upon it.

This, then, is a painting that negotiated a balance between a romantic desire for the wilds of the outback and an urban demand for order and comfort. In this respect, what the artist left out of his image of genteel middle-class recreation is just as significant as what he included. Streeton's view was directed away from the suburb of Heidelberg and the city beyond it, and towards the frontier of the horizon. He deliberately excluded the suburban reality of Heidelberg. At the time he was painting this image, Heidelberg was ripe for subdivision; speculators had already bought up land, and were waiting for the improvement of the rail link to the city that would allow them to reap their profits in a boom market. And of course, it was this same railway that allowed artists and tourists to escape to Heidelberg.

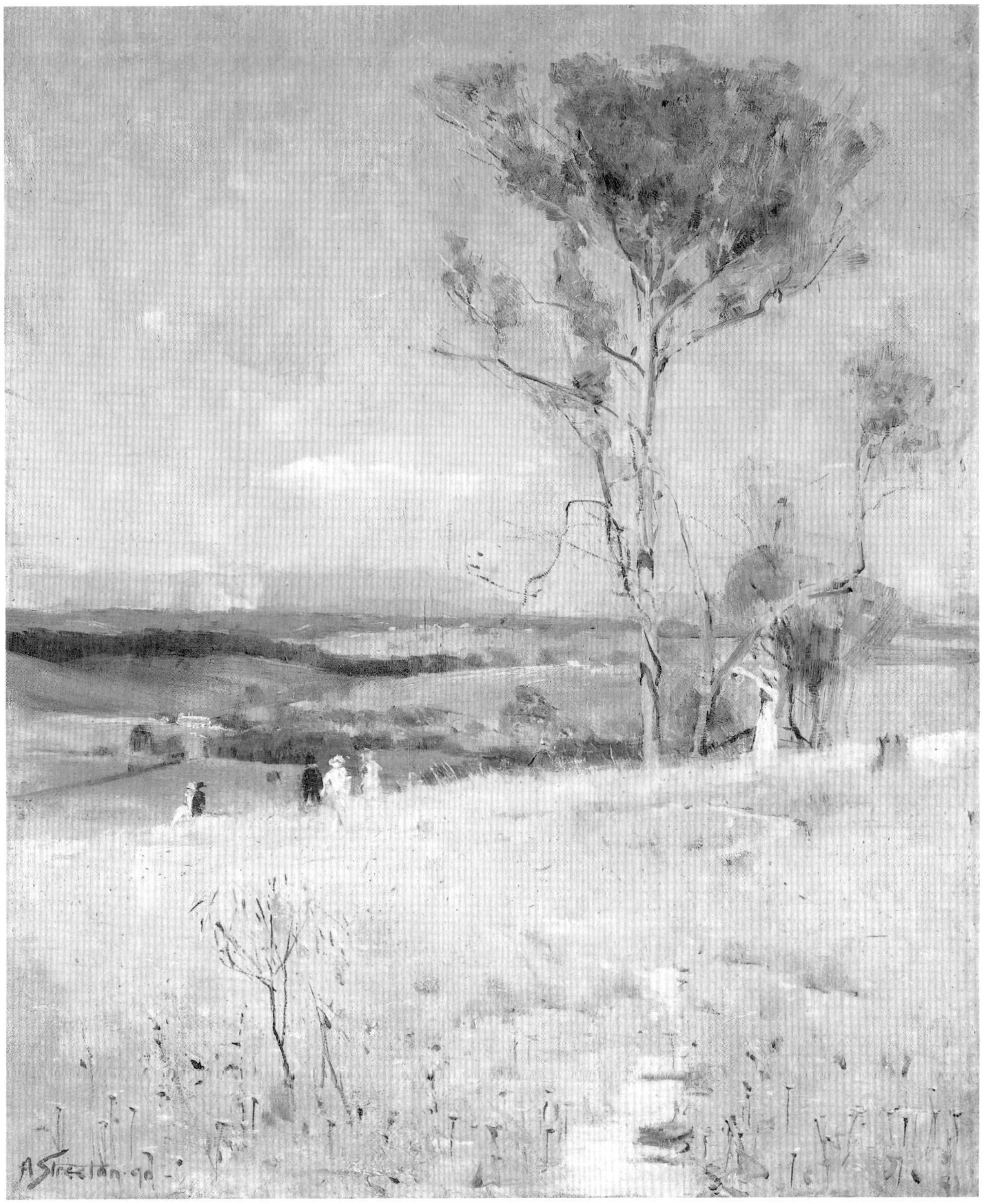

Arthur Streeton,
Near Heidelberg, 1890

The suburb sat on the margin between city and country, but its inhabitants still leant towards Melbourne. Indeed, at this time the most prized lots in Heidelberg were those that faced the suburb and city, not the bush. Significantly, the earlier plantings which were such an attraction to new settlers gave the appearance of a sedate English landscape, rather than rough Australian bushland.

Heidelberg, far from being a bush sanctuary, encompassed key urban ideologies: Capitalism, in the form of land speculation; Progress, in the form of the railway; and Arcadianism, in the form of a suburban balance of city and country. Streeton ignored all these, exploiting the temporary failure of suburban expansion (the railway wasn't improved until the turn of the century) to perpetuate the bush legend. The artist's relationship to the suburb was one of denial; to paint the suburb was to reveal a future, already imminent, that would necessarily relocate the heart of Australian culture from the bush to the city.

"A Walk from Kew to Heidelberg", *The Illustrated Australian News*, Feburary 1st, 1890

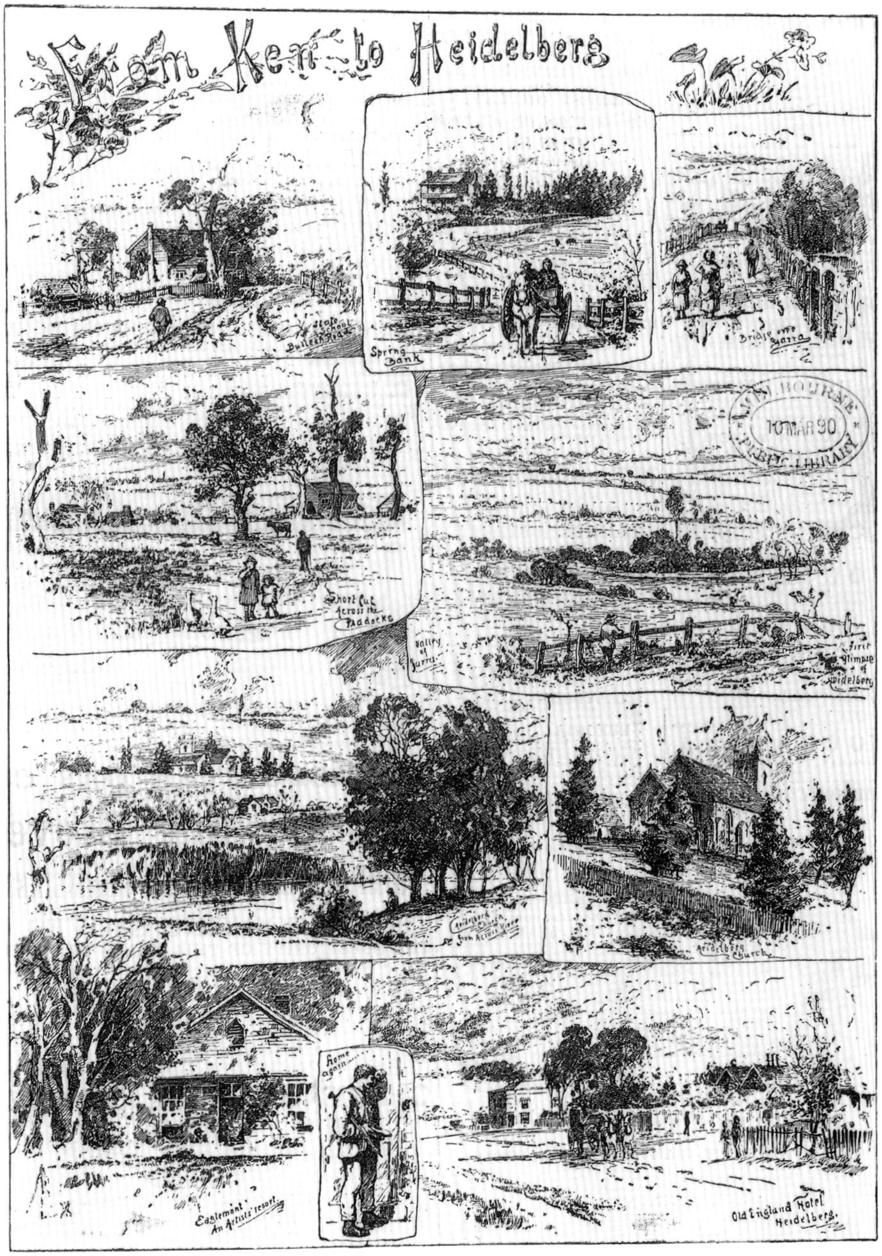

TWILIGHT OF THE PIONEER: FREDERICK McCUBBIN

This ambivalence can also be seen in Frederick McCubbin's *Winter Evening, Hawthorn* (1886)[Plate 2]. As the sun sets behind the distant spires of Melbourne, a workman, billy in hand, walks home to his slab hut. As was the case with Streeton, the painting contrasts city and country, and, by implication, past and future. The rural pioneer has founded the city, only to be overshadowed and supplanted by it. The sunset metaphorically signals the twilight of the pioneer and the dawn of urban Australia, a theme McCubbin also took up in his major work, *The Pioneers* (1905), and one common in the writing of Henry Lawson and Banjo Paterson.

But as with Streeton, McCubbin's metaphor rested on poetic licence and the evasion of contemporary urbanism. By 1889, Hawthorn was already a substantial settlement: its primary commercial activities were brickmaking, dairying and market gardening; it had a population of over six thousand; and it boasted hotels, churches, several railway stations, a town hall, schools, a library and a post office. The next year, electricity was connected to the area, and Hawthorn was proclaimed a city.

While the worker in *Winter Evening, Hawthorn* might be read as a 'pioneer' (a selector or farm labourer), it is more likely that he was a waged or day labourer. The artist implicitly acknowledged the

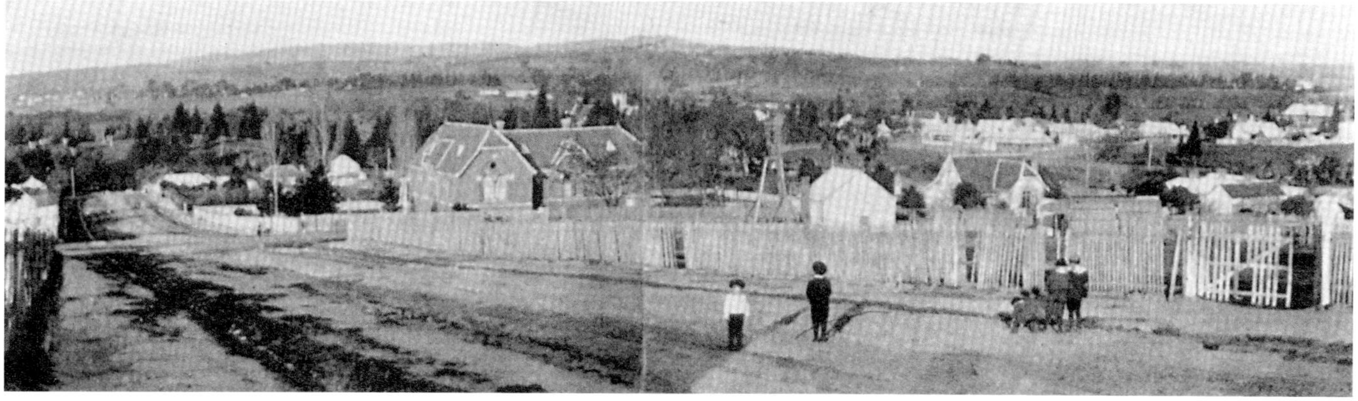

"A Picturesque Suburb" (Heidelberg), *The Australasian*, February 6th, 1897

reality of the suburb — the expanse of the city is evident in the background — but attempted to conceal, or at least defer, its existence beneath a nostalgic metaphor.

THE GENDERED LANDSCAPE

Even at this early stage in the history of white Australia, a key motif — the feminisation of the suburb — can be detected in the contrast between Tibbits and the Heidelberg School. The bush images of the Heidelberg School were executed in the authoritative, high-status medium of oil paint: Tibbits's urban scenes were painted in watercolour, a medium associated with amateurs, and particularly with women. The scale of Heidelberg School paintings was heroic: Tibbits's was domestic, intimate. Their landscape spaces were expansive: his were enclosed. The figures in Heidelberg School paintings are independent and self-possessed: Tibbits's dream homes appealed to a growing status consciousness and social climbing.

Australia was touted as an environment that would generate a 'new man', but which was it to be: the man's man of the bush, or the domesticated, feminised man of the suburbs? In strictly geographical terms, the suburb is a border zone, on the margin between city and country. But it is clear that by the late nineteenth century the suburb

No European manufacturing city 'boasts' more hideous suburbs. Places like Newtown and Enmore, Paddington and the Glebe, are simply that congerie of bare brick habitations, which is just as much an arid desolate waste as the mid-desert ... Utterly unrelieved by tree or grass, they oppress the soul and shrivel up every poor little instinct and aspiration towards natural purity and beauty in man, woman and child. The shoddy contractor despotises here in his vilest and most hateful shape.

Francis Adams, from *The Australians: A social sketch,* 1893

and suburban life marked, in shifting and uncertain ways, certain ideological borders between masculine and feminine, industry and pastoralism, speculative capital and productive labour, past and future, myth and reality. The achievement of the Heidelberg School lies not so much in their development of an iconography of the bush legend as in their ability to conceal these oppositions.

suburb to suburbia

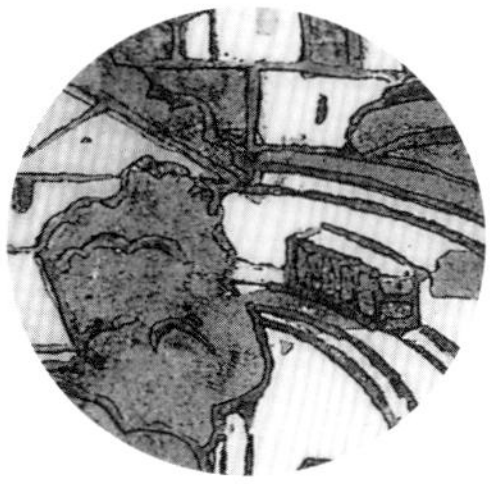

After World War I there was a popular sense that Australia had matured as a nation and was entering the company of more-developed industrial nations. Manufacturing industries grew, international corporations began establishing local branches, and Australia's average income was among the highest in the world. Cities and suburbs became increasingly prominent features of Australian life. In 1921, for example, just under half of New South Wales's population lived in Sydney, while Melbourne housed over half of Victoria's population. With the rural population declining, it seemed that cherished visions of Australia as a pastoral nation were becoming outmoded.

In discussions of national character, however, urban living had an ambivalent status. On the one hand, the growth and modernisation of cities was taken as evidence of Australia's prosperity and progress. On the other hand, modernisation brought uncertainty and instability; new ways of life, new forms of behaviour, and an increasing distance from the rural roots of the Australian legend. Definitions of Australia as a nation embodying the struggle, perseverence and self-reliance of a (white) pioneer population, settling and taming a rural frontier, were becoming an anachronism.

These uncertainties were exacerbated during this period by the dramatic social upheavals of depression and wartime. Great diversity is therefore evident in the urban imagery of these years. Artists such as John D. Moore, Clarice Beckett and Margaret Preston turned to the modern forms and debates of this period, while Sali Herman, Noel Counihan, Danila Vassilieff and Albert Tucker were among those artists who responded to the changes to the inner suburbs wrought by the Depression and World War 2.

The modernist home would be so designed and constructed as to best fulfill the requirements of a modern family which rides in modern motor cars, wears modern dress, eats meals cooked by modern methods, employs the modern machinery of the household, and is alive to the aspirations and impulses that stimulate this contemporary generation.

Building Industry Congress of Victoria, from "Modern homes for modern people", 1934

THE MODERN CITY

New suburban forms came to dominate Australia's cities in the decades after the war. In new or expanding suburbs such as Heidelberg and Preston in Melbourne, the terrace row gave way to the detached bungalow or villa. In planned suburbs like Daceyville in Sydney, street-planting and encouragement of gardening resulted in greener, more open streetscapes. Flats began to appear increasingly in suburbs — such as Melbourne's St Kilda and South Yarra, and Sydney's Kings Cross and Bondi.

Material prosperity could be seen not only in the growth of suburban housing, but also in Australia's embrace of new technologies such as the automobile, electrified railway, cinema and radio. The increased pace of urban life and the new values of consumer society were seen as a threat to traditional social structures; the jumbled landscape of the city and the racy lifestyle of its modern inhabitants were regarded as signs of loss and danger as much as of optimism and progress.

During the 1920s the planned suburban subdivision, heavily advertised as an ideal combination of city and country, became common. Such 'garden suburbs' became more widely available as the post-war resurgence in financial investment and credit put the suburban villa within reach of the upper-working and lower-middle classes. Workers earning less than £400 a year, such as skilled tradesmen and clerks, might have taken advantage of the Victorian State Housing Scheme, which offered manageable monthly repayments with a 10% deposit for houses under £800. Small scale 'spec' builders, such as A.V. Jennings, first appeared during this period, further expanding cheap housing options.

As the ideals of town planning became more prominent in public discussions of urban development, the growing suburbs came to be associated with regularity and regulation. The utilitarian impulse of town planning, the paternalist rhetoric of local councils and government, and the strict budgets of developers: all contributed to the sense that the new suburbs were controlled and regimented. Their street layouts and facades reinforced this perception, seeming to eliminate the individualism thought to be so central to Australian character.

This characterisation of suburban development remained dominant throughout the Depression and World War 2, with the persistence of decorative revivalist styles (such as Queen Anne, Spanish Mission and Tudor) and only occasional, belated interest in the International Modernist style of architecture. In the inner suburbs, the ongoing decrepitude of slums led eventually to the slum redevelopment campaigns of the war years.

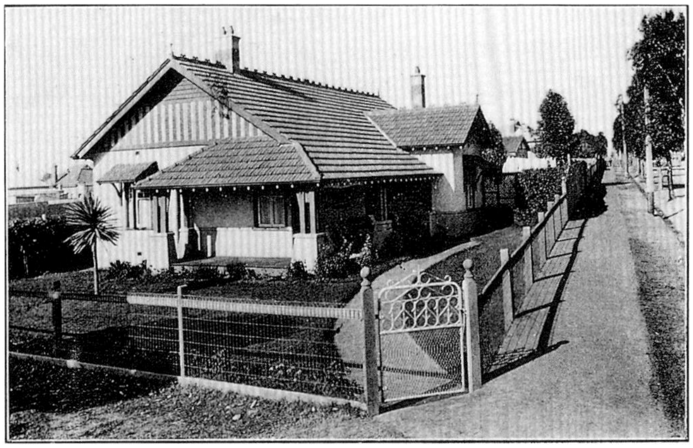

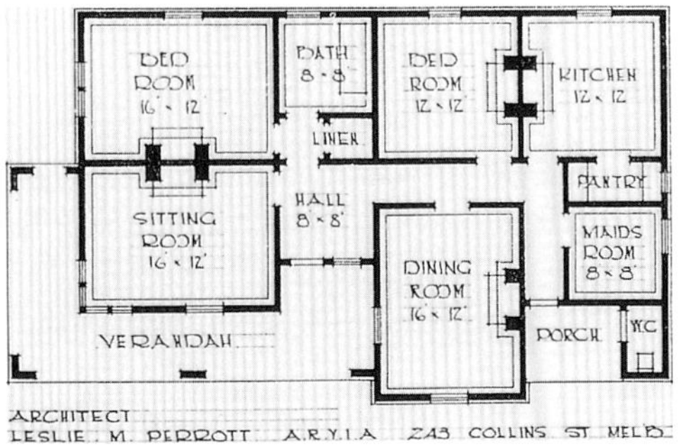

Concrete house, 1922

A HOME FIT FOR HEROES?

As the urban realities of Australia steadily overtook the bush in the 1920s and beyond, antipathy to the suburbs was both more pronounced and more complex than it had been at the turn of the century. While myth-makers like official war historian C.E.W. Bean fought a rearguard action, transforming the ethos of the bush myth into the ANZAC legend, cultural commentators saw the bushman irrevocably succumbing to the comforts of the city. At this time, words like 'suburban' began to be used in a disparaging sense. And if the city became more prominent in art, the images did not necessarily grow more positive. Even as modernist artists celebrated icons of urban progress such as the Sydney Harbour Bridge, many artists still understood the city in terms of nineteenth century conventions; for them, urban life still embodied congestion and filth.

Regardless of how the inhabitants of these new suburbs felt — there is evidence of strong satisfaction and a sense of community — writers and artists were quick to develop metaphors of uniformity, oppression, conformism and anonymity. The cynicism of writers applied regardless of political position. Those with left-wing political views saw in the suburbs a surrender of the radicalism of the 1890s to the creature comforts of capitalism. As early as 1911, playwright Louis Esson had described the suburbs as a "spiritual Sahara". "The suburban home must be destroyed," he wrote. "It stands for all that is dull and cowardly and depressing in modern life. It endeavours to eliminate the element of danger in human affairs ... It denounces Art, enthusiasm, heroic virtue. The Muses are immolated on its altar of respectability." Conservatives, for their part, regarded the alleged conformity of the suburbs as evidence that democracy was an anti-libertarian force; the suburbs, they claimed, levelled off the very individualism and independence that lay at the heart of the Australian character.

Australian artists of this period thus found a number of options available to them if they chose to depict the suburbs: they could persist with the nineteenth-century condemnation of the chaos, congestion and squalor of city life; they could pessimistically acknowledge the suburbs as evidence of the decline of rural values; they could negotiate a compromise in which modernity was given a subdued presence, balanced out by the conventions of landscape painting; or they could embrace the realities of urban life with all the threat of instability and promise of change — particularly in terms of women's role — that these brought with them.

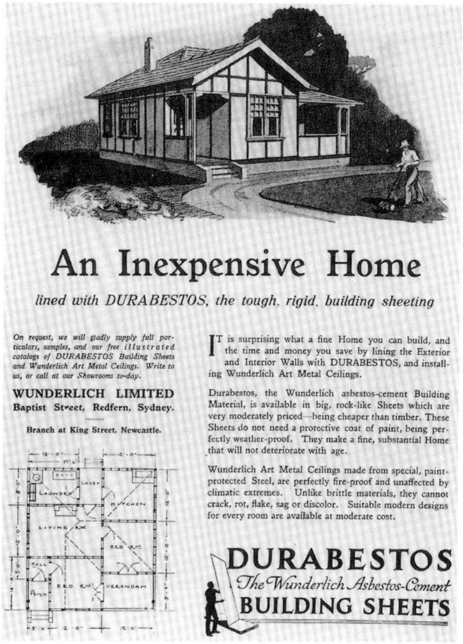

"An Inexpensive Home", c.1925

CHAOS: JOHN D. MOORE

So controversial was the suburb that it seemed almost impossible for it to fully satisfy any artist's vision of Australia: both the suburban expansion and modernisation of the prosperous '20s and the increasingly degraded inner cities of the Depression and the war could be recast in essentially nineteenth century terms.

John D. Moore's *Chaos* (1923) [Plate 3] shows a jumble of red tile roofs smothering the landscape. There is no evidence of the ordering principles of reason, of planning codes, of architectural regularity; no stabilising grid of roads, walls and fences.

Murdoch Street was an old sort of suburb, little squat bungalows with corrugated iron roofs, painted red. Each little bungalow was set in its own hand-breadth of ground, surrounded by a little wooden palisade fence. And there went the long street, like a child's drawing, the little square bungalows dot-dot-dot, close together and yet apart, like modern democracy ... The vacancy of this freedom is almost terrifying. In the openness and freedom of this new chaos, this litter of bungalows and tin cans scattered for miles and miles, this Englishness all crumbled out into formlessness and chaos.

D. H. Lawrence, from *Kangaroo*, 1923

However, the artist did not object to the suburb *in general* but only to the *unregulated* suburb. This is a didactic painting. Trained as an architect, and an adherent of the rationalist theories of Modernism, Moore hoped to convey the full horror of unchecked urban growth. It was not merely the randomness of the suburb that offended the Modernist's faith in order, simplicity and efficiency. The red roofs registered the suburb-dweller's determination to cling to the nostalgic and decorative symbols of the home. No 'rational' flat roofs or pure geometric forms could be found here. Moore preached the gospel of the French architect Le Corbusier, who had called the house a "machine for living in", but all Sydney offered were the nostalgic, decorative frills of the Queen Anne style.

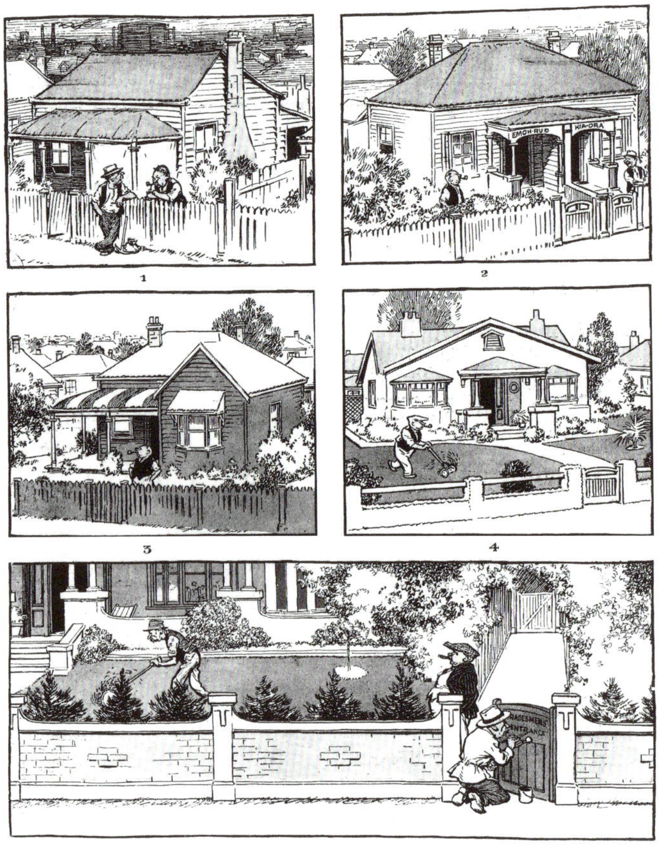

Percy Leason,
Getting On, 1927

Although it is generally assumed that an artist would object to the uniformity of suburbia, here the artist complained of an excess of individualism. Moore focused on the roofs of suburbia, one of the few architectural elements offering the possibility of variety in a geography of restricted plots and shrinking houses. He saw the problem in terms very similar to those expressed by D.H. Lawrence who also complained, in his novel *Kangaroo* (1923), of over-democratic and chaotic Australian cities.

Coming as it did from an architect's point of view, *Chaos* was unusual in the art of the 1920s. All the same, it pointed ahead to the images of the 1950s, laced as it was with misanthropy. Moore's work revealed how complex and confused the rhetoric of anti-suburbanism had become, for his work contained many seemingly contradictory qualities. Its ethos was both rationalist, in its demand for order, and idealist, in its dream of a perfectly planned city. Its spirit was humanist in its desire for a better world, and yet anti-humanist in the anonymity of the dwellings. While its faith in the ameliorative powers of the built environment suggested a materialist approach, its condemnation of unfettered development was anti-materialist. In style, it reflected modernist architectural principles, but it was painted in a conventional tonal-realist style rather than suggesting modernist abstraction.

Underlying Moore's and Lawrence's attitudes is a sense of the suburb that was inextricably, but very subtly, linked with class. Even in the nineteenth century it had been understood that one's residential address confirmed one's social status and could be used to improve it. But if appearances were a means of demarcating class, they might also confuse it. Moore and Lawrence adopted the position of a middle-class intelligentsia; condemning the housing of the *petit bourgeois* for being in poor taste, their complaints were perhaps social rather than aesthetic.

What was threatening to them was not simply kitsch houses but class mobility. As Percy Leason's contemporary cartoon from a 1927 *Table Talk* suggested, social mobility meant that one could no longer judge a book — or a home owner — by its cover. Improved housing was often advocated as a means of staving off social unrest and even revolution, but with the rise of the suburb, a different form of anarchy loomed — unchecked social mobility.

CONGESTION AND POVERTY: NOEL COUNIHAN AND THE SOCIAL REALISTS

With the depression of the '30s, and the looming clash of fascism, communism and democracy in Europe, some artists turned their attention to the inner suburbs, with their workers cottages, ageing terraces and boarding houses. In response to these overcrowded and impoverished neighbourhoods, Social Realist artists such as Yosl Bergner, Noel Counihan and James Cant depicted a barren environment of claustrophobic alleys, bleak corners and run-down tenements, peopled by emaciated and hollow-eyed workers.

Superficially these grim images of inner suburbs might reinforce the late-nineteenth-century belief that the city should be left behind for the comforting shelter of the outer suburbs. But the Social Realists presented the inner suburbs not as an evil in themselves but as a sign of the heartless neglect and self-interest of capitalism. For all their documentation of the ills of the inner city, they were careful to avoid stock responses. They did not suggest that slums be razed, although liberal reformers increasingly demanded

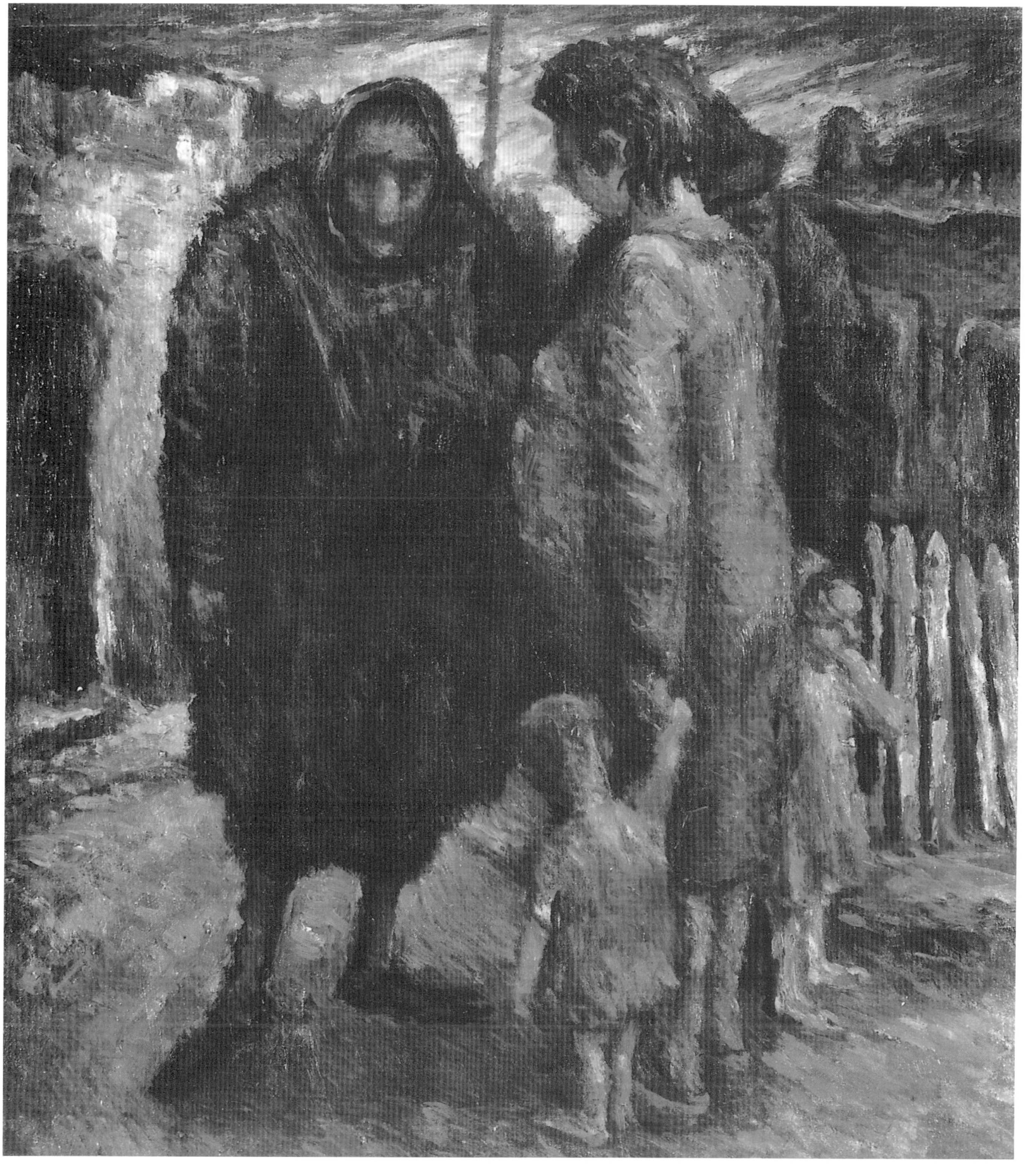

Noel Counihan,
At the Corner of Nightingale Street, 1944

this, for that would mean loss of community and self-determination for their inhabitants. Nor did they traffic in the moral panic peddled by the daily press and evangelical crusaders. Instead they sought to establish solidarity with the working class, being careful not to simply register them as somehow abject. Counihan's *At the Corner of Nightingale Street* (1944), for example, combines the actuality of the St Kilda street in which he was living, with memories of community life during the Depression.

Still, the word 'realist' must be used advisedly in discussing these works, for they are not without their own forms of myth-making. The depredation of the inner suburb was occasionally presented as a measure of the nobility and heroism of the working class. Some of Counihan's contemporaries complained that his was a middle-class view of working class life; too eager to emphasise the downtrodden, and unable to register adequately the vitality of working-class political aspirations or their own vision of themselves as 'battlers'.

All the same, Counihan and the Social Realists signalled a significant shift in the depiction of the suburb; they focused on the people who lived there, rather than the architecture surrounding them. In sharp distinction to the implied misgivings about class mobility suggested by Moore, they insisted that suburban cultures and identities were inextricably linked with class.

The "Images of Modern Evil" came directly out of wartime Melbourne. Beer and sexual contests along Swanston Street, all along St Kilda Road from Princes Bridge, down to Luna Park at St Kilda ... I was still the outraged Edwardian puritan.

Albert Tucker,
interviewed by James Mollison, 1982

SQUALOR AND VICE: ALBERT TUCKER

One other approach with its source in nineteenth century Europe was the use of metaphors of sex and gender to describe city life, particularly the image of the female prostitute used to suggest the threatening instability of the city and modernity. Albert Tucker's "Images of Modern Evil" series of paintings portrayed Melbourne's inner suburbs of East Melbourne and St Kilda as dark, damp environments populated by lascivious, mutated mannequins. These areas, on the fringe of the central city, were imagined by Tucker as places where the corruption or immorality hidden in city life overflowed and became visible.

Sensual, especially sexual, gratification was the motive force of these areas, according to Tucker, a self-confessed moralist. Darkness, sexuality, women and the city came together in these images in a veritable encyclopedia of turpitude. Throughout the series, Tucker clearly struggled with these themes; repeatedly attracted to them, he used his paintings to both exorcise and condemn the immorality he attributed to the modern city. And yet, by the artist's own admission, there was an anachronistic quality to his condemnation of the inner suburbs; if evil was to be attributed to the city, it would, by the late 1940s, be more immanent, less lurid.

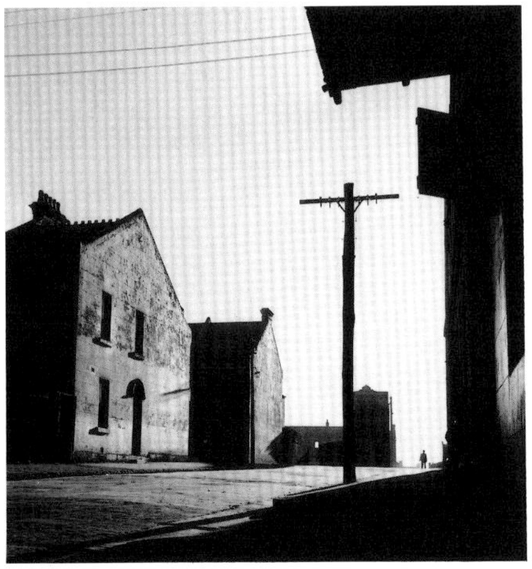

David Moore,
Surry Hills Street, 1948

CITY LIFE, VILLAGE VALUES: SALI HERMAN; DANILA VASSILIEFF

If the Social Realists, particularly after the Depression, used the inner suburbs as a symbol for all that they felt was wrong with Australia — poverty, class inequalities, oppression — Sali Herman and Danila Vassilieff found in them the virtues of village culture, an essentially pre-industrial ideal of community, mutual assistance, interdependence and familiarity.

An image of the suburbs is not merely a record of Australia as it is or was; it is also a plea for what Australia might be or a lament for what Australia is seen to have lost. Sali Herman's images of the inner suburbs of Sydney are all of these. On a superficial level his works documented the topography of Woolloomooloo and other working-class suburbs, recording the humble traffic of everyday life with a sensitivity for the human scale of their space and architecture. Even doing this, however, meant entering into existing cultural debates, for Herman explicitly counterposed what he saw as the reality of his city paintings to the 'fantasy' of what he derisively dubbed the 'gum tree school'. When his 1944 painting *McElhone Stairs* won that year's prestigious Wynne Prize for landscape, it triggered surprised debate. It was still difficult for some to accept that the city could be regarded as a 'landscape' in the artistic sense of the word.

Yet while Herman insisted upon aesthetic modernity — a new world generated a new art, he claimed — the weathered walls and mysterious alleys of his canvases imply that only the patina of age, and an 'old world' ambience, constituted a genuine urbanism. In his *Suburbia* (1947) Herman pointedly contrasts the human scale of the suburb with the modern city — complete with radio tower — in the background. Although this approach acknowledged that the bush was an increasingly distant and unrealistic measure of national character, the city did not offer any ready substitute. Herman seemed satisfied with Sydney only after filtering it through the centuries-old European genre tradition, which provided artists with a formula for the picturesque portrayal of peasant life.

While Woolloomooloo and Glebe, the most frequent settings for Herman's work, were reputedly squalid, Herman found character and community there, precisely the qualities said to be lacking in the new, outer suburbs. This gave a certain ambivalence to Herman's suburbs: they were modernist in ambition but nostalgic in mood; an Australian vista legitimated only through an appeal to a European model; the inner suburbs rehabilitated but reaffirming the ills of the new, outer suburbs.

All the same, the genre tradition allowed artists to develop a positive vision of the suburbs. Artists like Herman and Vassilieff began to consider the suburb as a site of

I had no 'philosophy of slums'. I painted houses, because houses are parts of people and people parts of houses.

Sali Herman,
interviewed by Elwyn Lynn, 1958

Sali Herman,
Suburbia, 1947

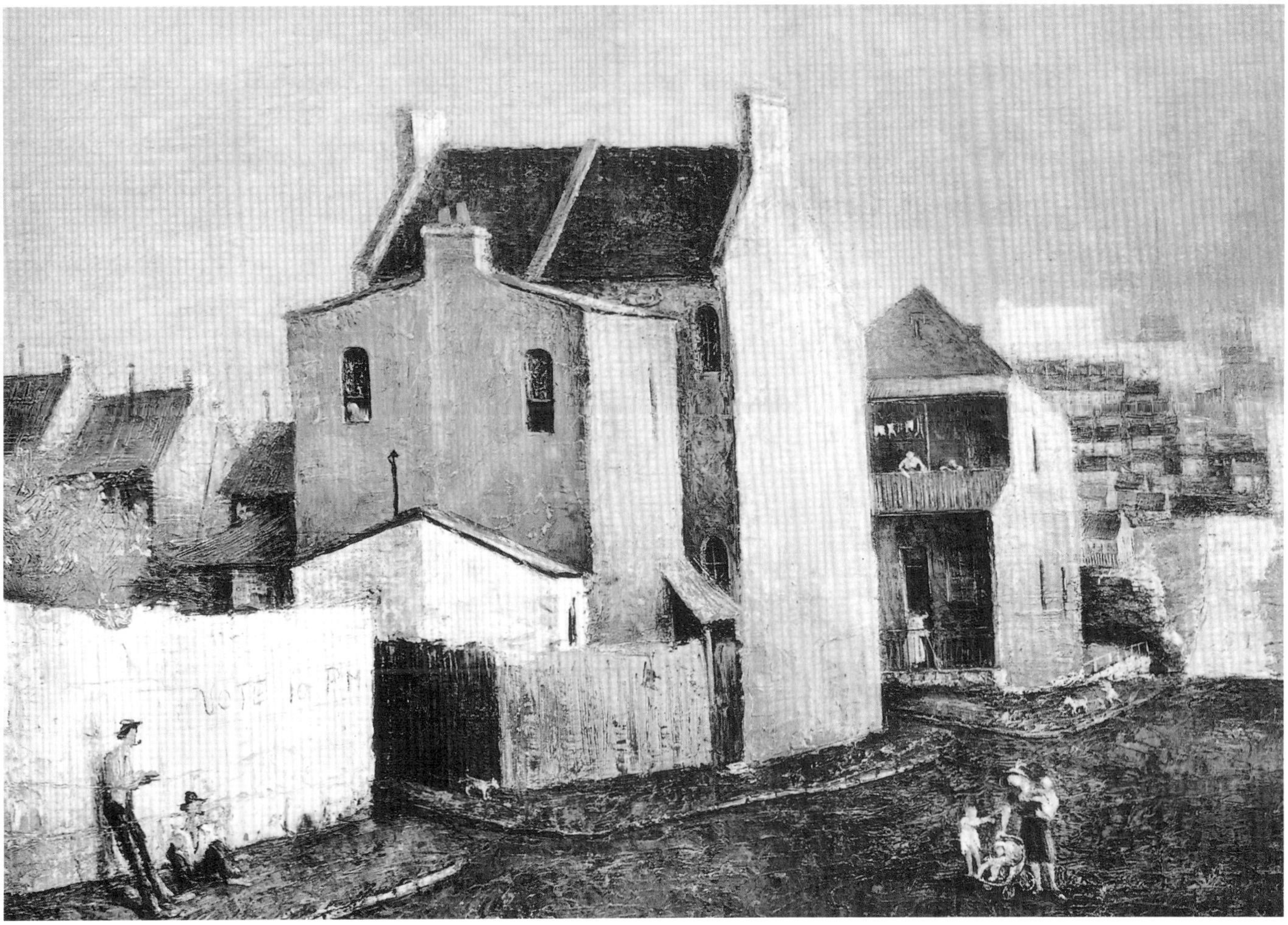

lived experience, rather than simply a built environment, a map or a terrain: that is, they developed an understanding of the suburb as a *place*, not simply a *space*. Many fine examples of this can be found in the work of Vassilieff, whose images of Melbourne's Fitzroy, executed in vibrant colours and energetic brushstrokes, convey a sense of life, even joy, in scenes of children playing, women shopping and neighbours chatting [Plate 4].

Even as moral crusaders decried the corrupting conditions of slum life, Vassilieff found childlike innocence, mutual respect and support in the inner city, depicting these with a light line and decorative colour without concealing the real struggles of the population. Yet the division between inner and outer suburbs remained; the genre tradition allowed Vassilieff to revalue the suburb — but only the *inner* suburb.

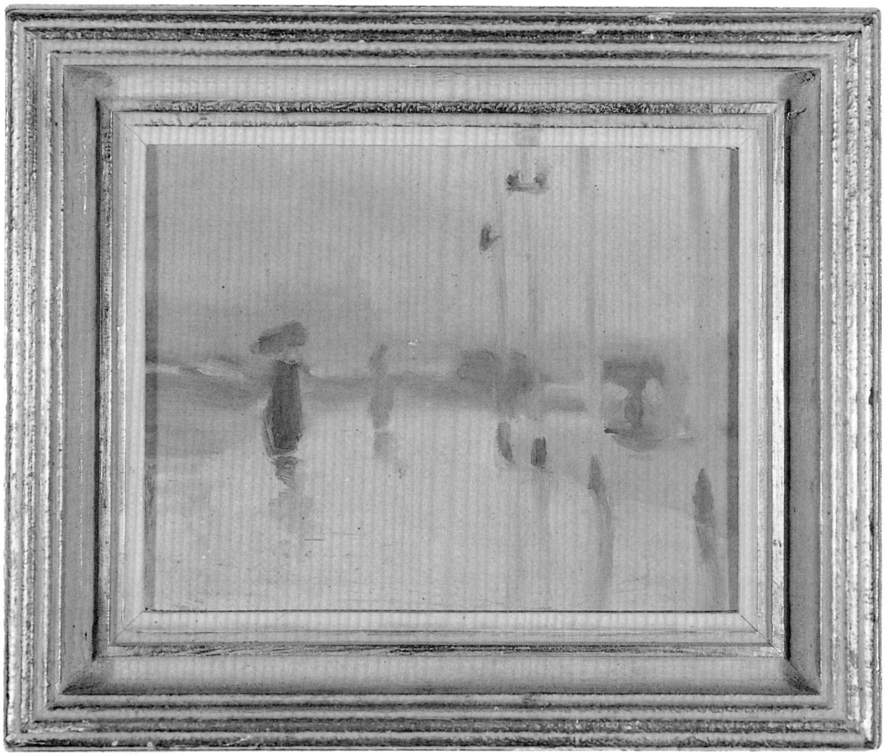

Clarice Beckett,
Wet Day, Brighton, 1921

PASTORAL REPOSE AND MODERNIST MOTION: ROLAND WAKELIN & ROY DE MAISTRE; CLARICE BECKETT

It is difficult to separate the suburb (a physical site) from suburbia (the states of mind associated with living at that site). The planning, promotion, settlement and habitation of suburbs are processes that produce material places but also social, ideological and psychic spaces. Yet for many years artists tended to concentrate on the physical features of the suburbs, leaving the less tangible psychic spaces implicit. Only as the patterns of suburban life became more commonplace, and its characteristics more explicitly articulated — particularly in literature and the mass media — did artists begin to address suburbia more specifically.

Even in the 1920s and '30s, when the post-World War 1 resurgence of suburban development, coupled with the growth of what is now called consumer society, made the lifestyles of suburbia a more conspicuous aspect of Australian culture, some artists still preferred to approach suburban lifestyle indirectly. Roland Wakelin and Roy de Maistre, for example, chose to evoke the suburban ideal of *rus in urbe* (the country in the city) by applying the artistic conventions of the pastoral landscape to the harbourside suburbs of Sydney. Theirs was a vision of undulating hills, inviting inlets and discrete houses nestled amongst lush growth. Their paintings displayed a tonal and compositional stillness that evoked the dream of quiet gentility. These views of the garden suburb mapped its ideal form but showed little of its life.

Clarice Beckett's views of bayside Melbourne likewise traced the appearance of the garden suburb; roads, fences and telegraph poles were everywhere in evidence, but were always held in check by towering trees and dense shrubs [Plate 5]. But the former elements threatened the garden suburb. Roads, fences and wires brought with them a geometry that straightened out the curves of the garden city, and signalled a demand for technological amenity that eventually saw utility take priority over the picturesque (a phenomenon still current in the recent outgrowth of cellular telephone antennas across the cities of Australia).

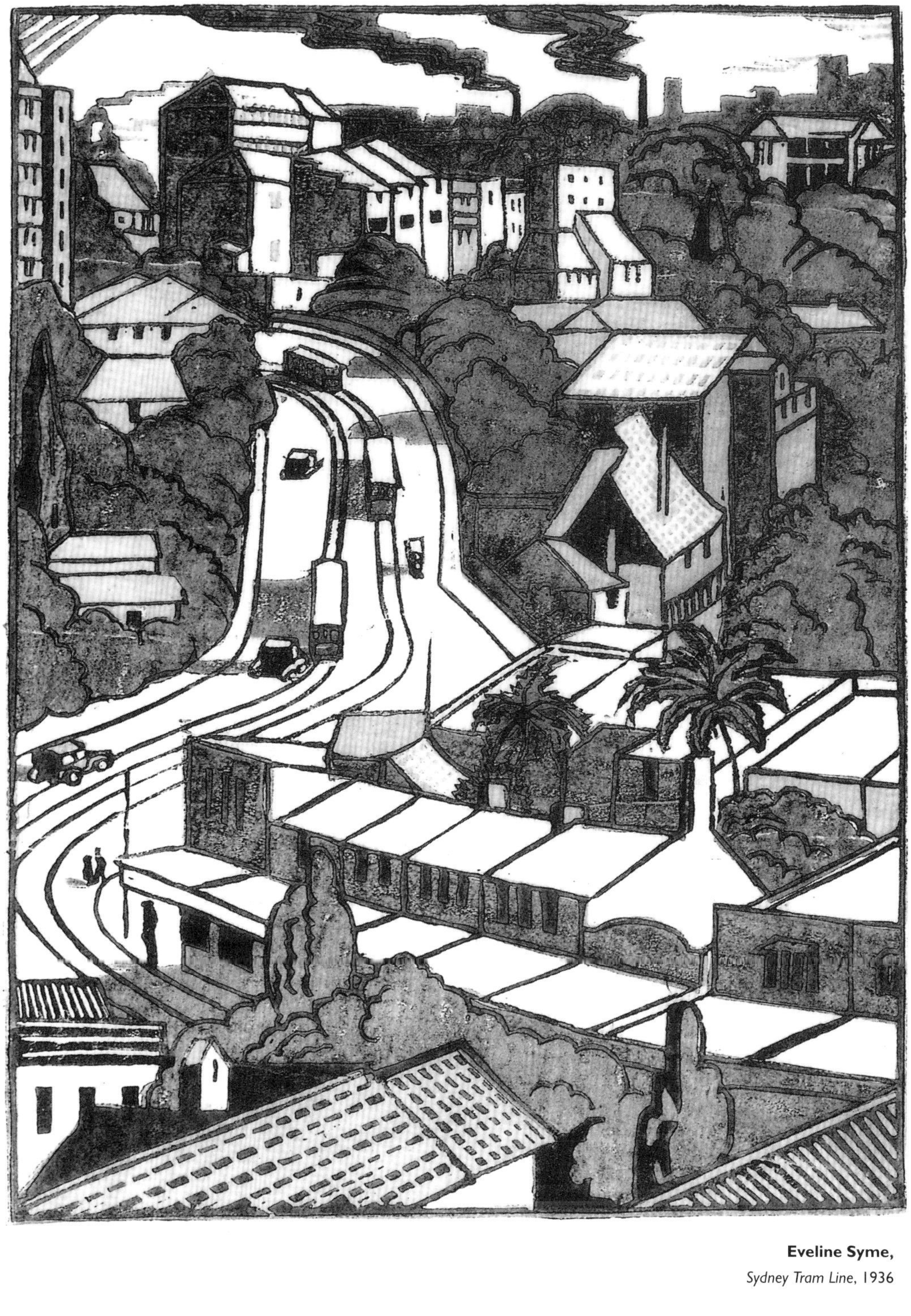

Eveline Syme,
Sydney Tram Line, 1936

The repeated motif of the car heralded a new version of the suburb — the 'auto-suburb'— which would replace the garden suburb with highways, car parks and garages. In fusing the automobile and the landscape, Beckett pointed ahead to the new urban geography of the second half of this century, in which the tranquillity of the garden suburb gave way to the politics of mobility; the city was no longer dwelt in so much as traversed.

Like Beckett, Eveline Syme conveyed a sense of urban space as being both local and mobile. Her view over Woolloomooloo in *Sydney Tram Line* (1936) registered the particularities of specific places — the city centre, the industrial zone, the domestic suburb. In the prominence of the road, tram and cars, however, she also emphasised the possibility of moving freely through and between these areas.

EMBRACING URBANITY: MARGARET PRESTON AND THE NEW WOMAN

It is in images of the domestic interior that suburbia is first encountered more overtly. The domestic interior introduced three crucial elements of suburbia: the often fuzzy distinction between the public realm and private life; the centrality of ritualized consumption in suburban life; and the gendering of suburbia as feminine.

Western culture, particularly since the industrial revolution, has marked a distinction between public and private life along gender lines. The public world of politics, commerce and industry was a male domain; the domestic sphere (child rearing, cleaning, cooking etc.) was designated as 'women's work'. The growth of suburbia saw an even greater emphasis on woman as homemaker. With the aid of machines, heavy domestic chores could now be assigned to women (male responsibility for rug-beating, for example, became the female job of vacuuming), extending women's duties, while confirming their domestic status.

The new suburbs offered the homemaker such modern amenities as electricity, gas and new household appliances. All these amenities, however, were commodities, heavily advertised in the burgeoning mass media of the 1920s and '30s. As participants in a developing consumer society, suburban women were targeted in campaigns intended to consolidate their status as homemakers and to convince them to perform their domestic duties using particular products, such as vacuum cleaners, washing machines, refrigerators and electric ranges. A 'dream home' could not be achieved without these products, the advertisers argued.

Yet again the old restless feeling is bothering her. She feels that her art does not suit the times, that her mentality has changed and that her work is not following her mind. She feels that this is a mechanical age – a scientific one – highly civilised and unaesthetic. She knows that the time has come to express her surroundings in her work. All around her in the simple domestic life is machinery – patent ice-chests that need no ice, machinery does it; irons heated by invisible heat; washing-up machines; electric sweepers and so on. They all surround her and influence her mind ...

Margaret Preston, from "From Eggs to Electrolux", 1927

This direct linkage of consumerism with the ideal suburban home had significant consequences. Household appliances, while promising relief from the drudgery of housework, only bound women more tightly to their domestic roles. The suburb, already seen as a feminine sphere because of its emphasis on home and family, was all the more emphatically cast as the antithesis of the public, male sphere. And so, in the consumerism of the inter-war years, the seeds of a series of oppositions still with us today were sown: the suburb as private, domestic, passive, consumerist, conformist — as feminine; the city (or bush) as public, active, self-sufficient and individualist — as masculine.

That said, it cannot be assumed that every image of a domestic interior was a suburban image, nor that all women were willing to accept the domestic roles broadcast in the media.

An image of an interior went beyond the domestic to the suburban when it addressed more than the simple appearance of the home; that is, when it incorporated ideology and class in images of modern consumption and display.

Typically this amounted to an emphasis on the particular forms of femininity constructed by the new imagery of the mass media. Femininity took on symbolic forms distinct from the traditional material activities of the domestic sphere. Sites associated with the public display of femininity (the dressing table or dining table) supplanted the private femininity of labour (the kitchen or the laundry).

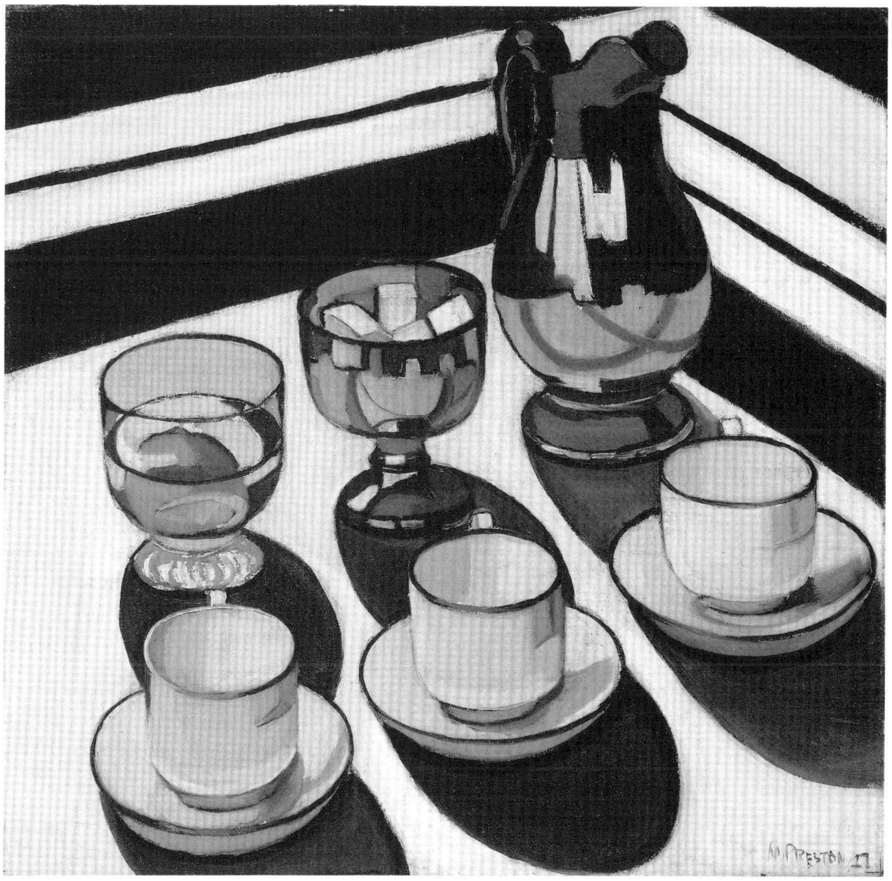

Margaret Preston,
Implement Blue, 1927

Margaret Preston's *Implement Blue* (1927) is a modernist still life in terms of style and at a social level. Stylistically it melds the traditional compositional sobriety of the classical still life with the spatial play of modernism. Objects are clustered in firm, architectural groupings with a careful echoing of shapes across the canvas. At the same time, the painting has a modernist's insistence on the two-dimensionality of the canvas. The backdrop is insistently flat, playing off against the volumes of cups, saucers and jug. A social modernity is evident in the emphasis on custom and consumption; the painting dwells on the implements and rituals of entertaining.

That women artists chose to depict areas designated pejoratively as 'women's space' does not mean that they accepted such ideologies unquestioningly; the formality of the tea party is, after all, disrupted by modernist spatial ambiguity. And indeed, artists such as Preston, Thea Proctor and Grace Cossington Smith were active in the public life of the Sydney art scene. Likewise, their versions of the domestic interior were stocked with the trappings of modernist consumption, featuring the latest appliances, fabrics, furnishings and interior design styles. In this sense the domestic interior became a site of ideological conflict and confusion.

Conservative male critics, unwilling to accept the strength of such art but unable to deny it, attempted to marginalise Preston, Proctor and Cossington Smith by using the bogey of a modernist, feminine domesticity to defend anti-modernist art. On the other hand, the artists themselves took an active part in the promotion of consumerist values, apparently seeing no threat in the linkage of gender, modernity and domesticity.

THE SUBURBAN HOUSEWIFE: DAVID STRACHAN; HARALD VIKE

If evidence that women artists had a particular vision of domestic culture is needed, it can be found by comparison with a male vision of the same sphere. In *The Gossips* (c. 1937) David Strachan invoked all the stereotyped negative qualities used to belittle the gendered suburb. In an environment of almost identical houses and faceless inhabitants, woman's role is that of idle gossip; a stark contrast to the productive and public role attributed to men. Unlike Vassilieff, Strachan showed no interest in particularizing the suburbs or their inhabitants, choosing instead to render both generic in the interests of a predictable anti-suburban rhetoric.

Later to attain a profile as one of the leading lights of the Sydney 'Charm School', Strachan made his drawing while studying in Melbourne at the George Bell School. While Bell encouraged students to apply modernist principles to everyday motifs, Strachan eventually turned away from city life towards dreamlike neo-classical figures and serene still lifes.

An untitled work of 1947 by Harald Vike on the theme of the feminised suburb demonstrates the extreme lengths to which artists had to go in order to come up with metaphors for suburbia [Plate 6]. As a concept rather than a physical environment, 'suburbia' was a good deal more difficult for artists to deal with than the suburb, which led them to develop symbolic or metaphorical vocabularies in order to convey complex and shifting meanings.

Borrowing from Renaissance paintings of the Enthroned Virgin, Vike depicted the contemporary housewife as a kind of Everywoman/Madonna. In spite of this sacred reference, this housewife's status is ambivalent. Enthroned though she is, her rule is a secular plebian one: a humble mop takes the place of the regal sceptre; over her head hovers not the dove that symbolised the Holy Spirit, but a winged purse; behind her not the plains of heaven but a small park and housing estate.

Vike's elaborate, even convoluted, solution to the demand for a suburban imagery tended to preserve, rather than resolve, its complex and contradictory status. This image might be read as one of either strength or subordination; the child evokes both the power of maternity and the 'barefoot and pregnant' status attributed to the housewife. Likewise, the double-edged sword of suburbia is in evidence; the tools of housework may evoke domestic drudgery but this negative is counterbalanced by the amenity of the park and the majesty of the woman herself.

Vike's, and other artists', efforts to reduce the suburbs to a determinate meaning were repeatedly thwarted by the symbolic overdetermination of suburbia within art and mass culture. Every attempt at defining the suburb within an art image was challenged by the new meanings given them within the mass media and, indeed, by the lived experience of their inhabitants.

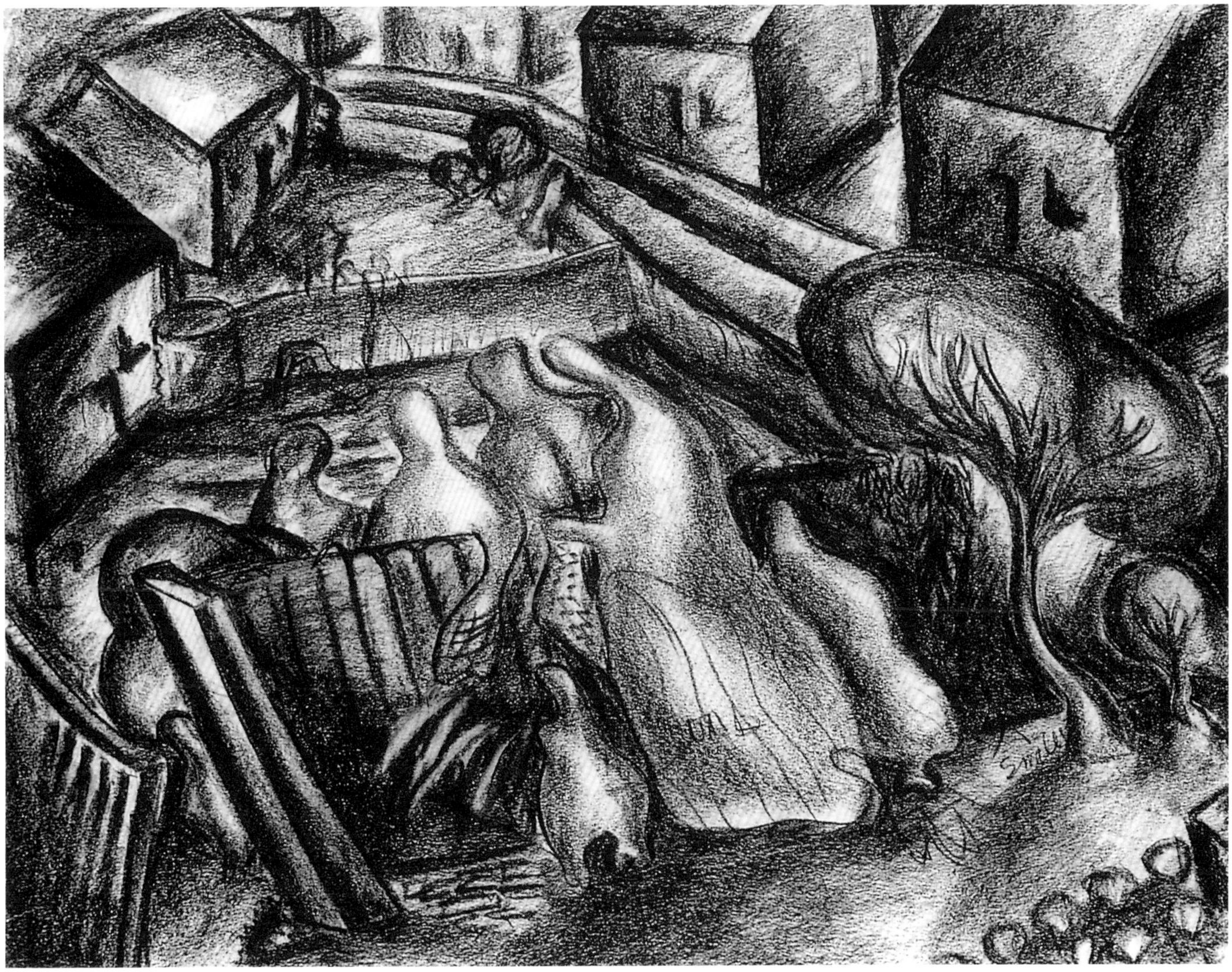

David Strachan,
The Gossips, c.1937

SUB

siren song

DIV

of the

ISI

subdivision

ON

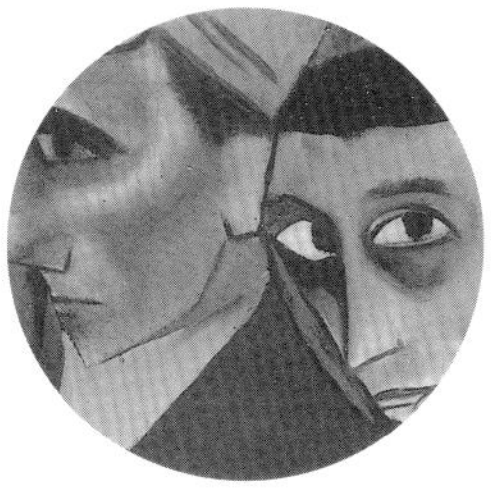

The 1950s was a period of dramatic modernisation in Australia. Urban expansion, migration, the growth of the mass media and consumer society: all thrust the bush legend further into the past, forcing Australians to accept that their future lay in the confusing realm of global consumer society. However, the nature of national identity remained a central concern for Australian artists and cultural commentators, even as the increasing diversity of Australian society threatened to confuse and complicate it.

The suburbs figured strongly in the new versions of Australian identity generated in the 1950s and early 1960s; both the fact that they appeared in art, and the way they appeared, were important symptoms of the crisis of identity in this period. For artists John Brack, Charles Blackman and Robert Dickerson the suburbs, and the rituals of suburban life, were a central preoccupation in their work during these years.

MODERN AUSTRALIA AND SUBURBAN DREAMS

In general terms, the increased prominence of the suburb in Australia after World War 2, especially the outer suburb, can be attributed to its centrality to post-war reconstruction. During the war, building had been restricted by rationing and shortages. The disruptions caused to family life during the war years by active service, evacuations and billeting further delayed housing construction, even as they increased the desire for it. The pent-up demand for housing that resulted was amplified by the baby-boom and large-scale migration of the post-war years.

The material home represents the concrete expression of the habits of frugality and saving 'for a home of your own'. Your advanced socialist may rage against private property even whilst he acquires it; but one of the best instincts in us is that which induces us to have one little piece of earth with a house and a garden which is ours ... My home is where my wife and children are; the instinct to be with them is the great instinct of civilised man.

Robert Menzies, then Opposition leader, in his radio broadcast "The Forgotten People", 1942

In practical terms such a demand meant that in the '50s new housing estates in the suburbs flourished and sold well. But the attraction of the suburbs had a more abstract, symbolic character. A new suburban home symbolised the reunion of the family, or a chance to begin one. It brought with it a sense of security, a return to order, and a chance to revive plans interrupted by the war.

As early as the nineteenth century, the spacious suburban home, with its promise of privacy and amenity, had been the goal of home-buyers. This dream had been noted by historians, cultural commentators and novelists. The status of this dream was exaggerated after World War 2, not simply because it had been denied to so many for so long, but because government policy and economic factors made it central to popular visions of Australia's future.

Government itself seemed to have accepted the suburban dream as an Australian right, and to have made it a key plank of economic policy. Suburban development was actively encouraged by government as a solution to a housing shortage estimated to be as high as 300,000 dwellings. Regulation of interest rates increased access to housing loans for home buyers, while an influx of public housing projects, long delayed by depression and war, increased rental stock for low-income earners. Cheap loans for returned servicemen had the appearance of a reward for those who had fought the war.

Highly publicised metropolitan planning schemes suggested that the suburbs were the approved model of Australia's future, while frequent references to industrialised building techniques and materials placed the suburbs at the heart of the modernisation of Australia. Home ownership, then, was not simply a matter of putting roofs over heads. Housing construction amounted to a significant proportion of national wealth; home ownership was — and remains — the largest single investment made by individuals. New housing seemed to embody modernity.

Yet for all the economic, political and individual will devoted to the construction of new, modern homes, the dream of an ideal suburban home was not easily achieved, nor

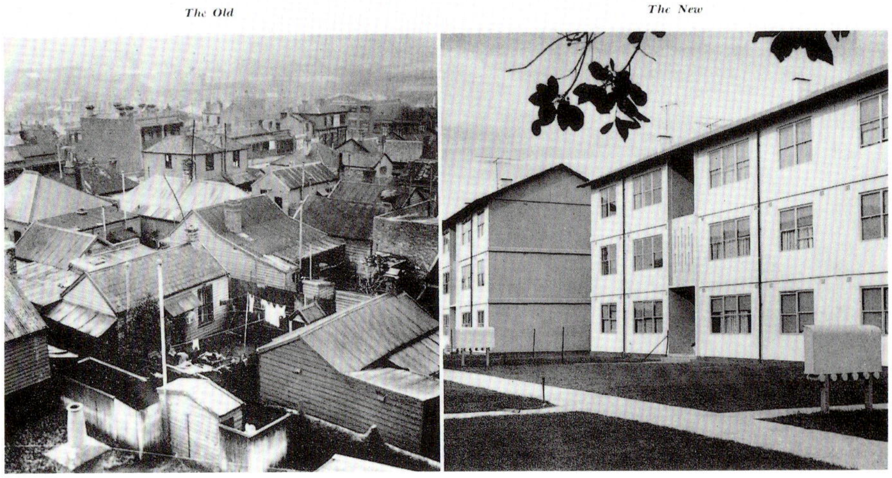

"The Old, The New"
Housing Commission of Victoria housing estate, 1958

was it without its drawbacks. Security, prosperity and independence were the attractions of the suburban dream, but persistent rationing of materials meant that in practical terms the dream was not easily realised. If home buyers hoped for a modern, high-quality house adequate to their present and future needs — this, after all, was what government and advertisers alike promised — they often had to settle for something less.

Rather than being a dream, the new house raised the spectre of compromise, of a long-term patching together of a home as supply and finance permitted. In the rush to build houses, infrastructure such as sewerage, roads and public transport was

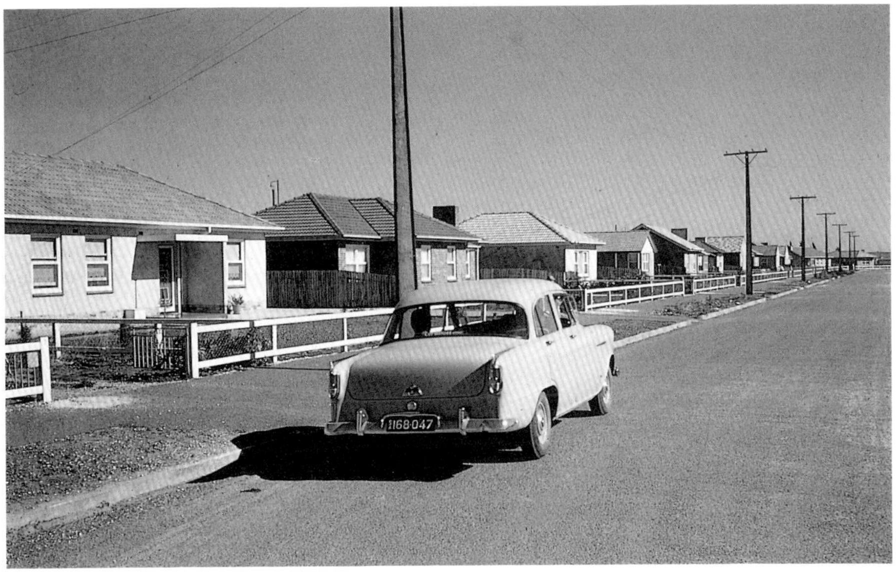

South Australian Housing Trust villas

delayed, leaving new-home owners struggling in poorly serviced developments. Yet even compromise and forced economy had a symbolic allure; the large numbers of Australians who economised by designing or building their own home generated a popular image of the suburban owner-builder as the new pioneer.

The relationship of the new post-war suburbs to the dream of home-ownership and to national identity was a complex one. The security and status of home ownership had an appeal evident even in the previous century. This sense of security was perhaps heightened by the linking of housing to post-war reconstruction. Likewise, the rhetoric of modernisation that coloured discussions of new housing suggested that the suburbs were crucial to Australia's future prosperity. At the same time, the post-war suburb was entrenched in an economy whose structures were increasingly global in form, bringing with them the threat of a dilution or destabilisation of Australian identity.

Writing on the period, Alastair Greig has noted the heavy emphasis on consumerism in housing. The 'suburban imperative' amounted to a package of house, household appliances and car, locking suburb-dwellers into a new global economy of advertising and consumption. Housing had, of course, always been a commodity, though most had preferred to think of it as an investment or as owning a stake in one's country. Now the commodity status of housing suggested that the very bastion of Australian society, the home, was to be subordinated to a consumerist economy.

Adelaide Flats, South Terrace

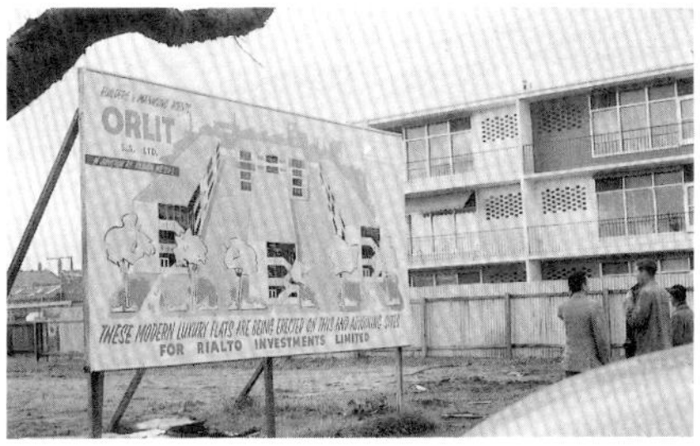

ARTISTIC IMAGINATION AND THE SUBURBAN DREAM

By the 1950s, the suburb was a disturbing presence for artists. Popularly considered to be one of the foundations of social stability, it had already attained a proverbial status as the epitome of uniformity. Some artists attempted to wish away the suburbs, playing

In a land of rolling plains and wide blue skies, a race of cheerful agoraphobes grew up in little weather-sealed boxes ... Out at the end of the Australian suburb, where raw new houses stood in shadeless yellow grass beside the rutted tracks, one seemed to suffer all the disadvantages of city life and enjoy none of the advantages ... What has happened to the spirit, the gusto, the faith? The twentieth century seems to have tamed and deadened and cheapened the Australian character ... The Wild Colonial Boy is selling used cars.

Robin Boyd, from *Australia's Home*, 1952

elaborate games of evasion or concealment. Others spoke directly of the suburbs but questioned the value of the suburban dream, suggesting that behind its promise of an ideal life lay the threat of dehumanising acquisitiveness and conformity.

In the artists' hands, slices of 'real life' turned into metaphors for disorientation, anxiety and bitterness. If artists sought to explore national identity they had to address suburbia, but in doing this they had to confront not only the deceptive promises of the suburban dream but also a clash between two of the conventional wisdoms regarding Australian culture: that art should reveal an essential national identity, and that Australia was fundamentally an urban nation.

The suburb was seen as the site of domesticity, conformity and consumerism, and these qualities were regarded as the antithesis of both genuine culture and of the legendary Australia of the outback. For artists, then, the suburb was marked as the enemy of art and Australianness alike, even though it lay at the heart of both. Even if artists avoided depicting the suburb, this very evasion, and the sense of unfamiliarity that outback imagery held for an urban audience, always preserved the city as an implicit presence.

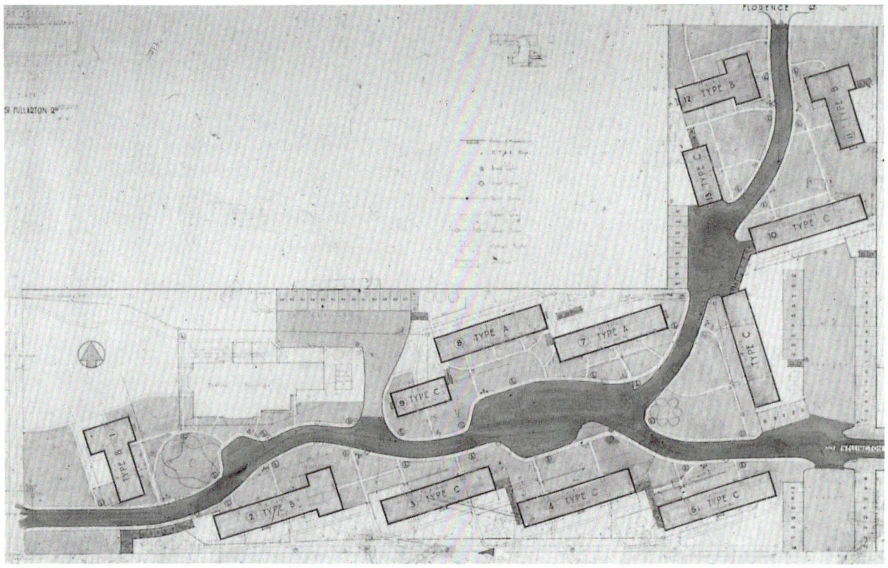

Plan of "Stow Court" development, South Australian Housing Trust, 1957

For Australian artists — who frequently addressed the suburbs, directly and indirectly, in the 1950s — the very ambivalence of the motif was productive. It forced them to confront distinctions between genuine and artificial culture, mythical and actual identity, historical dreams and everyday life. With grudging unease, a new generation of artists began to accept the suburb as the dominant reality of Australian culture.

While Albert Tucker still saw the city as the site of 'modern evil' and Sidney Nolan dreamt of an Australianness rooted in an outback mythology of explorers and bushrangers, the anachronistic qualities of such imagery must have been increasingly apparent, as post-war reconstruction steered Australia away from a rural, pastoral economy towards urban, manufacturing industries. But the 'problem' of the city remained, and was perhaps even exacerbated. If earlier artists had solved this problem by ignoring the city, or cloaking it in the visual styles of landscape painting or Social Realist art, the artists of the 1950s confronted it more directly, producing images marked by a wry, even bitter, resistance to what they saw as the cultural void of the suburb.

THE WEIRD MELANCHOLY OF THE SUBURBS: JOHN BRACK

Melbourne artist John Brack gave most attention to the suburbs, returning to the motif again and again. In many respects Brack's work embodied attitudes that were to dominate discussion of the suburbs from the post-war period and well into the 1960s.

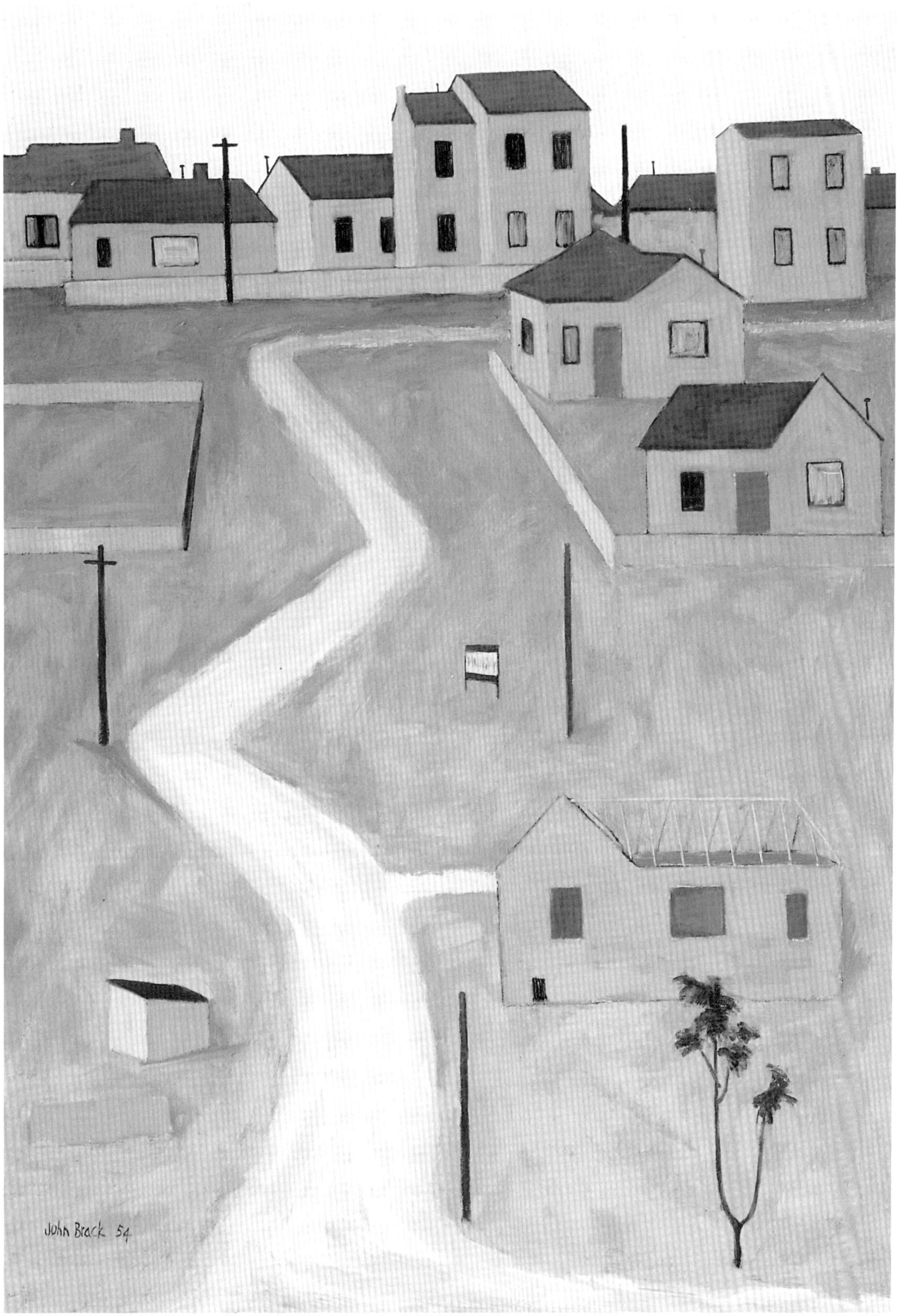

John Brack,
The Unmade Road, 1954

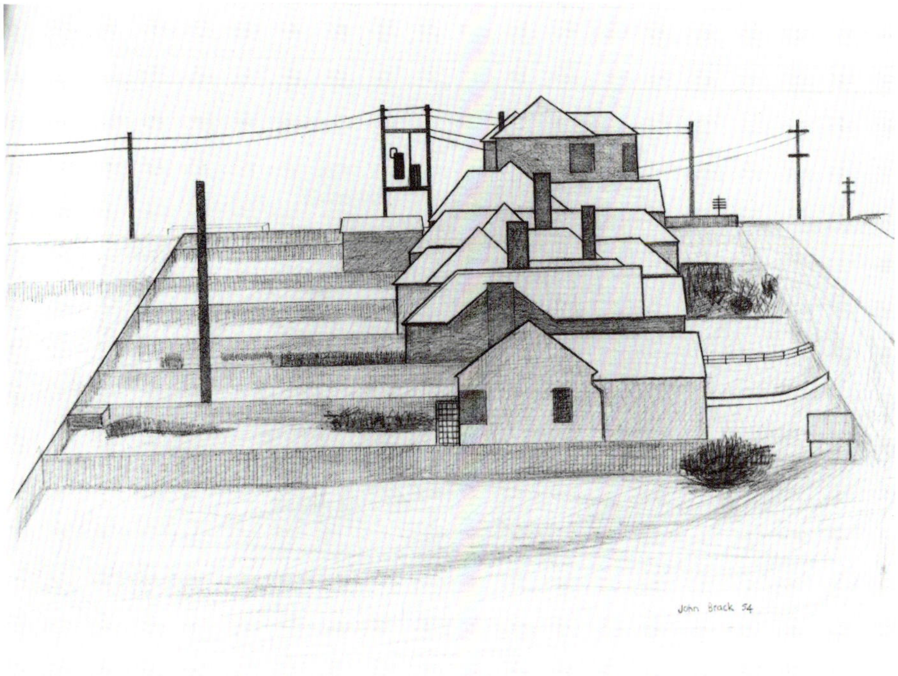

John Brack,
New Houses, 1954

Brack's art differed markedly from the dominant landscape imagery of the day, but his rejection of the outback iconography of artists like Drysdale and Nolan did not mean that he saw the suburbs in a positive light.

His suburbs were depicted as bland, uniform and lifeless; an existential wasteland. This was the suburbia that was also coming under attack — and would continue to be attacked well into the '60s — from novelists, humorists and architects. Particularly damning were novelist George Johnston, whose *My Brother Jack*, published in 1964, though set in the suburbia of the Depression and war years, is shot through with a typically post-war venom; influential architect and columnist Robin Boyd, with *Australia's Home* (1952) and *The Australian Ugliness* (1960); and Barry Humphries, with his '50s stageshow and record *Wild Life in Suburbia*.

What seemed particularly disturbing to Brack was the sense that nothing concrete had replaced the kinds of identity previously offered by the bush legends. In his canvases the urban landscape took on a pessimistic mood; the suburbs were depicted as flat, compressed spaces populated by hollow humanoids, all charted with a spiky line and a parched palette of browns and creams.

I had money in the bank and unshakeable self-confidence, my prospects were excellent: so it is not surprising that, with the benevolent assistance of the hire-purchase system, we committed ourselves deeply and eagerly to the panoply that was in keeping with our new standing ... The house was furnished in severely modern palewood furniture, and she chose sophisticated Indian mats and scatter rugs instead of wall-to-wall carpets ... She bought for the walls reproduction prints of the right modern paintings, both the van Gogh chair and his cypresses.

George Johnston, from *My Brother Jack*, 1964

There is more to Brack's pessimism than the waning of the bush legend, however. His paintings dwelt on a new Australia, or, more specifically, an Australia that had existed since colonization but could no longer be ignored. Drawing inspiration from the novels of Henry James, Brack's ambition was to distil the temper of a society into a forceful image derived from the observed world. He used an almost diagrammatic style to construct social archetypes whose sober clothing, fixed facial expressions and mechanical, ritualistic behaviour embodied Australia's anxiety about the suburbs.

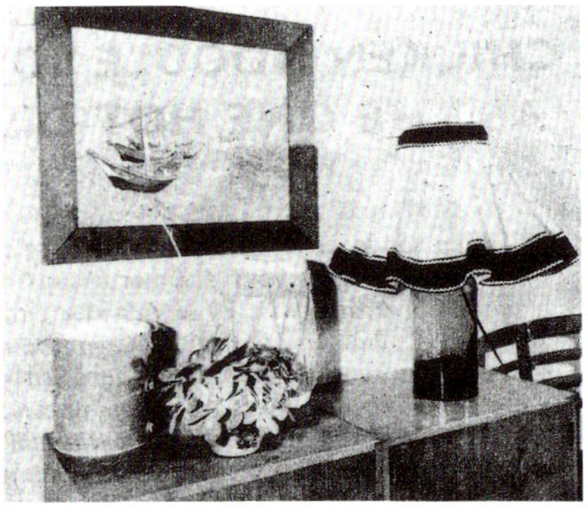

"Four Decorative Pieces", from *The Australian Womens Weekly*, July 22nd, 1953 showing van Gogh's *Fishing Boats on Beach*, 1888

The New House (1953) [Plate 7] shows cultural aspiration reduced from heroic nationalism to mere acquisitiveness. The happy couple, bursting with pride, can see no further than the domestic comforts offered to them by a world of subdivisions and hire-purchase. 'Real art', in the form of a van Gogh reproduction hanging above their mantelpiece — as advocated, for example, in the home decorating pages of the *Womens Weekly* — is regarded merely as decoration.

In this image, suburbia is made to stand for the loss of both a national myth and the possibility of authentic artistic culture. The world of the suburbs has none of the vibrancy, spontaneity or even texture associated with art; Brack's muted tones and evenly applied paint attributes a banal flatness to the suburban spirit. The contrast with van Gogh is poignant and highly personal, for Brack was inspired to become an artist after seeing a van Gogh print in a Melbourne bookshop. The taming of van Gogh in the suburban home illustrates the root of Brack's fear of suburbia: he saw it as an attack on his artistic calling.

The spectre of the feminised suburb compounded this fear. *The New House* represents suburbia as a woman's realm as distinct from the male domain of public work, often in the city centre. Once more the domestic interior, locus of feminine activities, repository of consumer goods, has man — in this case quite literally — in its clutches, the siren song of suburbia emasculating the husband and, by extension, the nation. Recent feminist readings of women's domestic role in the 1950s have treated the housewife more sympathetically, remarking on the struggle of women to find empowerment in their domestic skills even as domesticity itself hemmed them in. Such an interpretation, of course, had not been developed when Brack painted this work.

In several works Brack stressed the marginal 'borderline' status of the new, outer suburb, registering its crucial role in marking out Australian identity. Compositions were sharply divided between clustered suburban houses and the desiccated landscape into which they spread. An aerial point of view reduced the motif to a schematic contrast between city and country. Titles such as *New Houses* (1954) and *New Subdivision* (1954) emphasised the newness of these suburbs, insisting on the suburban future of Australia and almost sadistically reminding viewers of the demise of an identity tied to the bush. Here was the Australia that Streeton and his peers could not confront, now unavoidably, matter-of-factly, present.

In the nineteenth century, Marcus Clarke had famously described the 'weird melancholy' of the Australian bush. Brack now spoke of the weird melancholy of the suburbs. At the same time, the categorical uncertainty of these fringe suburbs — half city and half country — mirrored the growing uncertainty as to Australian identity: 'Home of the Bushman' or 'Cocacolony'?; outpost of empire or multicultural melting pot? For Brack, suburban geography could signal both the loss of the past and the uncertainty of the future; wedged between the two, the present was a realm of hollow ritual and meaningless repetition.

When he turned to the inhabitants of the suburbs, Brack represented suburbia as the triumph of a consumer culture with all its trappings; regularity, conformity and time–work discipline. Picturing suburban life as a kind of desperate holding pattern, he echoed the popular conception of suburbia as an existential wasteland. The peak-hour rush of *Collins Street, 5pm* (1955), the fleeting camaraderie of the pub in *The Bar* (1954), the carefully planned family outings in *The Car* (1955): all these rituals of suburban male experience revealed an acceptance of regimentation that was the antithesis of both the larrikinism of the bushman and the bohemianism of the artist.

Street after street of ugly, liver-brick tradesmen's cottages built in the 1930s, Roseberry is a respectable, working-class suburb further out... Wall-to-wall carpets, cream lace and brocade curtains hanging heavily at all the windows, blocking off the air — but there is a back garden with a lawn and two peach trees with fruit fly. A line of cypresses with a resident possum marks the back fence. We buy two white leghorns and I hang a print of van Gogh's *Cypresses* on the dining-room wall.

Dorothy Hewett, recalling 1950s Sydney in her autobiography *Wild Card*, 1990

"Wild Life in Suburbia", record sleeves, 1958-59

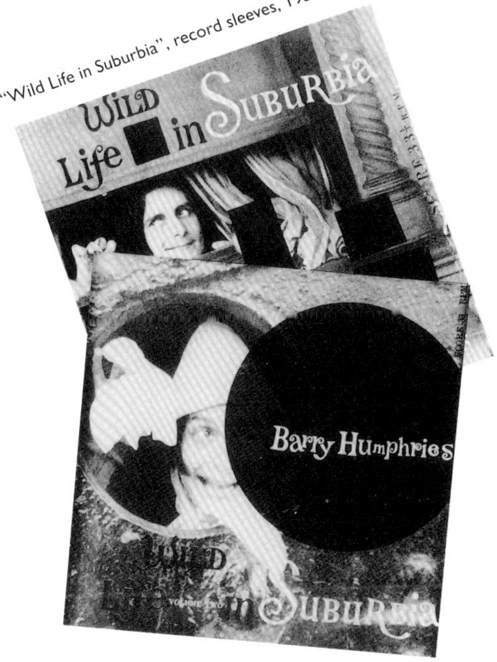

The shows were *South Pacific, Paint Your Wagon* / The claret gurgled from a Wynvale flagon / Espresso coffee and the ballpoint pen / The FJ Holden and Old Spice for men / The rage for square dancing, the new kool mints / The first ducks up the wall, the van Gogh prints ...

Barry Humphries, from "Prologue to the Fifties", 1984

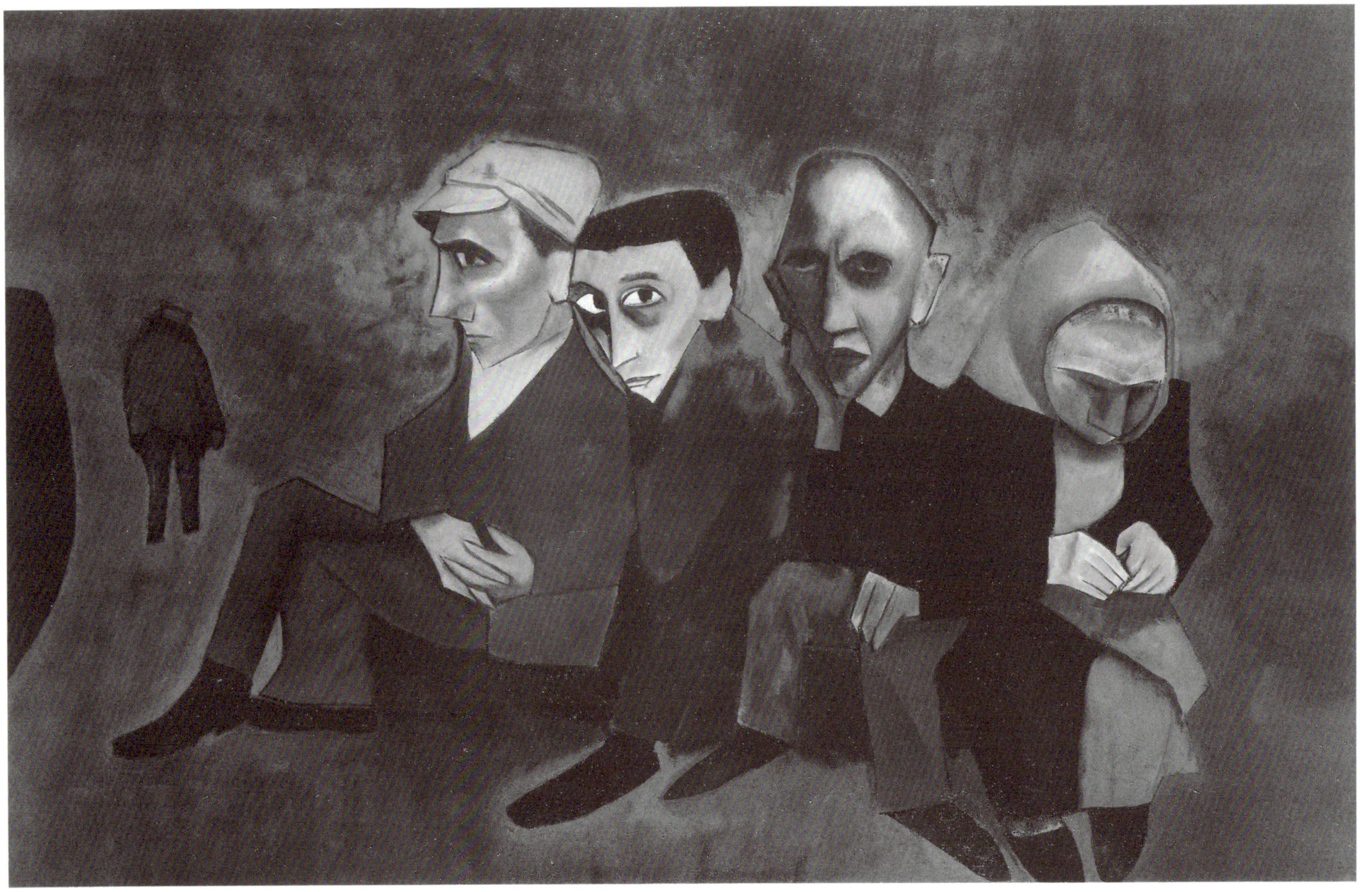

Robert Dickerson,
Wynyard Station, 1959

ADRIFT IN AN ANTIPODEAN WASTELAND: CHARLES BLACKMAN AND ROBERT DICKERSON

A similarly pessimistic vision of urban life can be found in the work of artists such as Robert Dickerson and Charles Blackman. The city is depicted as an existential desert; flat, parched and claustrophobic. Its denizens appear as hunched paranoiacs, frozen agoraphobics and downtrodden victims. In Dickerson's *Wynyard Station* (1959) a group of commuters huddle on a bench, brought into close physical proximity but making no social contact with each other.

As was the case with many of his works from this period, Dickerson seemed to see the city as something that drained the life from his figures, rendering them anaemic, even soulless. Blackman perhaps injected more emotion into his paintings of city life, but they were no less disquieting for it. His series of images of schoolgirls in Melbourne streets exuded a sense of innocence under threat, as if some physical or psychological danger lurked around every corner of the neatly laid out streets or behind the facades of sedate homes.

In such works by Blackman and Dickerson the classic anti-suburban themes are in evidence. The isolation of the figures and the emptiness of the streets point to a decline of community. Blank eyes, hollow cheeks and muted colours speak of a loss of spirit and spirituality. Inactivity or rote activity — commuting, in particular — suggest an absence of vibrant culture. The passivity of Blackman's and Dickerson's figures suggests more than spiritual decay; the loss of agency and loss of public life imply a fear of an emasculated, feminised modernity.

In 1959, as signatories to the *Antipodean Manifesto*, Brack, Dickerson and Blackman proclaimed the need for Australian artists to develop a new national imagery that would speak of regional experience in opposition to the increasing dominance of international abstract styles. But if their motives seemed positive, what they produced was an iconography of conformity and spiritual decline. Their images spoke of a loss of history and identity.

AUSTRALIA: A SUBURB OF NEW YORK?

The blame for this supposed loss of identity was attributed to the suburb. This reflected, if not the actualities of suburban life, then at least the fear suburbia generated among cultural elites. Worse still, suburbia appeared to artists to eliminate any possibility of generating symbols of national identity to replace those on the wane. For the uniformity of suburbia operated at an international as well as local level. It was not just that the suburbs made all Australians the same; they made Australians the same as everyone else in the Western industrial world.

Ladies! Your coach will shortly be crossing Hawthorn Bridge and entering the garden suburbs of Hawthorn and Camberwell. Here are to be found many stately and historic home units in the idyllic setting of lawn and flowering shrub. The many convenient shopping centres in this vicinity offer every amenity and facility to discriminating purchasers and housewives.

Barry Humphries
(monologue as Jeff Pritchard), 1959

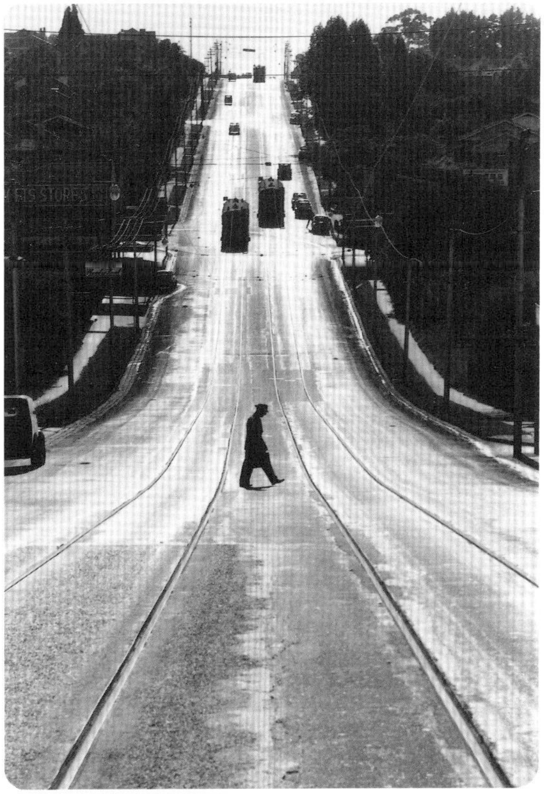

Mark Strizic,
Riversdale Road, Camberwell, c.1960

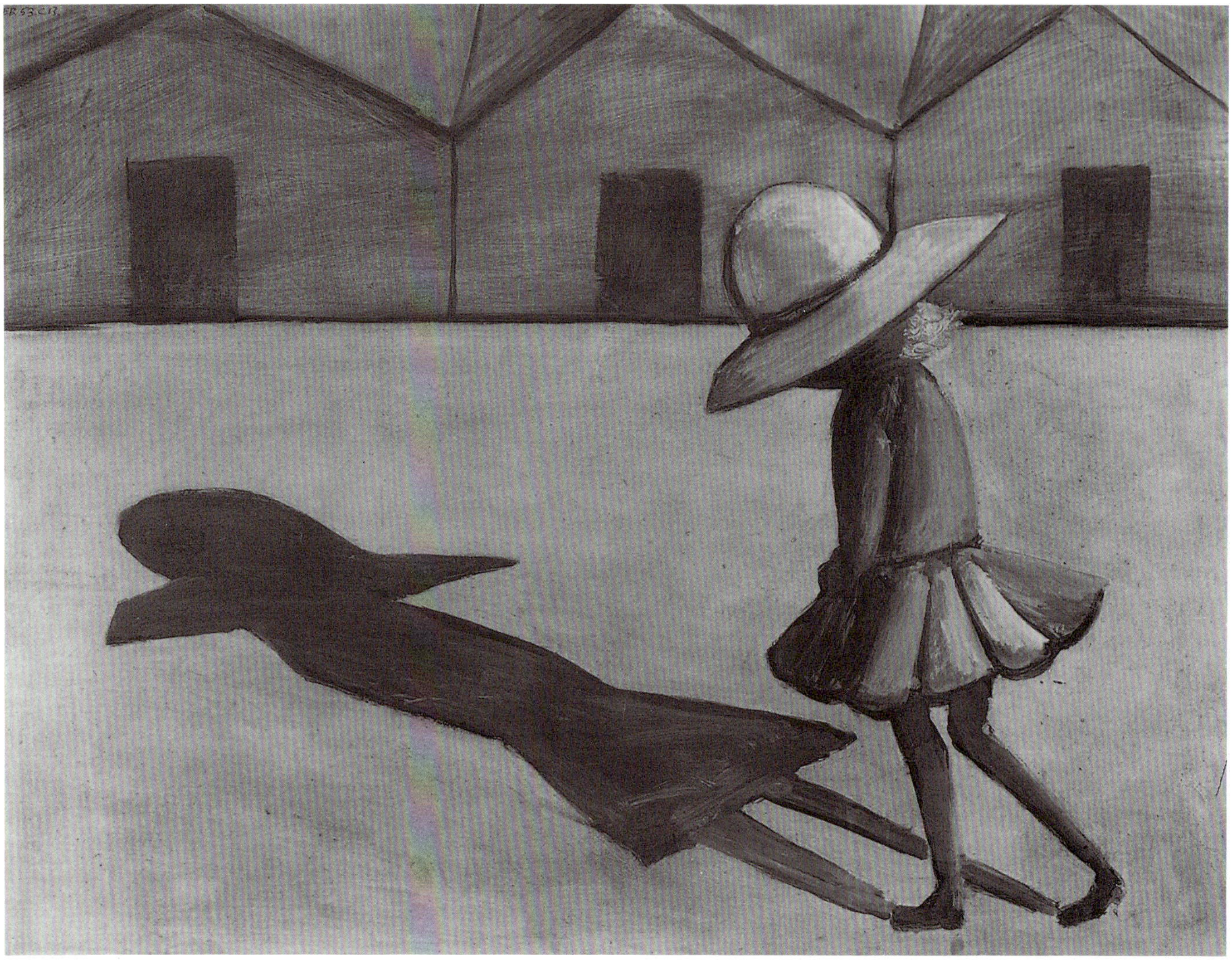

Charles Blackman,
The Shadow, 1953

This sense that Australia had become part of international culture at the expense of regional identity pervaded Australian art and culture in the 1950s and 1960s. It was articulated in the so-called 'provincialism' debates that raged well into the 1970s. Australian art was discussed metaphorically in terms of city, suburb and country. In emulating international trends, it was argued, Australian artists would become provincial copyists of metropolitan styles; Australia would merely be a 'suburb' of New York. On the other hand, if international trends were ignored, Australian art risked being seen as the product of a provincial backwater. The difficulty for Australian artists, and for Australian culture in general, was to negotiate some resolution of the conflicting demands of regionalism and internationalism.

Because it stood as both an emblem of the international and as a symbol of the passing of a certain version of regional identity, the suburb became a potent, but profoundly ambivalent sign for the dilemmas of post-war Australia. This may well explain the generality of the images of the suburbs painted by Brack, Blackman and Dickerson in the 1950s (or even Michael Shannon in the 1960s). They painted a generalised 'suburbia' rather than images of particular, recognisable suburbs.

The suburb was depicted as generic because it stood not for a particular *place* but for a particular *culture*. This culture was, in turn, understood as having no particularity; it was the uniform, universal culture of consumer society. Likewise, the lack of incident in the paintings. Nothing is seen to happen in the suburbs, not because nothing does but rather because, since it happens the same way everywhere, the possibility of distinctiveness — and distinction — is lost. This was, perhaps, the most galling point for these artists: the suburb — having defeated the bush legend, having come to embody bland, international culture — was no longer banished from Australian painting but in fact symbolised its very essence.

The street that I live in ... buildings at dusk with an old woman strolling in it, which is an event which takes place every night for this woman. Our street is full of poetry.

Robert Dickerson, from a letter to John Reed, 1953 (in Jennifer Dickerson's *Robert Dickerson: Against the tide*)

truce & tolerance

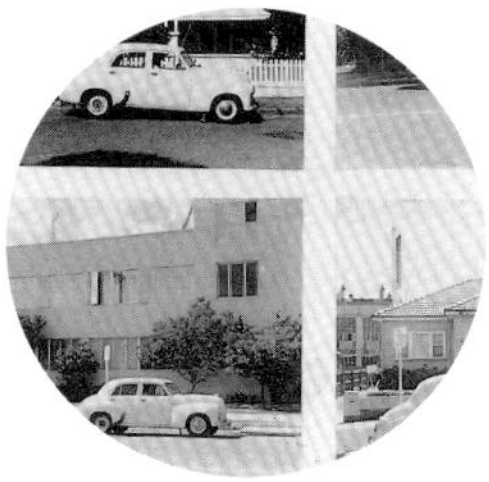

In many respects, the 1960s were a turning point in the history of the Australian suburbs. Not only did the architecture, geography and lifestyle of the suburbs change, so too, however slowly, did attitudes towards suburbia. Changes hinted at, or just begun, in the 1950s took root and consolidated. The significance of the automobile was now fully apparent; the relative autonomy that was to characterise the suburbs in later decades had been established.

A younger generation of '60s artists emerged, prepared to negotiate the demands of an international art world with reference to a local culture. Though their responses varied, Ian Burn, Dale Hickey, Victor Majzner, Ti Parks and Robert Rooney each found the suburbs a rich source of images for their critical explorations of art-making.

The new priorities of 1960s urbanism were made clear at the end of the decade, when in May 1969 the Victorian branch of the Royal Australian Institute of Architects conferred the title of best building of the year not on the newly opened National Gallery of Victoria, in the city centre, but on the Southland Shopping Centre, in suburban Cheltenham.

CAR CULTURE AND SOCIAL MOBILITY

Commuter culture, which had originally separated workers from the city centre, now developed into the lateral movement that saw more suburb-dwellers working, shopping and socialising between suburbs. Suburban growth linked to the automobile changed attitudes to urban space in ways that were to have a significant impact.

The introduction or proposal of the freeways and ring roads essential to automobile culture raised the spectre of destruction of large areas of land, sparking reactions that were later to blossom into the urban conservation and Green Belt movements of the 1970s. Popular conceptions of the nature of a home — a cultural and psychological vision of security very different from the simple material qualities of a house — continued to sit awkwardly with the ambitions of urban planners and the realities of Australia's demography.

The Australian suburb has been consistent in its ignorance and emotional immaturity for a century ... There can be no serious doubting about the fate of the suburb as we know it. Its days are numbered, even if it is a little early to start the countdown. There can also be no doubting if Australia will be able to tear itself away from the suburban dream. The pressures of extended driving and the burdens and boredom of suburbia have already been rejected, it would seem, by many young people ...

Robin Boyd, from "Waking from the suburbia dream: Australia's first substantial revolt against suburbia", 1970

The inner-city high-rise flats erected by state Housing Commissions in the 1960s could never hope to conform to the popular image of the detached villa or bungalow. However well-intentioned, such high-rise housing was soon regarded as an urban blight and, later, as having caused the wanton destruction of the picturesque character of nineteenth century suburbs.

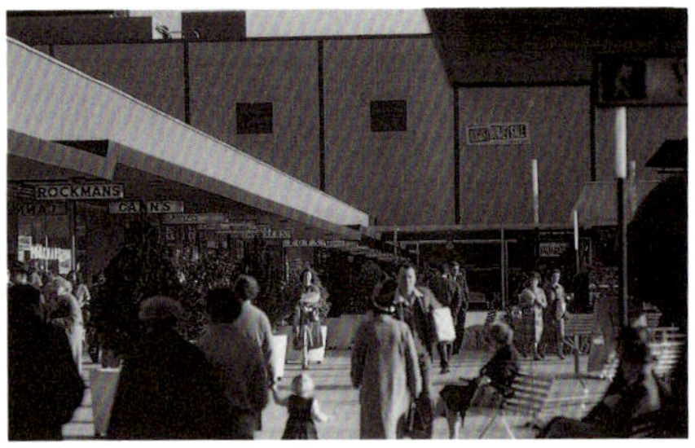

Chadstone Shopping Centre, Melbourne

At the same time, the standard suburban home, which continued to be built in numbers, was increasingly unsuited to significant shifts in the character of domestic life. As the children of the baby boom grew and left the parental home, the suburban sprawl seemed increasingly wasteful of space and resources. Returning to the inner city to live in shared houses, young Australians began to reinvigorate older suburbs, reviving their bohemian appeal and paving the way for the gentrification of the 1970s. Likewise, as social mores relaxed, the notion that a home would naturally house a nuclear family of heterosexual parents and their offspring became increasingly untenable. At the same time, architects increasingly called for the development of medium-density housing in the suburbs, for the relaxation of restrictive building codes, and eventually for more environmentally conscious planning.

So if the suburban dream of the detached home remained powerful, its terms were gradually modified to allow for a more flexible conception of domestic life. As a consequence, it became increasingly difficult to conceive of the suburbs in traditional terms and, more significantly, increasingly difficult to condemn the alleged uniformity and conformity of suburbia.

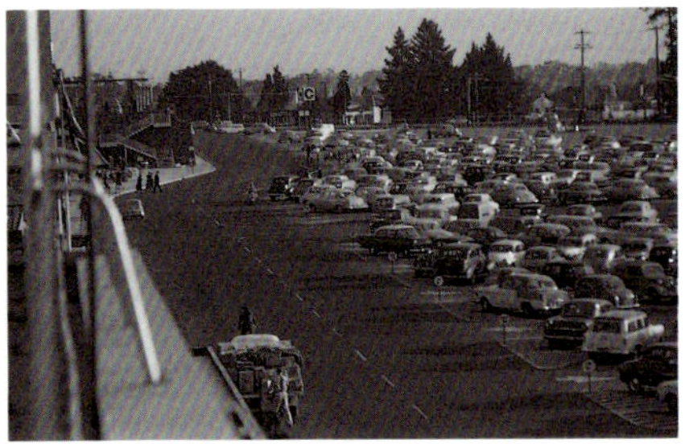

Chadstone Shopping Centre carpark

TOLERANCE AND REAPPRAISAL

By the mid 1960s, Australian commentators had begun tentatively to attribute cultural complexity, if not cultural value, to the suburbs. In his influential 1964 book *The Lucky Country*, Donald Horne berated those writers who belittled suburbia as the antithesis of the 'real'— rural — Australia, or 'genuine'— European — culture. In spite of this, Horne's own book is hardly a paean to the suburb, frequently dwelling on the complacency — the "triumphant mediocrity and sheer dullness"— of life in the suburbs.

Likewise, Craig McGregor, in *Profile of Australia* (1966), was uncertain in his assessment of the suburb. He struck a positive note when he argued that "those who dismiss

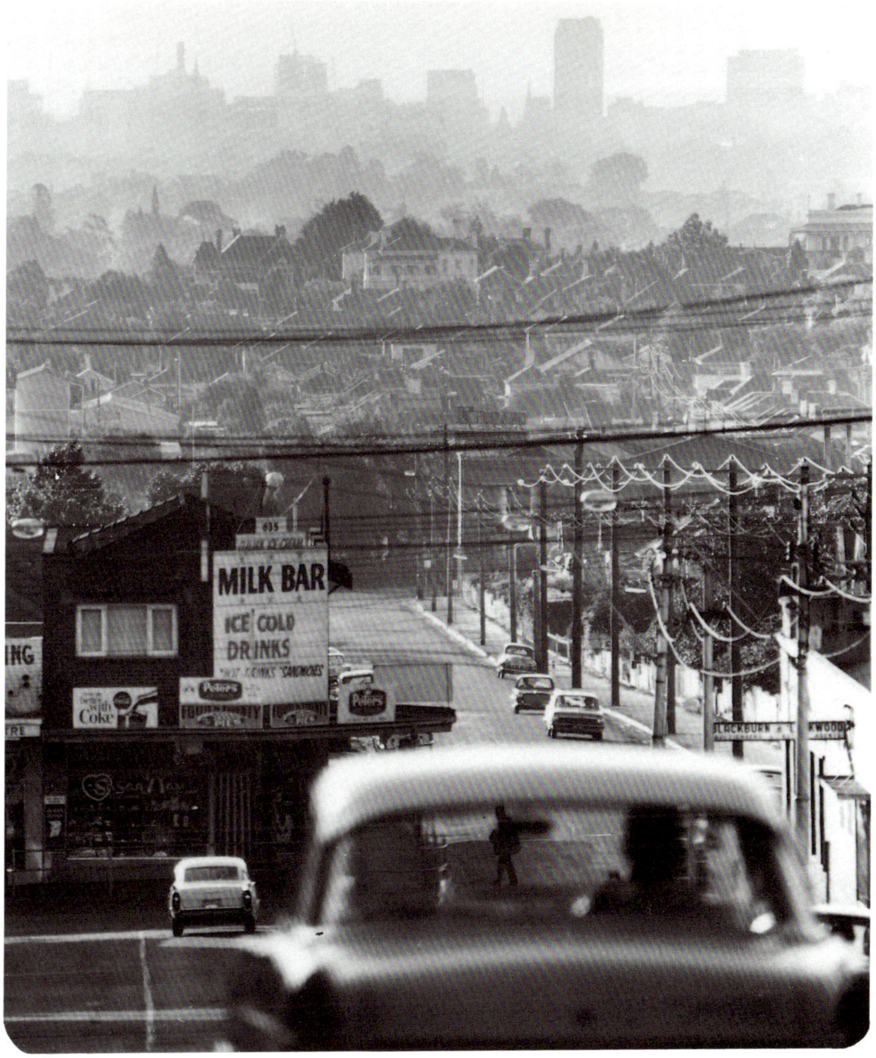

Mark Strizic,
The City from Prospect Hill Road, Canterbury, 1967

suburban life as dull and characterless miss some of its underlying strength". Yet, like Horne, he accompanied this plea for tolerance with the concession that "the dullness, the conformity, the lack of excitement or challenge" that the critics of suburbia catalogued, really did exist.

More generally, the new social ideals and attitudes of the 1960s also prompted a positive re-evaluation of Australian art and culture among artists. Coming of age in a decade of social upheaval and generational revolt, young artists intent on questioning inherited cultural structures developed new understandings of art and Australian identity.

The theme of life in a marginal culture was central to this reappraisal of art and suburbia. Younger Australian artists explored their peripheral relationship to the international centres of Europe and the United States, and found parallels to it in the marginal cultural status of the much-maligned suburbs. At first, the negative connotations of the suburb were preserved by artists, used ironically to register Australia's marginal position. But later the suburbs came to be valued in their own right, pointing to a way beyond the anti-suburban rhetoric of earlier decades.

ABSTRACTING SUBURBAN CULTURE

Initially this rethinking was evident in subtle manipulations of the dominant styles of international art. By the late 1960s, the governing model of advanced art was formalism, championed by the influential American critic Clement Greenberg. Formalism proposed that the task of artists was to locate and display the 'formal' properties unique to their particular medium. Colour Field Abstraction was the exemplary formalist style; with abstract structures of flat areas of colour, it abandoned representation and concentrated on painting's specific formal properties — colour, gesture, scale and two-dimensionality.

The authority of formalism created a new dilemma for Australian artists. The formal properties of painting were more or less the same the world over. If the artists were to overcome their marginal status they had to engage with formalist abstraction, but if they did, any possibility of a specifically regional expression would be denied them. Worse, given the so-called 'tyranny of distance', Australian versions of the New York style would only ever be pale, out-dated imitations of the work developing in the metropolitan centre. This left local artists with an extreme self-consciousness about the tensions between regional and international imperatives.

In the midst of this dilemma, Dale Hickey, Ian Burn and Robert Rooney began to incorporate suburban motifs into their work. On the surface, their work took up the New York styles of Minimalism, Colour Field Abstraction and Conceptual Art, but they also incorporated regional motifs. By developing a hybrid form combining appar-

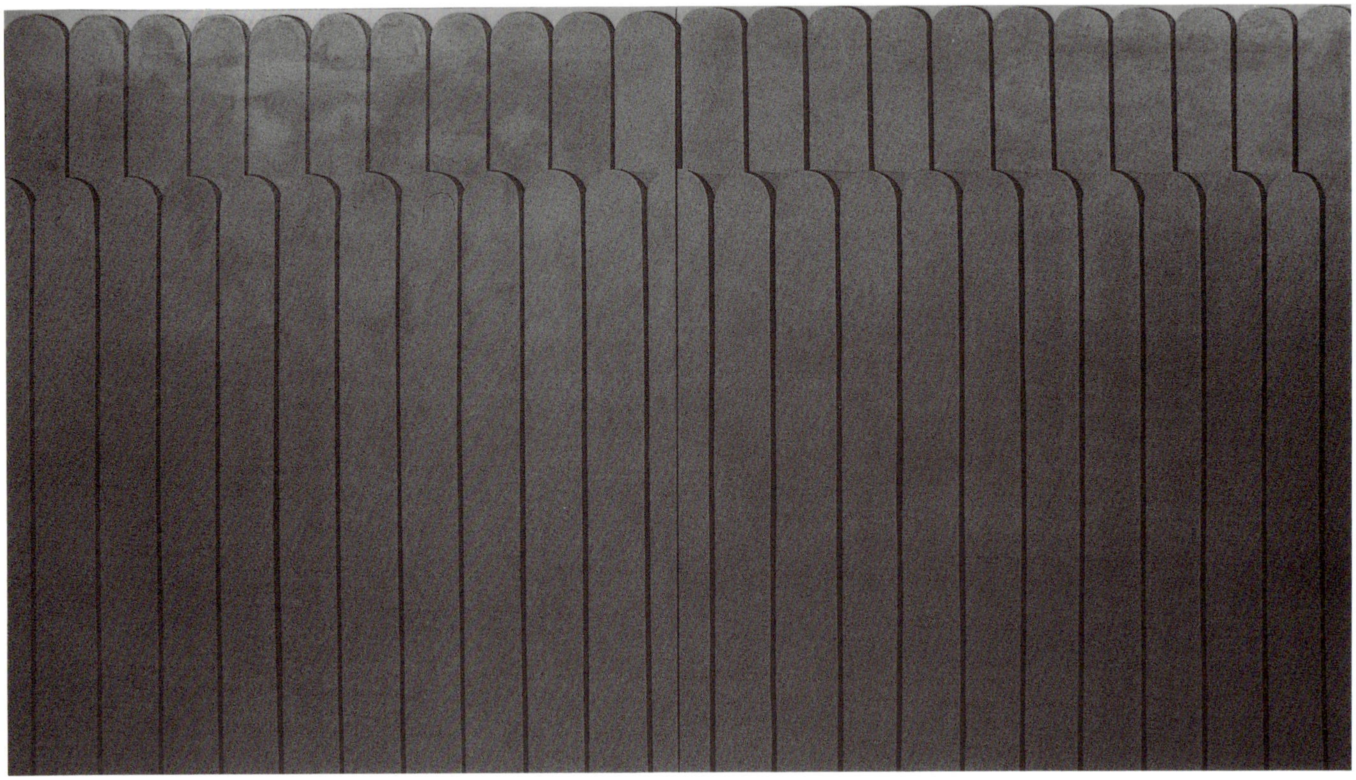

Dale Hickey,
Untitled, c.1968

ently neutral international styles with such symbolically loaded regional motifs, the artists suggested that marginality could involve sophisticated aesthetic dialogue, rather than passive consumption.

One crucial tactic was to present the suburb as both the epitome of banality and the site of a substantial regional culture. Their fascination with the 'minor languages' of suburbia suggested that denigration of the suburbs might be replaced by an appreciation of their culture. In this they reflected a broader trend in cultural commentary at the time, a 'relativism' that measured the value of cultural activities within the context of their own milieu, rather than against an abstract, high cultural benchmark. By maintaining a dialogue between margin and centre rather than opting for one or other side of the equation, these artists contributed to the rehabilitation of the suburb.

I remember being very bored at a teaching seminar I went to ... and I drew three pipes ... Those pipes directed me to objects which had a similar structure, and in my own environment, that is, my house environment ... we had an eiderdown, or a quilt ... which was sewed into patterns. A series of pillow shapes, very geometric, but with rounded forms, and I used that particular quilt or eiderdown to make another painting ... So, having arrived at that point, I did a number of paintings which were based on that type of formal thing; around Malvern and St Kilda.

Dale Hickey, interviewed by Hazel de Berg, 1969

THE SUBURBS SPEAK BACK: DALE HICKEY

Dale Hickey's large-scale non-objective paintings, built on repetitive structures of near flat, geometric forms, were highly regarded by formalist critics. For example, discussing Hickey's *Untitled 67–68* (1967–68) [Plate 8] Patrick McCaughey suggested that, "The painting becomes a thing in itself … It transmits no secret message or symbols; it does not seek to comment on the universe or the world around it. The painting communicates no message but itself: an implacable, paradoxical presence whose garish drabness is both amusing and menacing."

Hickey himself, however, felt that art *should* deal with the world around it. Inspired by Aldous Huxley's *The Doors of Perception*, a book about psychedelic and spiritual experiences, he believed that the artist's task was to find a powerful combination of pictorial substance and metaphysical worth in the most banal, everyday items. *Untitled 67–68*, like several other works executed at this time, was derived from a suburban artefact — in this case a mass-produced quilt.

The work is a deliberate hybrid: it combines art and the suburbs; realism and abstraction; a unique painting and the mass-produced goods of consumerism; American formalism (crisp areas of flat, bright colour) and European Op Art (a shimmering spatial motion generated optically through the subtle manipulation of colour and tone). Hickey's introduction of the 'non-art' banality of suburban motifs into formalist abstraction occurred at the very moment when formalist theory was beginning to be persuasively challenged.

As Hickey showed, rather than constricting Australian culture, the suburbs could be used ironically to engage in a debate with international styles. Suburban motifs were used to parody international style abstraction and to break its rules. *Untitled* (c.1968) is a life-size depiction of two overlapping paling fences. The work breaks two of the cardinal rules of formalism: it is an illusionistic representation of an object, and the superimposed fences introduce three-dimensional space into the flat field of the canvas. Ironically, the repeated vertical stripes of the palings, all aligned frontally across the canvas, all perfectly parallel to the edge of the canvas, are reminiscent of

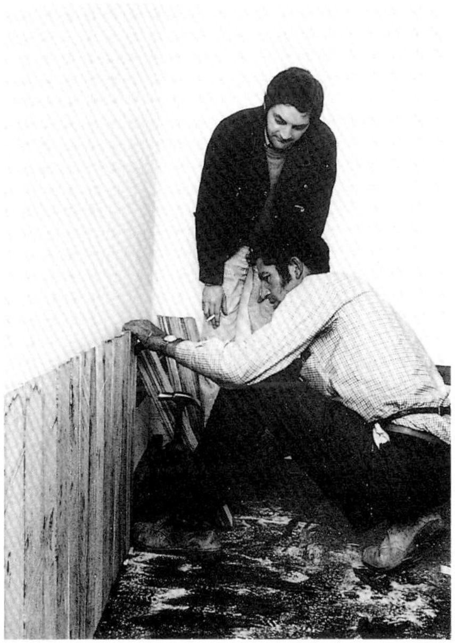

Dale Hickey watches Jim Emmins construct a fence inside the Pinacotheca gallery, St Kilda, October 1969, as photographed for *The Age*

In the past, I have been mainly creating illusions, by painting. Now, this here is going into actual objects. Almost three years ago I did a 12 foot x 6 foot painting of a fence. But if you're going to paint it, why not build it?

My interest in paling fences (repetitive, basic geometric shapes) arises, among many other factors, from the fact that I see them in my everyday commuting. They are part of the chaos of my everyday experience. They are neither meaningful nor meaningless — they persist in the mind despite the detached observation of the commuter.

Dale Hickey, quoted in "A fence is a fence is a fence, or was it?", *The Age*, October 23rd, 1969

the monochrome stripe paintings of the American Frank Stella, then regarded as the epitome of minimalist abstraction.

The association is not accidental. *Untitled* (c.1968) suggests a Stella abstract deliberately botched up by the introduction of illusionism and corrupted by the taint of marginal culture. It is as if Hickey has deliberately pandered to the expectation that provincial Australian artists would get it wrong. The use of a suburban motif to introduce illusionism reinforced the provincial resonance and heightened the parody of this approach.

Hickey made the friction of opposing cultures the motivating force of the canvas. The old provincialist positions — vilification of the suburb as a cultural wasteland, slavish emulation of international styles, or xenophobic celebration of regionalism — were left behind, as was the formalist rejection of mass culture and everyday life. A painting of a suburban fence in Melbourne embodied the worst fears of all camps.

Hickey used the motif to attest to the sophistication, not the banality, of regional culture. He demonstrated that Australian artists were willing both to re-evaluate their own cultural discourses and to engage critically with those of the major international powers; the suburbs could speak back to the metropolitan centre.

In 1969, Hickey took his engagement with the suburbs one step further; he had three paling fences constructed in the Pinacotheca art gallery by a professional contractor. A distinction that had underwritten artists' images of the suburbs for most of the century — attributing significant cultural value to art and none to the suburbs — was questioned. He presented a suburban fence on the same terms as an abstract artwork; a fence builder on the same terms as an artist. It was no longer a matter of merely assessing the *merit* of suburbs; like the fences, they were just *there*.

Hickey did not want to make the fences into art, nor did he want to turn the art gallery into a suburban plot; instead, he wanted to stage a situation where the *fluidity* of such readings was apparent. While Hickey's *Untitled* (c. 1968) exploited distaste of the suburbs for its effect (the suburb corrupted abstraction and allowed the artist to undermine the dominance of international styles), the installation of 1969 valorised the suburb.

Hickey's fence installation developed out of the strategies of the international Conceptual Art movement; it questioned the relevance of authorship, the art object and the gallery system. But it was avowedly local in its construction. The vernacular of the suburban fence, spoken within a society that reviled the suburb as the antithesis of genuine culture, gave Conceptual Art a regional accent. What Hickey did arose not only from his idea of the metaphorical — even metaphysical — role of art, but also from his status as a resident of suburban Melbourne (and certainly not by his ability to divorce himself from that context). Indeed, Hickey considered himself a commuter as much as an artist.

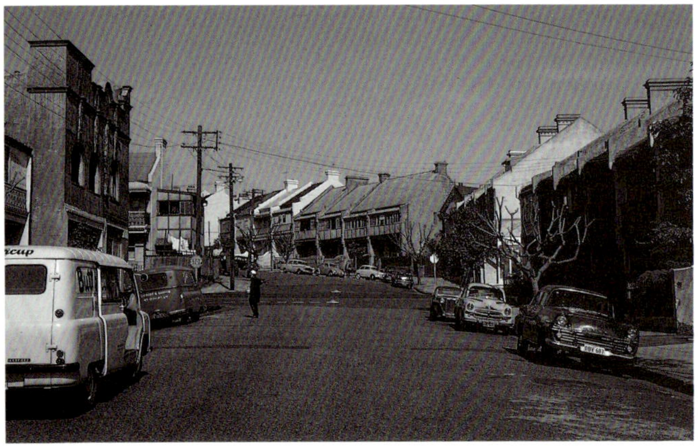

Paddington Street, 1960s

THE FASCINATION OF THE BANAL: ROBERT ROONEY; VICTOR MAJZNER; TI PARKS

Hickey was not alone in using the suburbs to parody formalism, nor in being intrigued by the banal patterns of the suburban landscape. Robert Rooney's 'hard-edged' paintings of the late 1960s included a series of abstract works based on knitting patterns and toys cut out from cereal packets . His use of disguised suburban, domestic motifs served to corrupt the principles of Colour Field Abstraction. The paintings looked the part, but their titles (*Superknit*, *Canine Capers*, *Cereal Bird Beaks*) deflated their formalist pretensions. In *Cereal Bird Beaks II* (1969) [Plate 9] Rooney parodied formalist abstraction by basing the painting on a source found on the supermarket and kitchen shelves of the suburbs. The geometric forms of the painting

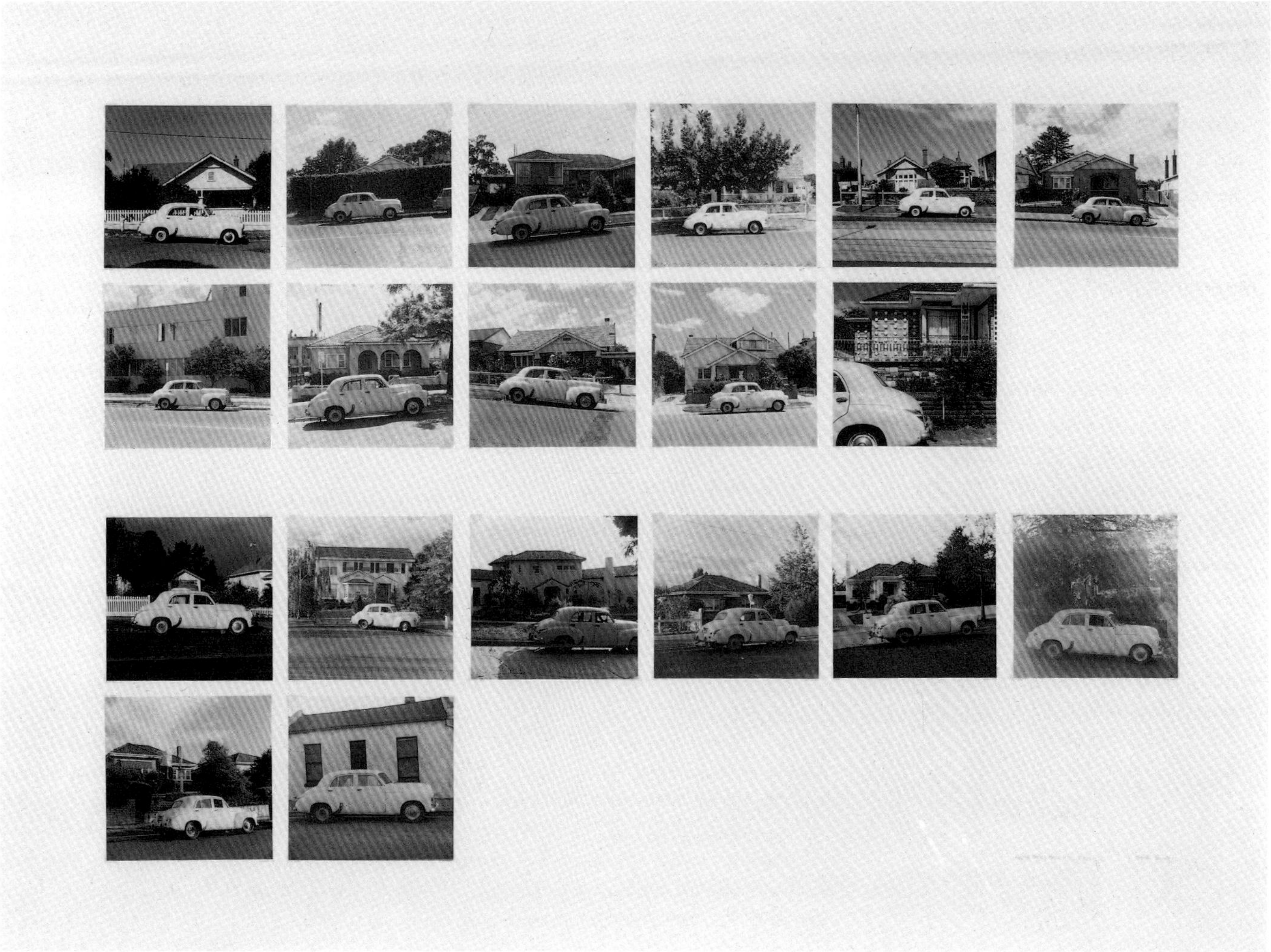

Robert Rooney,
Holden Park 1 & 2, May 1970, 1970

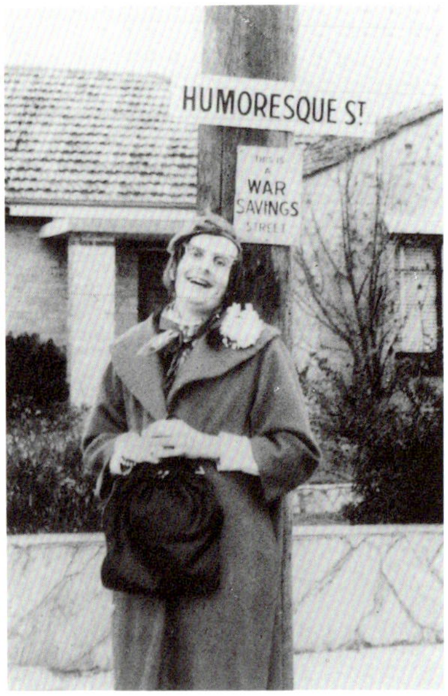

"Edna in Humoresque Street, Moonee Ponds, 1961"

were derived from a cut-out toy printed on a breakfast cereal package. Repetition of the forms allowed Rooney to mimic the all-over effect of a formalist canvas, but also to trigger a pun — cereal beaks became a 'serial' pattern. As was the case with Hickey's early work, the tainted status of suburbia was preserved so it could act as a virus eating away at 'high' art and good taste.

Rooney's fascination with suburbia continued into his later work, but his acceptance of the binary opposition of (high) culture and (low) suburbia ended with his photographic works of the early 1970s. In these works, Rooney documented the repetitive framework of suburban life; sleeping (*AM–PM*, 1974), dressing (*Garments: 3 December 1972–19 March 1973*, 1973), strolling (*Luna Park: St Kilda 8 January 1975*, 1975), and driving (*Holden Park 1 & 2, May 1970*, 1970) in gridded arrays.

The repetition of deserted streets, banal motifs and flat colours suggested an anti-suburban attitude; as if Rooney had wed John Brack with Conceptual Art. But the emptiness of Rooney's photographs is of a peculiar kind, similar to that which John Cage utilised in his silent composition '4'33"', which required a pianist to do nothing for the nominated period of time. Cage's score, bereft of notes, created a silence that was then filled with the ambient noise of the environment; shuffling feet, muffled coughs, rustling programmes. Likewise Rooney's depopulated streets resounded with the ambient signals of the city; the languages of domestic architecture, the textures of brick, the styles of gardens, advertisements, automobiles, local landmarks and litter. They are like empty stages, ripe with the sensation that something has just happened, or is just about to. What happens may not be exciting (although the works have a forensic quality, as if they document the scene of a crime) but it constitutes activity, narrative, memory and sensation all the same.

The street signs Rooney photographed for his booklet *War Savings Streets* (1970) cannot be seen merely as a set of signs after all, for they show that ideals (patriotism, thrift, self-sacrifice), as well as streets, thread through the suburbs. Rooney took up the lessons offered by Cage — inclusiveness, refusal of hierarchies, the impossibility of emptiness — and forged a new approach to the suburbs, neither a fulsome embrace nor a sweeping condemnation.

Other artists based in Melbourne also used suburban motifs in sly parodies of formalist abstraction, subverting its emphasis on recondite visual effects with the supposedly empty visuality of suburbia. In a 1970 exhibition, Victor Majzner produced flat, laterally striped canvases echoing the work of American artists like Kenneth Noland and Gene Davis. Majzner's stripes were not a product of the formal imperative of the rectangular canvas, however, but were based on venetian blinds.

Victor Majzner,
Green Vent, 1970

For formalists the flatness of the canvas was a refusal of illusionistic depth, but for Majzner it was as much a metaphor for the resistant, almost fortress-like enclosure of suburban facades. The parodic effect was amplified by stretching flywire across some canvases, which generated a shimmering *moiré* effect that both conformed to formalist principles in its use of purely optical effects and corrupted them by allowing the intrusion of the everyday world.

Ti Parks's *St Kilda Street* (1967) similarly parodied the minimalist reliefs of Americans such as Donald Judd by disguising the frame of a suburban window as a minimalist construction. If the official abstraction of the 1960s insisted that a painting should not be regarded as a window onto an illusionary world, both Majzner and Parks used actual windows to point out how far formalism had drifted from the real world. However, for all the humorous effect they achieved, the mute and resistant quality of their windows left no doubt that the real world of suburbia might equally be lacking in the human touch.

A CONCEPTUAL CRITIQUE: IAN BURN

Meanwhile, in New York, another Australian artist was incorporating images of suburbia into a practice based on Conceptual Art attitudes. Driven by the New Left and countercultural politics of the 1960s, Ian Burn, like many of his peers, was intent on developing a critique of the accepted conventions of art. His series of "Systematically Altered Photographs"— *The Suburbs*, *The Kitchen* and *Kangaroos* (all 1968) — were produced as part of an attack on formalism, representation and nationalism. In this series, Burn took reproductions from *Australian Panorama* (an Australian News and Information Bureau pamphlet), photocopied them, and then repeatedly photocopied the photocopies until only a foggy trace of the original remained.

The 'naturalness' of the original photographic image, its apparently transparent truthfulness, was undermined by the very process that allowed it to circulate as propaganda — mechanical reproduction. The original and its reprocessed echo were framed together, presenting an ideal image of the Australian suburbs, alongside its deconstruction into dots and blurs. In comparing an 'effective' and an 'ineffective' photograph, Burn hoped that viewers might recognise the conventions of photographic authority and propaganda.

The propaganda images of *Australian Panorama* attempted to sell the Australian way of life to the rest of the world, but, just like Australian art, they looked backward and parochial on the international stage. And, since such images represented Australia to itself as well as to an international audience, they were a reminder of the narrow, inward-looking aspirations of Australian society.

With both Hickey and Burn, the critique of the 'Establishment'— of the 'powers that be' in the art world and society as a whole — was tied to suburbia. In Burn's practice, however, unlike Hickey's, the suburbs were not redeemed. It is as if Burn needed the suburbs to be banal in order to emphasize his levelling off of the authority of photography. More than that, it is as if Burn could not afford to be generous in his

Imagery was reintroduced in ways which deliberately exposed its problematic status ... The original image was cut from a magazine. There was no sense of creating the image, only of recreating it within a new system. The source was a promotional publication put out for overseas consumption by the Australian government ... The clichéd character of the images was important.

Ian Burn, discussing the "Systematically Altered Photographs", 1988

approach to the suburbs, since they epitomised (metaphorically, at least) the complacency and provincialism that he left behind in migrating to the international culture of Conceptual Art.

While Burn managed to inject a regionalist flavour into Conceptual Art, in his work the suburb remained the opposite of both genuine culture and critical consciousness. In this respect his attitude to the suburb is similar to that of Barry Humphries, another expatriate critic.

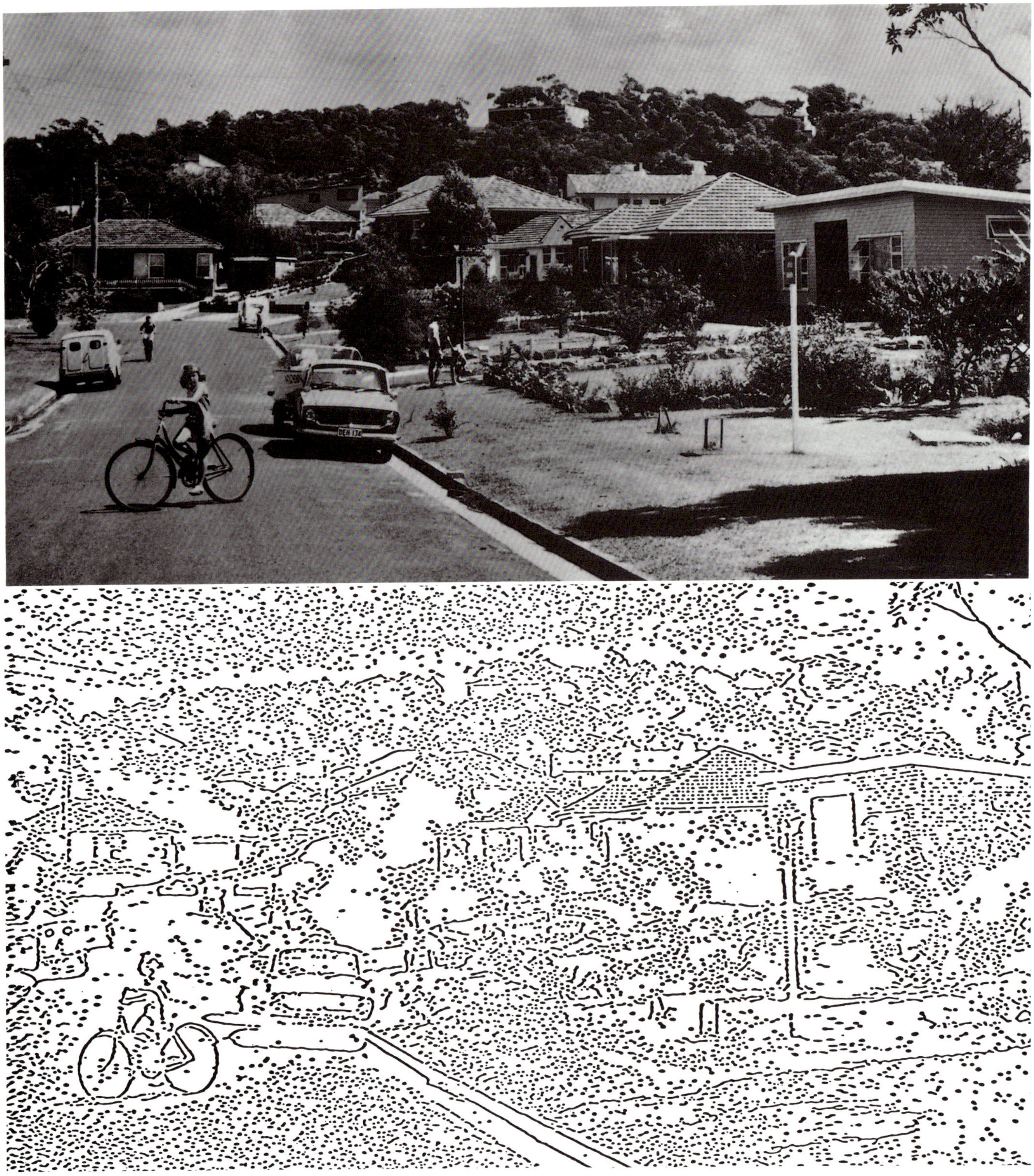

Ian Burn,

Systematically Altered Photograph:

The Suburbs, 1968

TRUCE AND TRANSITION

The work of Burn, Hickey, Majzner, Parks and Rooney indicates the ways in which the suburb enabled Australian artists to address issues of national and cultural identity in the 1960s. National identity, colonial status and cultural value could be discussed without recourse to the nostalgic and bucolic images of the Antipodean generation.

Furthermore, the suburbs allowed artists to engage critically with regional and international culture at a time when the interaction of the two was a key debate within the art scene. Suburbia allowed artists to take positions within the provincial/metropolitan debate without this being reduced to an issue of loyalty to an existing style.

Indeed 'suburbanism', one way or the other, is likely to be the target of practically all intellectuals. And since most Australians live in the suburbs of cities or in towns that, in a modified way, reflect the same values, this means that intellectuals hate almost the whole community ... Detailed recognition of the essentially suburban character of Australia has been slow, partly because old myths have remained virulent and partly because special factors in Australia such as the almost pantheistic love of outdoor activity have muddled the pattern of what — according to overseas authorities —'suburbanism' is supposed to be ... What is sometimes not realised by those who attack 'suburbanism' is that the entire gentility–vulgarity confrontation is out of date ... New generations are denying the old proprieties and stuffiness. The genteel have been vulgarized, the vulgar made more gentle.

Donald Horne, from *The Lucky Country,* 1968

In the history of Australia's love–hate relationship with suburbia, the period from the late 1960s into the early 1970s was a transitional one, as the differences between Burn and Hickey suggest. While Burn recognised that the suburb figured prominently in accounts of Australian identity, he still regarded it — or at least images of it — with some disdain. If Hickey saw the suburbs as being worthy of his attention, he still maintained an ironic distance.

What is important is that the artists found a way in which they could begin to reconfigure white Australian consciousness at precisely the site that had been previously represented as the lowest common denominator of such a consciousness. Identity, they demonstrated, was to be found in the demographic reality and everyday activities of Australian culture, not in its mythical pasts and futures.

Suburban subdivision, Broadbeach, Gold Coast

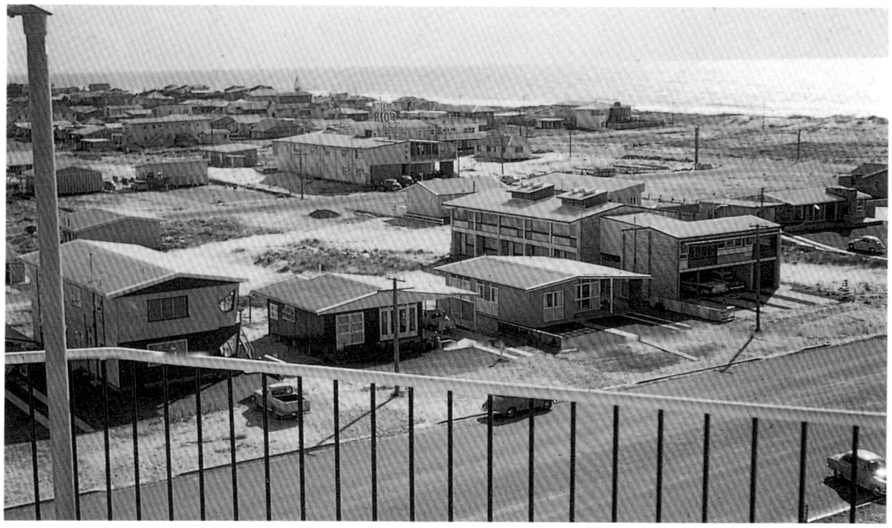

5 THE 1970s

LOCAL colour

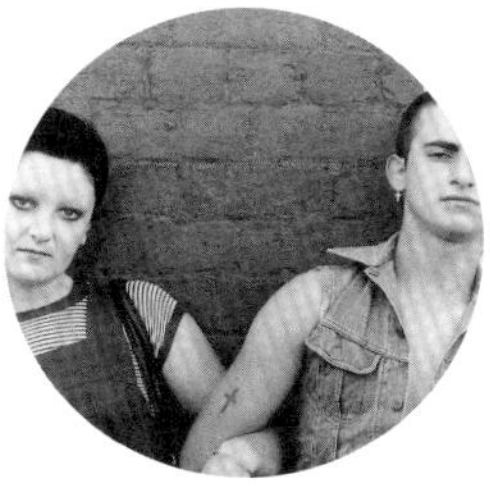

In the 1970s, technological and demographic change, and the increasing sophistication and pervasiveness of the mass media began to effect the face of Australian cities. The physical transformation of cities was further fuelled by a growing dissatisfaction with the technocratic uniformity of corporate modernist architecture. For residents, grass-roots politics of feminism, conservation, and the environment provided new models with which to analyse, understand and shape these changes as they affected local communities.

This transformation gave rise to what is often characterised as a 'postmodern' city; one in which the physical, industrial and economic relationships that had previously defined and structured the city became more fluid. With this fluidity came a new spirit of active engagement with the suburbs around them by artists such as Peter Kennedy, Carol Jerrems, Jenny Watson and Ann Newmarch. Increasingly, artists sought to capture the layers and contradictions of the suburbs in images that could encompass present realities and personal vision, as well as reflecting more broadly on culture, history and politics. The diversity and complexity of the resultant images mirrored that of the suburbs themselves.

THE POSTMODERN CITY

Sociologists, economists and historians have suggested that, in the years after World War 2, developed Western nations entered a post-industrial — or postmodern — phase. While opinion varies as to the exact forms that postmodern society takes, theorists consistently point to significant changes in urban and suburban space. These suggest the passing of the modernist city and the advent of a new sense of locality, identity and culture.

By the '70s the old concentrations of industry in inner city areas were dissolving, making way for economic restructuring, urban redevelopment and gentrification. At the same time, improved transport, infrastructure and information-processing meant that outer suburbs could be serviced locally to a degree that made them far less dependent on the city centre. Outer suburbs were now seen as self-sustaining communities, with their inhabitants less inclined to regard the city centre as the locus of activity or amenities. The defining relationship was no longer between centre and periphery but encompassed suburban regions, corridors or rings.

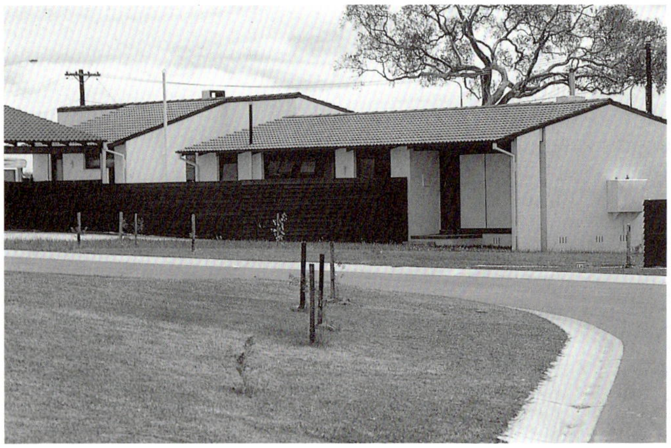

Prototype Radburn housing, Fisher, Canberra, 1971

New ways of living emerged, new types of household units, ranging from the quasi-collective households of youth subcultures through to increasingly diverse family structures. With the greater emphasis on administrative and service professions, new classes and power relations emerged, and concentrations of unemployment developed in those areas dependent on the declining manufacturing sector.

Postmodern society is distinct — but not entirely separate — from an earlier industrial culture in which the economy centred on manufacturing and the accumulation of capital, and urban space was shaped by the dream of an ordered, rational environment. It is argued that in the age of mass media and the computer, capital, labour and wealth take on less concrete forms, circulating in abstract and symbolic forms. Information and image are the cornerstones of this new culture, with labour directed towards servicing a mobile, information-hungry consumer society. The inhabitants of this new postmodern city are different, at least in the sense that new roles and forms of status are available.

Throughout the '70s, city dwellers increasingly sought out or constructed new lifestyles, whether based in the leisure and consumption of baby-boomers, the retirement activities of an ageing population, or adaptation to changing job roles and prospects. In a society where identity was equated with image, with its greater emphasis on lifestyle and on social mobility, a new consciousness affected the inward and outward vision of the suburb. Looking inwards, the self-sustaining character of the serviced suburb generated an internalised view, with an assumption that all desired amenities could be obtained there. At the same time, looking outwards, ambitious and status-conscious inhabitants might aspire to life in another suburb, perceiving it as a move up the social ladder. The postmodern city, then, can be characterised as more fragmented, more mobile, more diverse and more style conscious than the modern.

Not only were new classes or categories established but identity itself became more fluid. Where previously identity and status were assumed to be the product of a more or less straightforward linkage of individual to suburb — and suburb to class, occupation or ethnic group — this formula was now coloured by complex combinations of such variables as gender, race, sexuality, age and education. Suburb-dwellers were now identified on the basis of more-complicated, layered characteristics, and, significantly, were understood as having multiple, and transformable, identities.

COMPLEXITY AND DYNAMISM

In the 1970s, cultural nationalism had a profound impact on artists' perceptions of Australian society and their own role within it. Already the questioning of hierarchies that characterised the arts in the 1960s had weakened the 'cultural cringe', breaking the habit of evaluating Australian practices with received international standards.

The nationalism of the 1972–75 Whitlam government, the 1975 formation of the Australia Council for the Arts, the revival of the film industry, and the 1973 Nobel Prize for Literature awarded to Patrick White all added to the feeling that Australia's 'cultural cringe' might finally have been overcome, that Australian life could sustain substantial artistic practices. Although this cultural nationalism often dwelt on the past, particularly in the period films that dominated the cinema renaissance, Australia's urban present was regarded as a positive and dynamic subject, worthy of artists' attention.

This turn to urban Australia was accompanied by a new respect for the suburbs and a determination to explore the complexities of their culture. Artists became

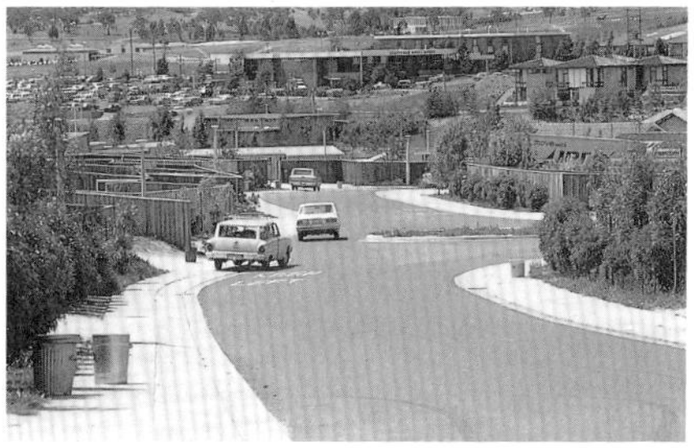

Radburn housing estate, Curtin, Canberra, 1971

In 1973 I walked about the streets of Thebarton and Mile End, photographing those bits of the past I thought were beautiful: the Rosella Sauce parakeet on a grocery wall, Hardy's grand house with its lacework trim on the corner of Dew Street and the lane, tiny houses the Pioneers might have come out of in George Street, the old gasometer on the corner of Maria Street; Moran's Corner and Hook the bootmaker's and the Daisy Dell milkbar on the Beach Road ... The Thebarton Primary School was being pulled down even then, and now everything on that list, and so many other buildings have gone too. It's happening everywhere; particularly if the suburb is still working-class and untrendy.

Barbara Hanrahan, from "Weird Adelaide", 1988

ethnographers, documenting the structures, appearances and behaviours of suburban life. New and reinvigorated political attitudes such as second-wave feminism, the New Left and environmentalism turned to the suburbs in their focus on social issues. The strategy of local activism established the suburbs as a focal point of political agency.

Interest in the suburbs was matched by a new dynamism in suburbia itself: green and alternative architecture; community activism; and the beginnings of gentrification, for example. Continuing migration, the mobility of post-war migrant families, and the shift to a service economy altered the previous ethnic, occupational and class characteristics of many suburbs.

The continued expansion of the urban sprawl, coupled with the growth of large shopping malls, resulted in suburbs that were more self-contained cities than subsidiaries of a central business district. Even the mass media found a hitherto unacknowledged diversity in the suburbs. If television persisted in contrasting city and country, in programs like *Matlock Police* and *Bellbird*, it also began, with series such as *Number 96* and *Certain Women*, to represent urban life as a heterogeneous mix of age, gender, ethnicity and sexuality.

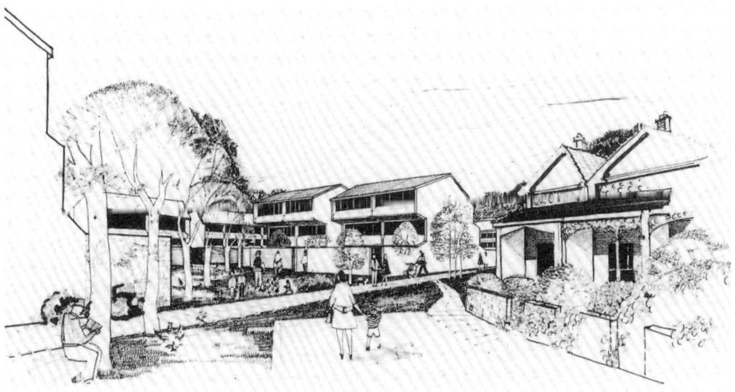

"Proposed re-development project illustrating integration of new with old," from *Housing is People*, Housing Commission Victoria, Melbourne, 1972

Likewise, popular music turned to the Australian suburbs for its imagery. Melbourne's Skyhooks took an ironic pride in suburban culture with songs such as "Balwyn Calling" and "Carlton". Their unbowing insistence on such local, suburban references was a radical departure within the local music scene, and they achieved record levels of sales in the process. In Perth, Dave Warner built his entire image, and a hit single, on the realisation that he was "just a suburban boy".

The idea of producing work through combined effort isn't new. Far from it! It's the norm of most people's daily lives and was, of course, common practice in Western visual art right up to the beginning of this century ... Formal values and daily life are intimately bound together and the recognition of this enriches both through the development of a dynamic interaction which accepts no arbitrary divisions, but sees differences as the foundation of artistic progress.

Geoffrey Hogg, from the "Australian Perspecta 1981" catalogue

THE COMMUNITY MURAL MOVEMENT

The impact of the anti-elitist attitudes of the 1960s on attitudes to the suburbs was most evident in the community-based art movements of the 1970s. From the mid-1970s, artists involved in the community mural movement sought to connect art with everyday life, moving out from the enclosed institutional and ideological spaces of the art world into the suburbs. Countercultural tactics such as collective action and consciousness raising were combined with the styles of Social Realism and the techniques of oral history. The task of these artists was to work with local communities in order to produce a public, non-elitist, artwork that explored the experiences and histories of local areas, and encompassed diverse, often marginal, social groups.

The mural movement heralded some significant changes in the relationship of the arts and the suburbs. Most evident was the fact that art now took place in the suburbs, rather than simply being about them. Whereas the artist had previously adopted the position of the aloof commentator, the producers of murals now spoke overtly of local experiences, to a local audience, in voices generated within that specific locality. Because community murals frequently focused on marginalised groups — migrants, Aborigines, women, the working class — muralists were the first visual artists consistently to attack the myth of a homogeneous suburbia.

The multivalent character of suburban culture was emphasised by the focus on the specifics of local history, which found synonyms in the past as well as the present, and the use of montage compositions, which visually conveyed a sense of multiplicity and variety. For all its idealism, the mural movement encountered vexing problems, including an emphasis on the communal production of art over the finished work itself, a sometimes unquestioning acceptance of realist styles, and difficulties in combining traditionally individualist artistic practices with collective ambitions.

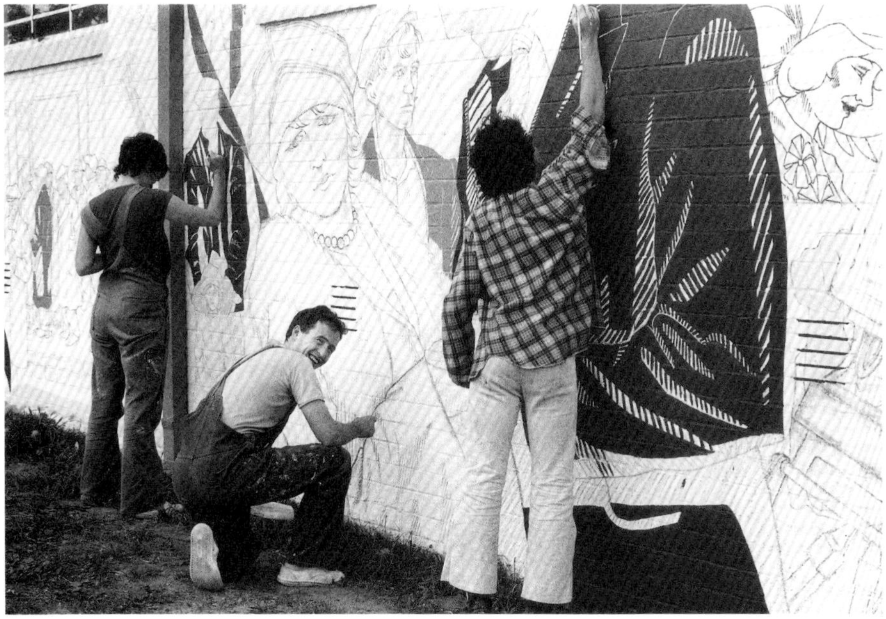

Geoffrey Hogg with Turana residents painting mural, Turana Youth Training Centre, Brunswick, 1980

In its focus on locality, the community mural movement might appear parochial in the extreme, a further product — and proof — of Australia's provincialism. Yet its proponents, buoyed by the new cultural confidence of the 1970s, argued that it combined both the regional and the international: historically and politically it reflected on the local and global history of capitalism; aesthetically it engaged with the modernist streams of collectivism, social realism and collage.

Muralist Geoffrey Hogg articulated this fusion of local and international in an exhibition catalogue for his 1980 exhibition at the Victorian College of the Arts Gallery. He argued that the ambition of the mural movement was to "produce a work that is modern, a work that expresses the uniqueness of the Australian situation and approaches its work methods in a manner suited to the last two decades of the twentieth century".

The movement negotiated a position between the modernist concern of a socially committed art and the recognition of the postmodern heterogeneity of the late-twentieth-century suburb.

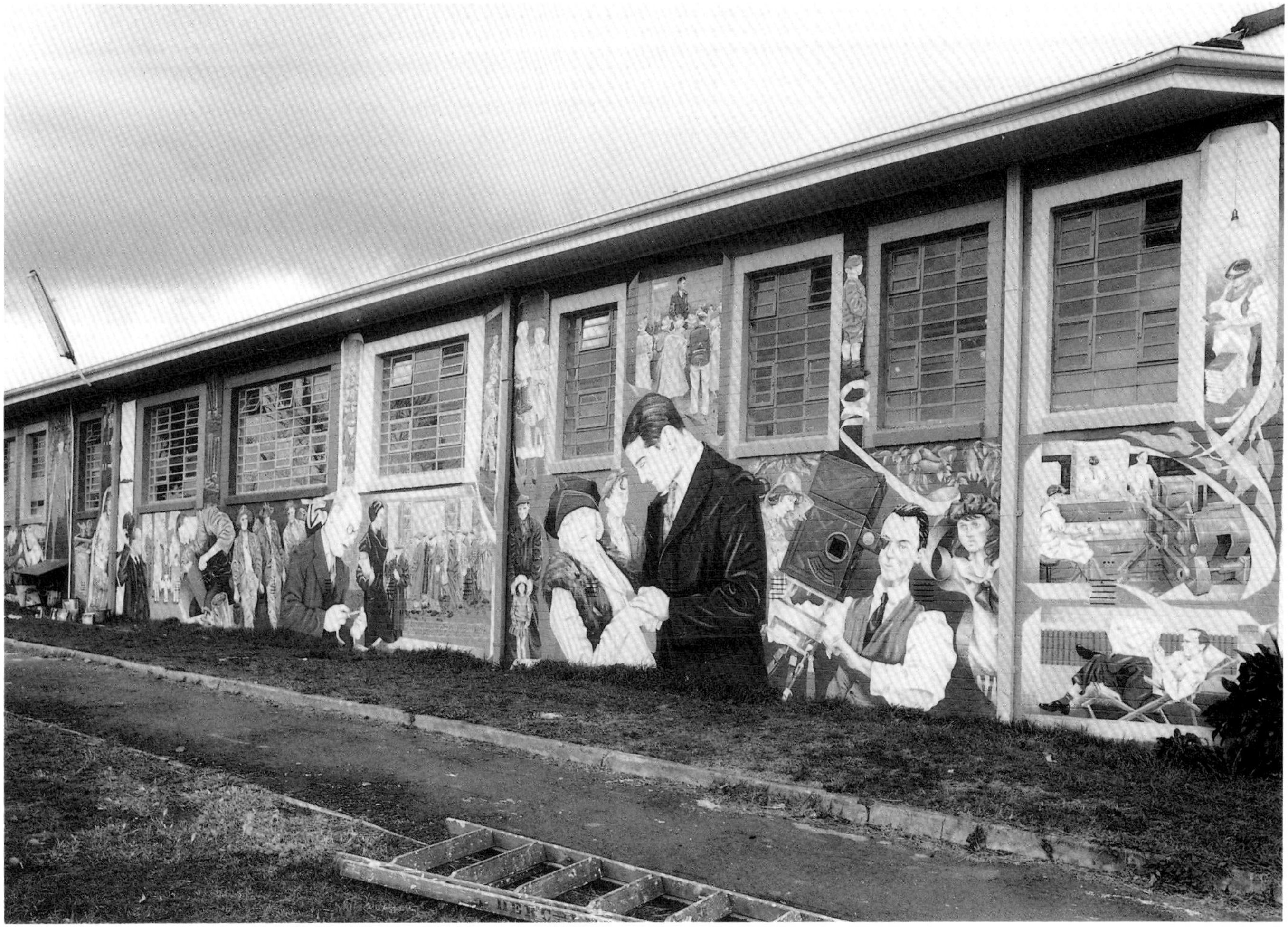

Geoffrey Hogg,
assisted by Jan Duncan, Gwenda Wiseman and Mark Wotherspoon,
Turana Youth Training Centre First Mural, 1980

The intention of the project relates to the idea of introducing each group to the other, so that each may relate to the other and enjoy insights to the other through the sharing of a common experience ... The introduction of members of each group to the other groups is effected, not through physical contact on a person-to-person basis, but through members learning of one another through the presentation of material in the exhibition, which is seen on the film.

Peter Kennedy, from "A description of the project", 1976

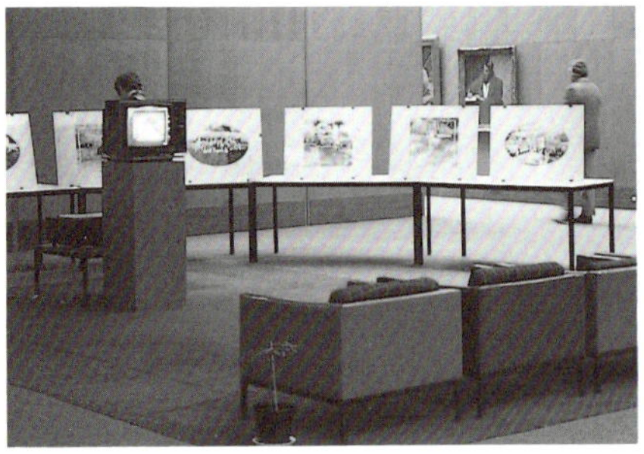

Peter Kennedy, *Introductions* (installation view, National Gallery of Victoria, October 1976)

SYSTEMS AESTHETICS: PETER KENNEDY

Where once artists had viewed suburbia as the epitome of bland conformity, they now recognised it as a complex social system. Influenced by philosophy, sociology and anthropology, the Conceptual artists of the 1970s viewed artworks as analytical propositions about the nature of art and the operation of culture. The view that culture was part of a social structure meshed well with the anti-elitist, local politics of the decade. Since the task of Conceptual Art was to identify the operations of cultural systems, artists began to ask why distinctions between high art and mass culture were made.

Peter Kennedy's *Introductions* (1974-76) [Plate 10] incorporated social action, videotape documentation and watercolour images. The artist's aim was neither to condemn the suburbs nor to document them, but rather to actively participate in, and contribute to, their culture. Kennedy introduced four suburban social groups — a Hot Rod club, an embroidery club, a bushwalking club and a marching girls' troop — to each other through videotape and watercolours of their activities.

Participants were asked to respond to the question, "Why are you a member of your club or group; what would be the first most important reason you would give?" Kennedy encouraged suburb-dwellers to speak of their experiences and their values in their own voices. Their replies revealed the ways in which they built and maintained a community.

The clubs chosen might appear, at first glance, to confirm preconceptions of the banality and gentility of suburbia, but Kennedy's work argued for a reconception of the suburbs as a site of political and cultural agency. The suburbs were shown to be a place where people organised their lives, evaluated their circumstances and even actively sought to change them. As had previously been the case, Kennedy approached the suburbs — as he stated in the description of the project to accompany its 1976 installation at the National Gallery of Victoria — as "an explication of the Australian social condition". But the populism and relativism of the 1970s meant that the suburbs were no longer held at arm's length. They were now, as Kennedy also acknowledged, "a metaphor for the social realities and aspirations of us all".

In another significant reversal, suburban culture was seen not as the enemy of artistic culture but as a means of attacking the elitism of the visual arts. Rejecting the role of art in supporting what he termed "official culture", Kennedy saw the incorporation of "real world" issues as a way of making art more meaningful and accessible to a wide audience while also raising awareness of the politics of cultural hierarchies.

THE SUBCULTURES OF THE SUBURBS: CAROL JERREMS

In the 1970s, as the work of Hogg and Kennedy demonstrates, Australian artists frequently approached the suburbs with a 'culturalist' attitude. This perspective abandoned the previous restriction of the term 'culture' to *high culture* and proposed instead that culture be understood as the meanings generated out of the whole way of life of a social group. Language, custom, ritual, popular culture and consumption were all therefore legitimate sources of social meaning, in addition to more-orthodox arts and institutions.

As a result artists became anthropologists of the suburb; their work explored the subcultures of suburbia, seeking local values and meanings rather than overarching generalisations or blanket condemnation.

Photographer Carol Jerrems, in her exploration of suburban youth culture, produced images that were, in this respect, significantly different from earlier explorations of the theme. Her primary concern was to register a local system of life and meaning. She did not seek either the moralising metaphors of Albert Tucker's "Images of Modern Evil" series or the heroic Social Realist archetypes of Noel Counihan's Fitzroy paintings. Jerrems's culturalism can be seen in her recognition of the social effects of costume, hairstyle or body decoration. She understood that these were the

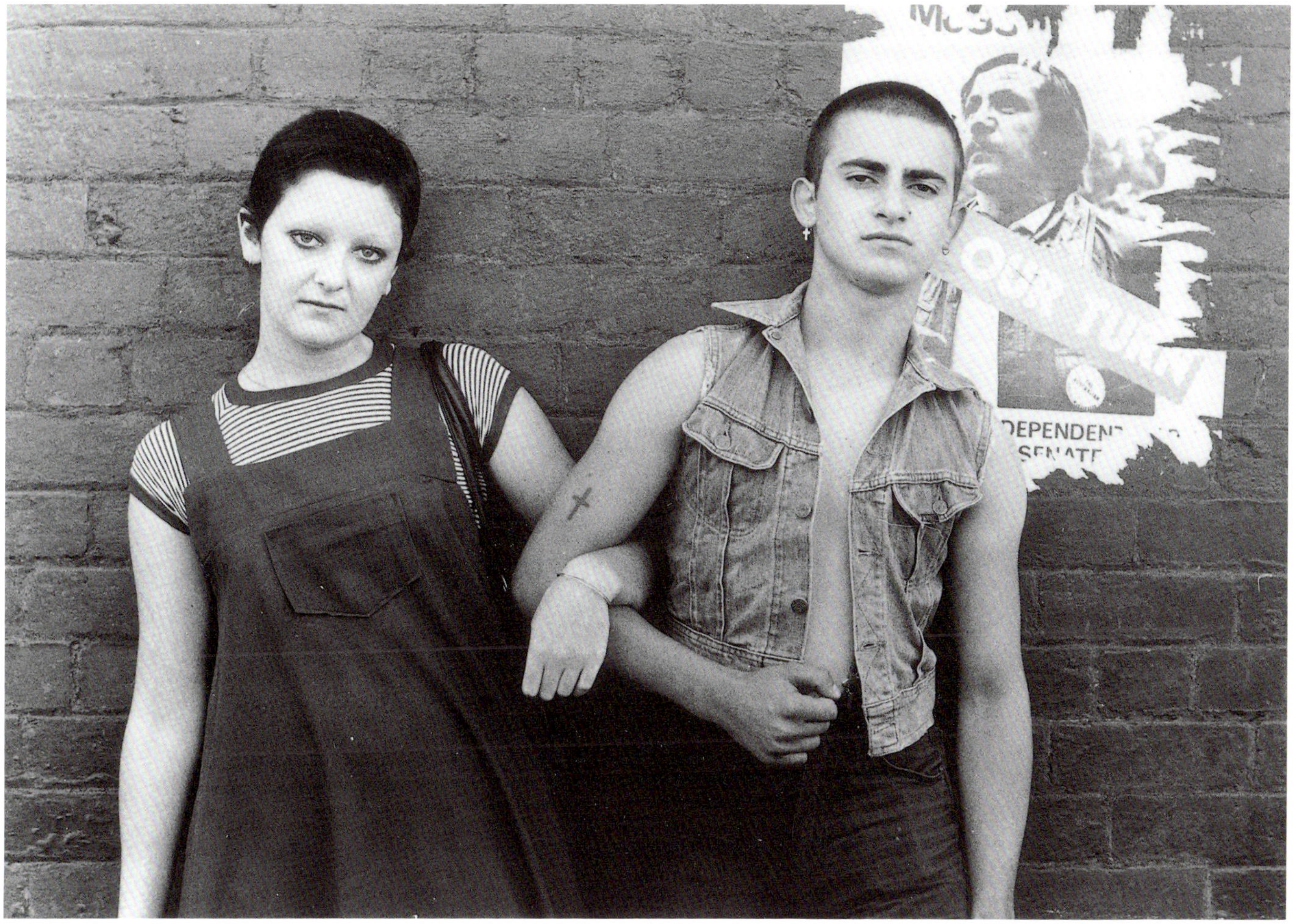

Carol Jerrems,
Sharpies, 1976

ways that youth cultures define themselves — *for* each other, and *against* the mainstream, or 'parent', culture.

Metaphorical readings of these photographs are still possible — particularly in terms of the power relations between genders — but Jerrems attempted to present suburban culture on its own terms. This is very different from presenting it at 'face value', for her photographs are carefully staged, often using her friends and art students as models.

The post-war tradition of 'street photography', which images such as *Sharpies* (1976) initially evoke, had appealed to notions of photographic realism in order to affirm the truth and authenticity of the image. The apparent immediacy of the snapshot was used to establish a surface appearance of 'truth'. But Jerrems's careful juxtapositions — of male and female, body and environment — suggest a different truth, one based on knowing contrivance on the part of both subject and photographer.

Jerrems's blunt, stripped down photographs risked presenting her subjects as specimens gathered on a field trip. But because she was careful to show the relationships between members of youth subcultures, rather than simply their relationship to 'mainstream' society, she avoided reducing the defiant stares of sharpies and street kids to a simplistic — and easily dismissed — stance of teenage rebellion.

ON THE STREET WHERE I LIVE: MICHAEL SHANNON; JENNY WATSON

The art of the 1970s made it clear that the proximity of the artist to the suburbs was a crucial issue. As long as the artist maintained a distance from the suburbs, even if this was intended as a critical distance, they could not hope to express adequately the substance of suburban culture. No amount of sympathy for the suburbs could overcome the absence of its inhabitants and the lives that they made for themselves.

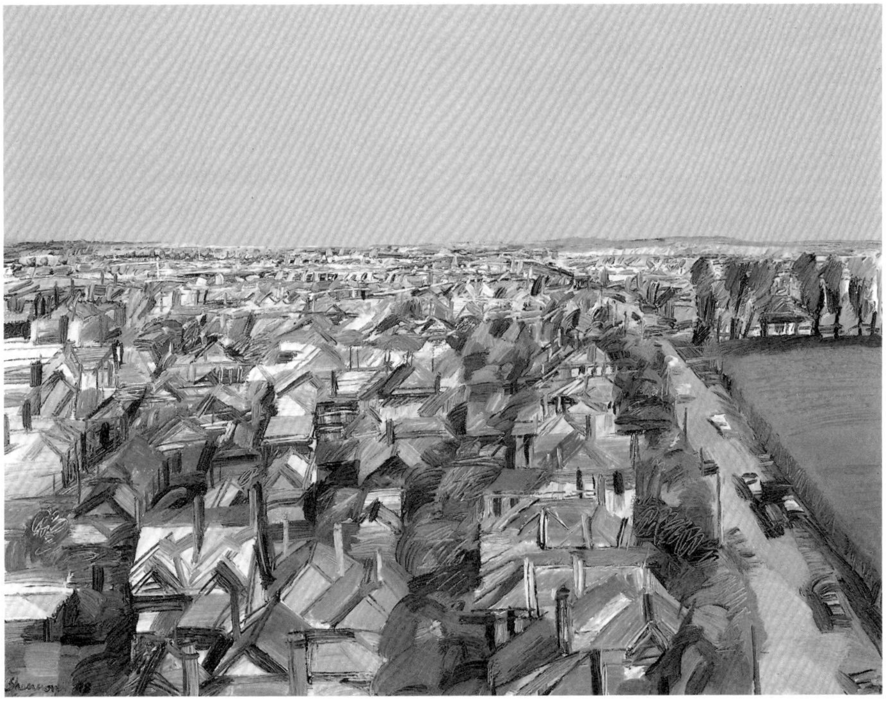

Michael Shannon,
Suburban Landscape, Melbourne, 1978

Michael Shannon's *Suburban Landscape, Melbourne* (1978) left behind his earlier depictions of desolate streets and fading communities, such as *The Corner Shop* (1965) and *Abandoned Footy Ground* (1971). Suburbia was now presented as a green and pleasant land, albeit one peppered with the red of roof tiles. The material and psychological advantages of the suburb — comfort and security — seem to outweigh the negatives — isolation and alienation.

Echoing the claims of recent sociology, Shannon implied that the suburb offered a negotiated security; the negative sides were recognised, but were deemed an acceptable price to pay for the positive aspects. Suburb-dwellers got what they wanted. But what cannot appear in the painting are the precise components of that negotiation or those groups who might find the price too high — non-working women and migrants, for example. The elevated point of view in the painting says it all; distant, sweeping and synoptic, it is innovative in its positive view of the suburbs but remains rooted in an earlier desire to understand the suburbs as a generic phenomenon.

In the 1970s, after years of setting themselves apart from the suburbs, artists were finally prepared to admit the obvious — that they lived there themselves. Rather than act as judge, jury and executioner, the task of artists became one of dealing with the complex layering of history, ideology and identity that accumulated in the suburbs. Images and practices that registered the diversity and fluidity of urban life had to be developed.

Jenny Watson's series of suburban diptychs, the "House Paintings" [Plate 11], was among the most successful responses to this challenge. This is primarily because Watson developed a way of painting the suburbs that incorporated reflections on art's conventional approaches to the suburbs while accepting that depicting that abstract concept *suburbia* might be beyond the capabilities of art.

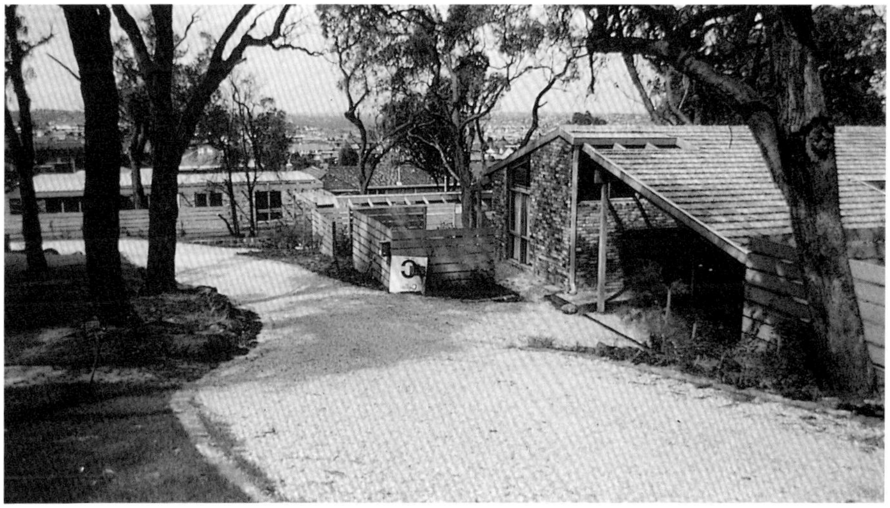

Merchant Builders, Conservation cluster housing, Doncaster, Melbourne, 1972

The artist painted the suburban houses in which she had lived. Each diptych consisted of a small Photorealist painting of the house, with its street address superimposed, and a larger canvas, an indistinct abstract work produced by gridding and enlarging the first. Embedded in the series were layered narratives: the chapters of the artist's life, the neighbourhoods of her youth, the memories associated with each house, and the subtle indicators of class implicit in the addresses. These competed with the frontal, photographic style of the paintings, as if two modes of interpretation — the empirical and the psychological — were in conflict (as indeed they often were in the sociology, and the art, of the day). As a result, the diptychs mapped both a personal history and the differing discourses applied to the suburbs by their interpreters.

This reflexiveness is typical of postmodern artistic practice; Watson presents not only a site — the suburb — but also the various means of *sighting* it — autobiography, photography, painting, geography, sociology. Her work was premised on a relativist realism; an effect that she later described — when interviewed by Paul Taylor in 1982 — as arising when "the work moves in and out of realism of every sort — observed reality … cultural reality, emotional reality". If all channels were accepted as real, all points of view given equal weight, then the social and intellectual hierarchies that belittled the suburb could be side-stepped.

In Watson's "House Paintings" series, meaning is rendered elusive or unstable, in contrast to earlier, pat definitions of suburbia. In large part this is due to her acceptance that painting, and consequently the viewer, could not make contact with its subject except in the most limited ways. In effect, the paintings are as much about what cannot be seen as what can. The public faces of the houses (their facades) reveal something of the social status of their inhabitants, but the private life of their interiors remains hidden. If the domestic sphere was regarded as woman's realm, Watson at least reclaimed it for herself, even if she did this by concealment.

This effect is amplified by the larger canvas in each pair. As a painting of a painting (of a photograph) it reinforces the sense that a commentary on suburbia always involves a gradual process of distancing oneself from the initial object of attention, leaving the artist suggesting an absence rather than depicting a presence. The process of enlargement dissolves the houses into grids of non-referential brushstrokes; the procedures of art and representation eventually lose their grip on the motif entirely. At the same time, Watson's expressionistic working over of the houses suggests that memory and emotion are woven into the buildings: each brushmark is a sign of her active presence on the canvas and, by analogy, in the house itself.

Furthermore, like Dale Hickey, she corrupted the formal integrity of the abstract canvas with the taint of suburbia. The maligned reality of the suburbs was used to destabilise the elite discourses of the visual arts. Suburbia, then, shook the confidence of art in ways that questioned painting's ability to mean, to represent and to maintain its high cultural status.

FEMINISM AND DOMESTICITY: ANN NEWMARCH; HELEN GRACE; MICKEY ALLAN

For artists associated with the resurgent feminist art movement of the 1970s and early '80s, the suburbs, and particularly the domestic sphere, were themes that allowed women to explore their position within the art system and the world at large. Ann Newmarch's *Backyard* (1975), a photo-silkscreen print showing two young children at play, depicted the home as the place of childrearing.

If childrearing is a woman's role, as was assumed at the time, the image registers both women's power *and* their lack of it. There is strength to be found in the daily struggles of mothers, and Newmarch emphasised this in her project "The House that Peg Built", which celebrated the skill and resilience of her aunt. But Newmarch was also conscious of the threat posed to children by forces seemingly beyond her own — or indeed any individual's — control, expressing such fears in a later series on the theme of uranium mining, radiation pollution and birth deformity.

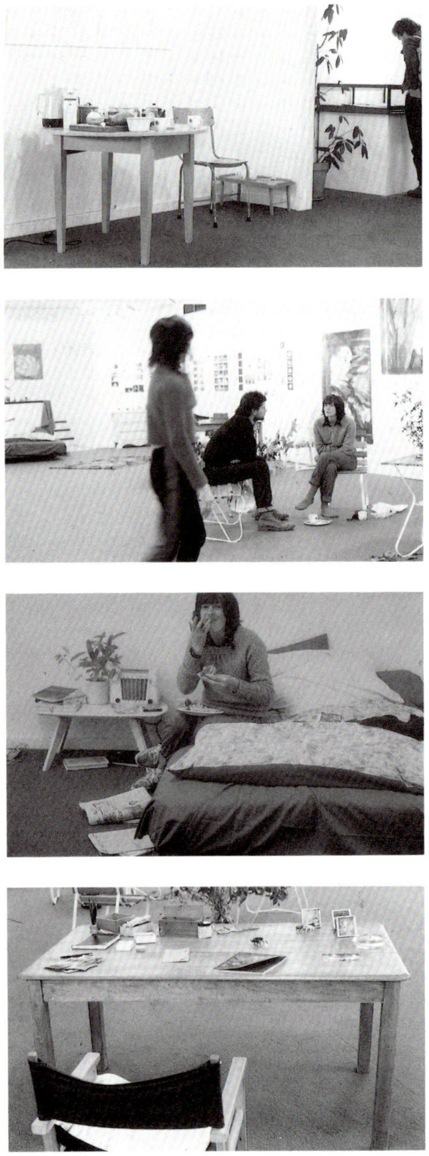

Micky Allan,
"Live In Show" (various installation views), 1978

The domestic image is double-edged, combining a despairing note with a call to action. In common with many feminist artists, Newmarch was also conscious of the ways in which preconceptions of women's domestic roles affected their status in the art world. Once again, the image of innocent children has a bitter twist, for the male authorities of the art scene frequently saw a woman's artistic practice as secondary to childrearing, as something that would be dropped when children arrived. Certainly many women did find that domestic duties — of many sorts — had a significant impact on the nature and quantity of the art they produced.

Helen Grace subtly combined two key elements of feminist artists' analysis of domesticity in her *Time and Motion Study #1 'Women seem to adapt to repetitive-type tasks'* (1980), exhibited in "The Lovely Motherhood Show" at the Experimental Art Foundation, Adelaide, in 1981. Her series of photographs of nappies drying on a backyard clothesline, one print for each day of the week, equated domestic labour with the repetitive mechanical tasks of mass production. The work argued against the regimentation of both activities, while also suggesting that domestic work ought to at least be recognised as an economic equivalent to industrial labour. At the same time, in using the same photograph for each day, rather than shooting a series on consecutive days, Grace suggested that her artistic practice might also be subject to the same constriction, repetition and mechanisation.

Moving beyond women artists' metaphorical reappropriation of the domestic sphere, Mickey Allan literally equated domesticity with art, in her 1978 "Live In Show". The artist moved her household furniture and belongings into the George Paton Gallery, on the campus of the University of Melbourne, in which her drawings and photographic works were being exhibited. She lived in the space for the duration of the exhibition, encouraging interaction with gallery visitors.

The desire for a union of art and everyday life had been expressed by male artists since World War 2, especially those associated with the Fluxus movement or working under the influence of John Cage. The domestic realm had, however, been conspicuous in its absence. It was as if this feminised domain lacked the substance of public culture. Allan's installation not only revalued the domestic but also pointed to a blindspot in the rhetoric of male artists who, for all their professed admiration for the everyday, still filtered it through patriarchal criteria.

CAPTIVE IN THE HOME:
MANDY MARTIN; KERRIE LESTER

Some women artists carried such feminist analyses into the '80s, creating images of the house as prison; the suburban woman as its presumed captive. Mandy Martin's series of photo-silkscreen images of houses in Queanbeyan, Canberra, uses a variety of formal devices to represent the home as a kind of prison — physically, socially and psychologically constraining women.

The flat, frontal compositions present impenetrable walls, which suggest that no interaction between the occupants and the outside world is possible. Women, they suggest, are held rigidly within a domestic role. Blank and shuttered windows reinforce this effect, and the fence palings in *Picket Fences* (1980) [Plate 12] become jail bars. Even the neatly clipped shrubs suggest that free growth and organic movement have been suppressed by the containing geometry of suburban architecture. The very demeanour of the house seems to hint at the psychological state of its inhabitant: withdrawn, defensive and agoraphobic.

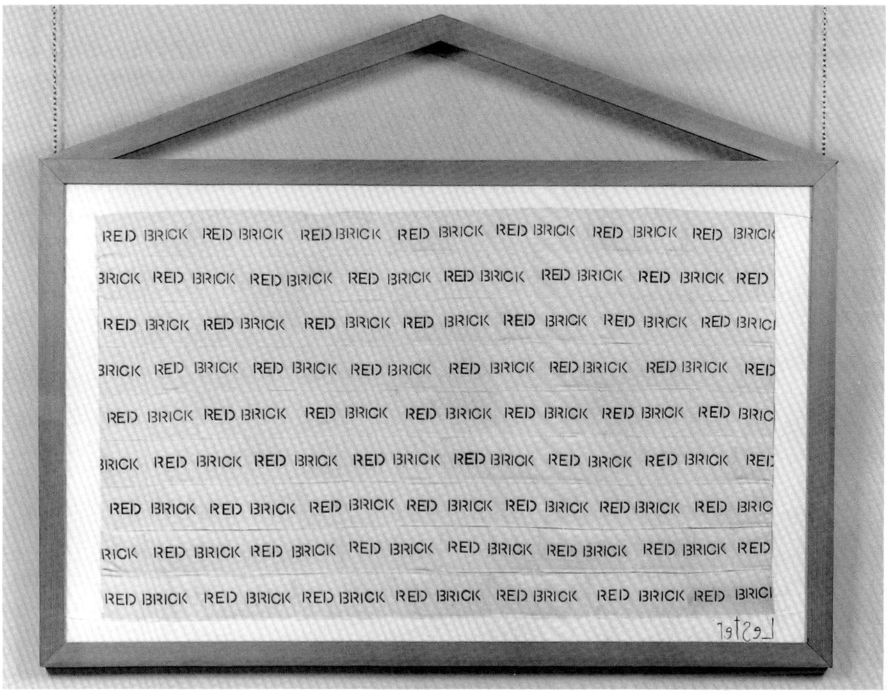

Kerrie Lester,
Red Brick House, 1981

Likewise, Kerrie Lester's *Red Brick House* (1981) suggests that the bland, repetitive facades of suburban architecture construct rigid boundaries around their inhabitants, fending off contact. The literal frame of the piece can be read metaphorically as a reference to the social frame that domesticity erects around suburb-dwellers. It emphasises the obsession with boundaries of suburban life and town planning. The surface of Lester's canvas itself is not a point of entry into a pictorial world but an impenetrable wall. The point of such work is that it does not offer contact with suburbia, instead it suggests that the refusal of contact is a characteristic of suburban life.

In the earlier work, I was dealing with the theme of women in suburban Queanbeyan and combined images of the women, with selected visual metaphors from their home environments: disfigured trees, windows, shadows. These reinforced the information given about repression, deprivation, neuroticism as shown in the women's tense faces, hands and postures. The present work indicates these social conditions in a different manner ... to create the feeling of human presence without actually incorporating the figure.

Mandy Martin, artist's statement, 1980

AN EERIE REALISM: RONALD HAWKE; CHRIS O'DOHERTY

A new realism was evident in images of the suburbs in the 1970s. For some artists, such as Ronald Hawke, this realism took the form of a crisp, evenly lit depiction of the suburbs which evoked a mood of barren despair. In *Hill's Hoist* (1975) the linear geometry of urban living comes off a poor second to the organic forms of the Adelaide hills that it has relegated to the background.

The Photorealism popular in mid-decade, which presented a world of pristine, sterile surfaces, was used by artists like Alan Oldfield and Chris O'Doherty to convey the eerie formality of suburbia. The carefully controlled geometry of their canvases — which frequently froze appearances within precise, frontal networks of verticals and hori-

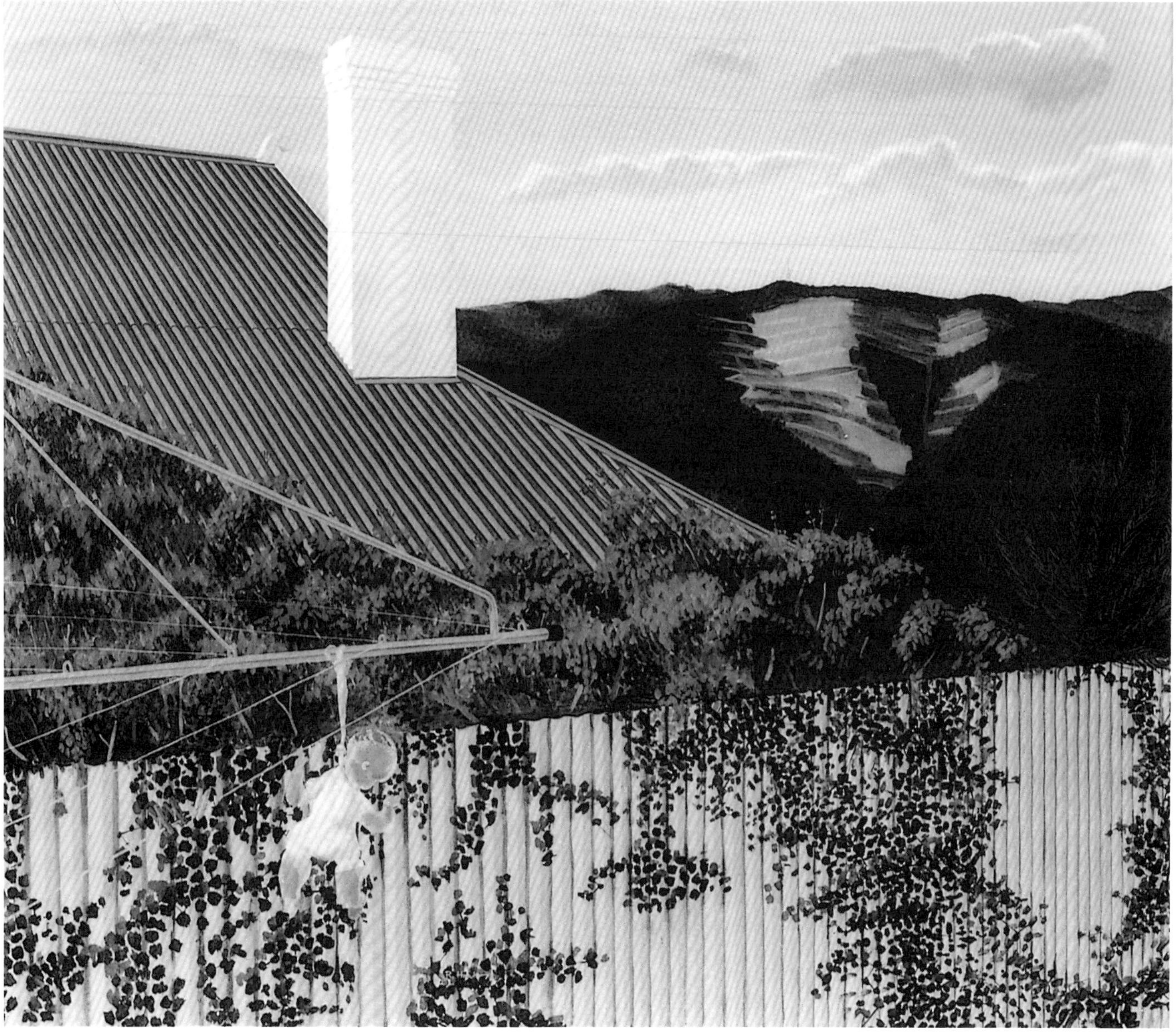

Ronald Hawke,
Hill's Hoist, 1973

zontals — mirrored the planned environment of the suburbs. The mood of restraint, in both composition and colour, echoed the psychological and social constraints of suburbia.

The very flatness of their images suggested a lack of interior life in the suburbs, both physical and spiritual. These works can be seen as the successors to the '50s melancholia of Brack. While Brack's '70s counterparts were not unsympathetic to suburbia, such realisms are markedly different from those of the culturalist and feminist artists who sought a positive engagement with the suburbs, warts and all.

THE EVASIONS OF POSTMODERNITY

Once again it becomes clear that, for artists, the suburbs and suburbia had more than intrinsic interest. They also offered a way to construct metaphors for Australia's national and cultural identity, or to explore theories of the visual arts. There is no question that the suburbs became a more acceptable motif in the 1970s, but it is also apparent that the increased presence of the suburbs in the visual arts did not necessarily mean that artists and viewers were brought closer to suburban realities. That is, the suburbs were still often used as a sign for something else, be it psychic anomie, the disappearance of nature, the passing of youth, or the waning of individualism.

Community-based art practices, such as those of Geoffrey Hogg and Peter Kennedy, attempted to bring the particularities of suburban life into art. However, the diversity of suburban cultures that they discovered made the suburbs, if anything, *harder* to define and comprehend.

Feminist artists like Ann Newmarch and Jenny Watson suggested that suburbia amounted to a complicated web of ideological positions which were alternately positive and negative, nostalgic and critical, empowering and oppressive. This mobile, reversible evasiveness of the postmodern suburb would continue to preoccupy Australian artists in the 1980s and '90s.

6 THE 1980s AND BEYOND

the **postmodern** suburb

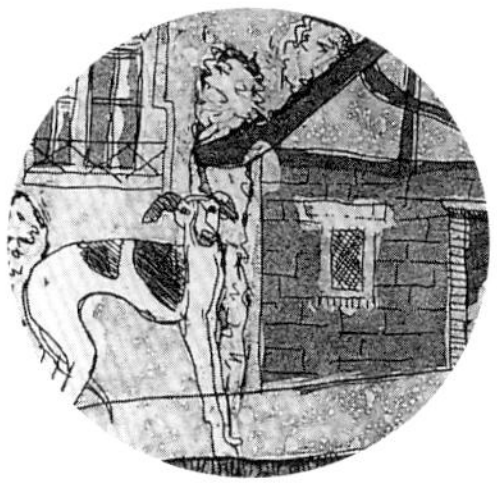

Economic restructuring and information technology have now produced multicentred cities in which suburbs are the core of employment and growth, stealing the limelight from the city centre. This development consolidates a pattern that commenced in the 1970s. In the '80s and '90s, the suburbs themselves became unstable sites, with policies of economic rationalism leading to the amalgamation of town councils, renaming of municipalities, redrawing of boundaries and redefinition of planning codes.

If the social and economic processes of postmodernism were operating in the 1970s, it was not until the '80s and '90s that artists consistently sought to come up with cultural metaphors with which to address them. Themes of mobility, complex communities, fluid and hybrid identities, and the interplay of personal, psychological and political realities within the suburbs have now been taken up by many Australian artists, among them Ken Searle, Lin Onus, Jon Campbell, Tracey Moffatt and Mikala Dwyer.

'POSTMODERNISM': A POPULAR CATCHPHRASE

Prior to the '70s, social change and mobility in the suburbs were counterbalanced by the prevailing cultural images of suburban stability, which artists themselves promoted in their condemnations of suburban conformity. In the '70s , artists undertook a reversal of this, championing the heterogeneity of suburbia as a means of contesting the homogeneity of the dominant culture. The '80s and '90s, however, have seen a more pervasive awareness of the implications of postmodernism, transforming a specialist analytical term into a popular catchphrase, even a cliché.

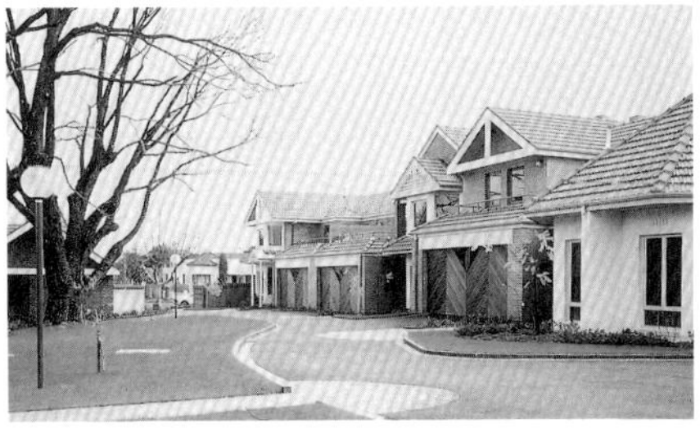

Tim Hurburgh,
"Ellesmere Court, Princess St, Kew, Melbourne"

In a postmodern culture, highly conscious of spatial and social mobility, the suburban state of mind becomes even more difficult to pin down. The suburb itself, while relatively self-contained, is not necessarily stable, its character shaped by notions of change, shifting lifestyle trends, and generational and class mobility. The archetypal urban figure — or urban myth — of the 1980s, the yuppie (Young Upwardly Mobile Professional), was by definition on the move, just as that other urban acronym, the nimby (Not In My Back Yard), was someone with strongly held beliefs as to what their suburb should be like. The suburbs are now meaningful in multiple ways and on multiple levels. While notions of the home and of amenity persist, they are coloured by a sense of potential change, of shifting image, and of malleable futures.

RE-READING THE SUBURBS

If the status of the suburbs was changing, so too were cultural attitudes towards them. In rejecting received cultural hierarchies, artists of the 1960s and 1970s such as Hickey, Rooney and Watson, had paved the way for an acceptance of the suburb as the crux of Australian life, and for a positive reappraisal of its merits.

Developments in international art and theory became increasingly useful to Australian artists. If Pop Art and the theories of the avant-garde composer John Cage urged artists to unite art and everyday life, it was developments in sociology that provided the crucial model for Australian artists. The English sociologist Dick Hebdige, based at Birmingham University, was particularly influential. Building a method of analysis that came to be called Cultural Studies — identified specifically as the 'Birmingham School'— he argued that the meanings of a culture were based on lived experience. In this sense any activity, even those previously considered banal and unimportant, could be regarded as having symbolic meaning and structure. The notion of style figured prominently in Hebdige's work, for it brought together the varied symbolic systems — language, behaviour, social ritual, aesthetics — that generated, broadcast and reinforced meaning. In its attention to everyday life, and its turning away from 'high' culture, this model could be readily applied to the suburbs.

The homogeneity of the suburbs discriminates against all sorts of groups. I'm interested in the way that the suburbs have developed with a kind of Anglo-Australian notion about how people live. The suburbs are still developing in the way that people thought they wanted to live in the immediate postwar period ... Now the suburbs are a least 50 per cent full of people from either first or second generation non-English-speaking backgrounds, and yet we still keep on building these houses as if everybody wants to live like the British always wanted to live. It's time we paid attention to what the different cultures want.

Sophie Watson, Professor of Urban and Regional Planning, University of Sydney, 1992

This new, style-conscious sociology of the Birmingham School conferred the suburban landscape with a hitherto unacknowledged sophistication and substance. Such thinking was reinforced by developments in American architectural theory, particularly the writings of Robert Venturi, Denise Scott-Brown and Steven Izenour. They argued, in their book *Learning From Las Vegas*, that the maligned, 'trashy' architecture of suburbs and shopping strips contained a complex architectural symbolism. They regarded facades as screens on which an overlay of signs could be draped, with each component, however tacky, given serious attention by the architects.

Artists' re-reading of the suburbs was not simply a matter of answering old, negative images with new, positive ones, or unhesitatingly applying insights gained from overseas theorists. Artists had to come up with new ways of understanding Australia's suburbs. The discovery of new meanings for the suburbs was not simply a product of the arrival of a different kind of suburb, but rested also on a new artistic consciousness, which in turn approached the making of art, and the forging of meaning within it, in novel ways.

LEARNING FROM SUBURBIA: HOWARD ARKLEY; IMANTS TILLERS

Since the late 1970s Howard Arkley has been cataloguing the appearance and lifestyles of suburbia in his many images of suburban streets, houses and interiors [Plates 13 & 14]. But it is not the mere presence of the suburbs in his work that is significant. The *way* they appear marks a change from an earlier insistence on the generic quality of the suburbs to a new recognition of the varieties of suburban style. Arkley's airbrush paintings and drawings trace a bewildering variety of facades, driveways, fences, gardens, screen doors and rooflines to document the styles of the suburban house. Far from the epitome of sameness, Arkley finds the suburb a source of difference. Individuality, his works imply, can be found in the manipulation of the codes and conventions of architecture and landscape. The decorative embellishments applied to suburban houses, which critic Robin Boyd condemned as 'featurism' in the 1960s, are celebrated by Arkley, who seems intrigued by the way these established codes can mark one house as an exotic Californian bungalow and another as a quaint English Cottage. Where Boyd found pathetic aspirations and bad taste, Arkley finds a fascinating and sophisticated complex of styles and signs.

Arkley's sympathetic view of the suburbs is not simply the result of a less stratified, more tolerant view of culture, although the example of earlier artists and writers who revalued the suburbs is obviously important. What also motivated his positive view of the suburbs was a new understanding of the ways in which meaning was generated, and the ways in which an artist could engage with such meanings. Arkley's delineation of the styles of the suburb is more the work of an anthropologist than a connoisseur or apologist. The photographic material on which his work is based was gathered on field trips around the suburbs of Melbourne, and his paintings mark out the styles of the suburban house as a linguist might catalogue the dialects of a tribal culture.

Arkley's anthropology of the suburbs is similar in spirit to Hebdige's studies of youth subcultures. His paintings emphasise the style of the suburbs, but rather than suggesting that such styles are shallow and meaningless, he insists that individuals and cultures can construct their identity through the styles of the suburban house. Venturi and his partners had argued for a shift from the 'Heroic and Original' architecture of modernism to the 'Ugly and Ordinary' architecture of postmodernism. While Arkley stopped short of such sweeping claims, his paintings were executed in a similar spirit of tolerance and iconoclasm.

Arkley's fascination with the suburb is also a veiled commentary on the status of art, because one cannot introduce the pop culture of the suburbs into the high cultural realm of art without triggering some reflection on their relative rank. If his sympathy for the suburbs and his insistence on their complexity elevates them, it still seems that the paint and canvas of the art world carry more weight than the bricks and tiles of the suburbs. The mere incorporation of the everyday into art is not going to iron out their differences.

Like Arkley, Sydney artist Imants Tillers also set in train this sly reversal of status. In 1980 Tillers produced a video — for the National Gallery of Victoria's 'Survey'

The use of the rural landscape as a metaphor for the Australian experience is fictional and romantic; it's not true. It's always amazed me how few artists have used the real Australian experience; that is, the Australian suburban landscape as a source ... People often choose to think that I'm being cynical or sarcastic or witty about the houses ... That's not what I think at all! I'm not saying this is bad, it's just a question of what is ... At the same time, it's not that I'm admiring it either.

Howard Arkley quoted in
Richard Brown,
"Spraying the Suburban Dream",
Tension, no.18, October 1989

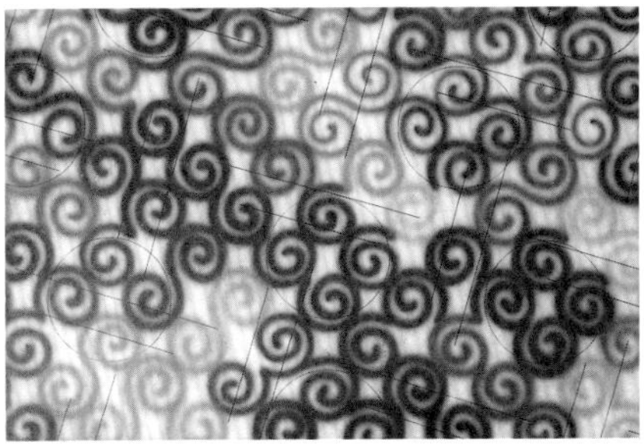

Howard Arkley,
Secession (detail), 1979

The blocks are huge. Big brick buildings, one after another. This could be Balwyn, could be Burwood, could be Vermont. Could be Mitcham. Maybe if you grew up around here all the space might mean something to you. East, west, south, north, the city of Melbourne blurs into itself. Concrete on concrete, brick veneer on brick veneer, weatherboard on weatherboard. Walking through the suburbs, I feel like I'm in the ugliest place on the planet.

Christos Tsiolkas, from *Loaded*, 1995

series — which consisted of slow pans across suburban facades in western Sydney. Whatever its pretensions, Tillers seemed to be suggesting, the art world had a lot in common with the suburbs: both were highly style-conscious; both were obsessed with appearances; both were intent on keeping up with the neighbours; and both were shot through with territorial rivalry and snobbery. This gesture of reversal, in both Tillers's and Arkley's work, moves art towards the suburbs rather than elevating the suburbs to the status of art. In the process, the differences between the two are not so much eliminated as converted to an equivalence; art and the suburbs, these artists suggest, have a family resemblance.

While Arkley's suburban paintings have a certain analytical quality — cataloguing the symbolic languages of the suburbs — he is also careful to suggest that the suburbs remain beyond an artist's comprehension. The postmodern artist, like the modernist, believes that art can offer knowledge of the world; the difference is that the postmodernist would never claim that this knowledge is absolute or infallible. Arkley's airbrush technique produces strong black lines whose edges have fuzzy penumbrae. These lines, while bold, are difficult to hold steady visually, especially as they approach each other or increase in density. This blurry effect, coupled with intense, sometimes fluorescent colours, results in visually disturbing, unstable images. It is in fact quite difficult to look at an Arkley painting for any length of time. The flaring and flickering effects of line and colour have a metaphorical resonance; it is as if the suburbs escape our gaze. They can be painted, drawn and viewed, but not pinned down.

So while Arkley suggests that an artist might approach the suburbs as an analytical anthropologist, they still slip through his fingers; one cannot 'picture' the suburbs adequately in the realm of art. After decades of art condemning the suburbs, Arkley implies that the suburbs defeat art. This defeat is not that which the artists of the anti-suburban '50s feared — that the mass culture of suburbia would swamp the high culture of art — but rather a recognition that the suburbs reveal art's efforts to make sense of the world to be necessarily limited.

IRONY AND MONOTONY: ALEKS DANKO

Aleks Danko also goes about exploring sets of conventions — the suburbs' and artists' — in works which humorously register the norms of suburbia but also suggest that art has oversimplified the issues. His 1991 installation *Day In, Day Out (Second Version)* bluntly evokes the conformity attributed to the suburbs — row after row of identical houses, turned out on a production line, are laid out in a neatly ordered grid. Within modernist art, the grid had been established as one of the foundations of abstraction. It imparted to art a sense of structure from which such wild variables as the artist's subjectivity had been eliminated. As such, the grid was a ready metaphor for the dehumanising abstraction of suburban geography.

Aleks Danko,
Day In, Day Out (Second Version) (detail), 1991

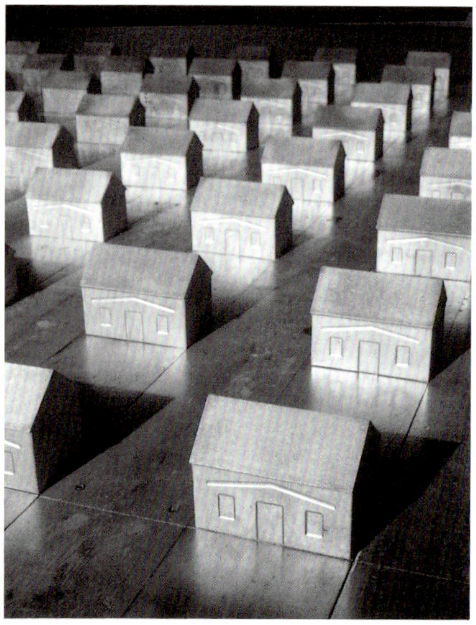

However, postmodern art is concerned not only with the problem of representing contemporary life but also with the weight of existing systems of representation that bear down on the artist. Not only have the suburbs been represented as conventional, the artistic means by which this was done have become conventions themselves. To depict the suburbs, as Danko is aware, also involves investigating and questioning the received ways of depicting them. In *Day In, Day Out (Second Version)*, the suburban desire for order and regularity is fulfilled. A rotating gel on a theatrical spotlight bathes the houses alternately in darkness and light, giving the viewer a sense — in the language of daytime TV — of the 'days of our lives' passing 'as the world turns'. The suburbs, according to Danko, are not for 'the young and the restless', but for the aged and resigned. The monotony of the installation suggests a pessimistic view of suburban life as a place where nothing really happens and life is a time served, a sentence fulfilled.

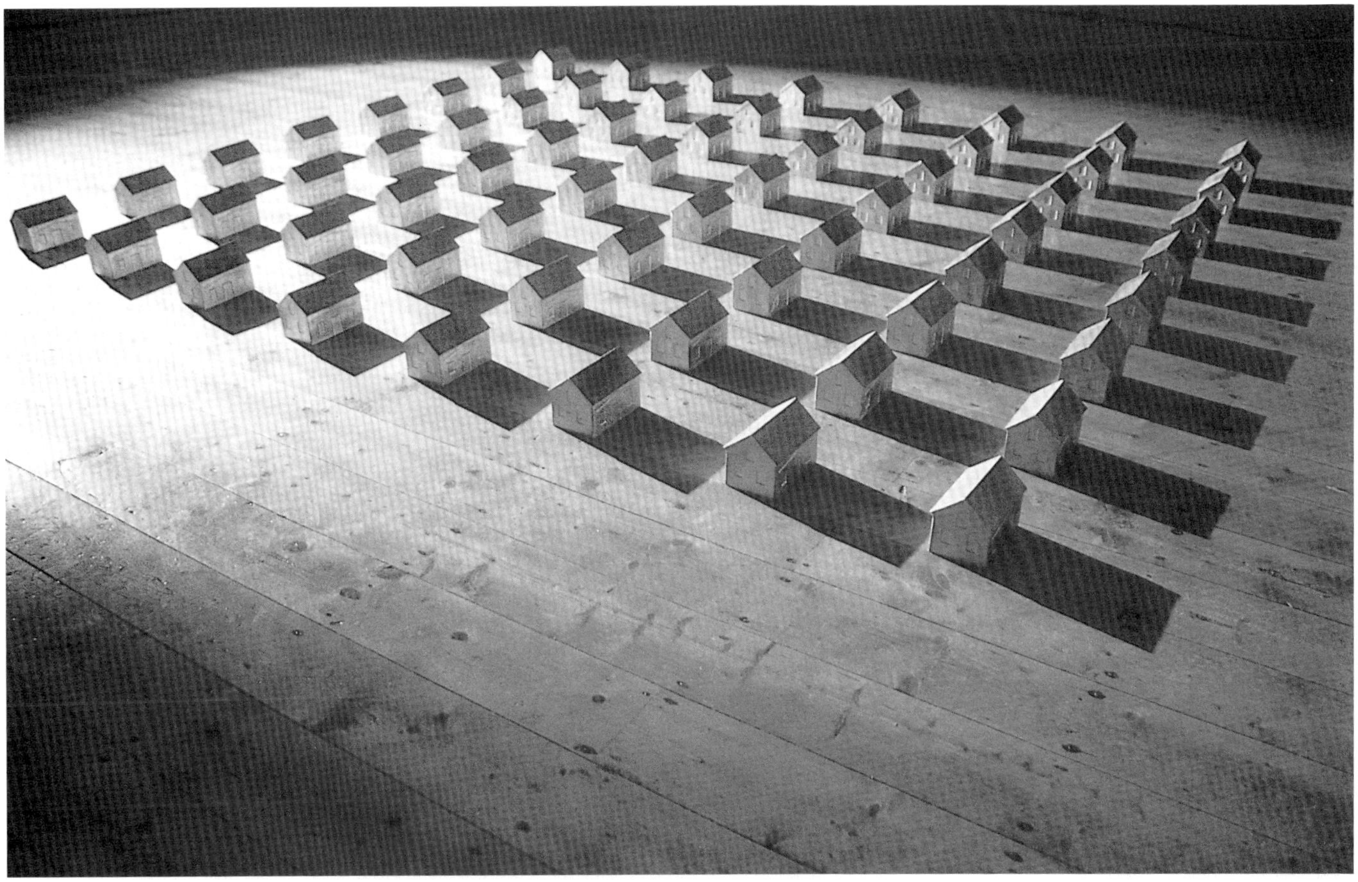

Aleks Danko,
Day In, Day Out (Second Version)(installation view), 1991

The theatricality of *Day In, Day Out (Second Version)* emphasises Danko's dual goal of depiction and critique. The regularity of suburban geography, the repetitive forms of suburban architecture, and the regimentation of suburban life are all in evidence. But these are so exaggerated that art's formularised anti-suburbanism is also glaringly apparent.

The very predicability of the suburbs may, however, be a positive quality — the unflappable suburb-dweller may have attained a Zen state in the heart of materialistic culture, accepting everything and finding value in it. This fatalistic resignation is evident in a statement that Danko attributed to his father: "As you know, we are pensioners, day in day out, twenty-four hours closer to death".

What we want now in Adelaide are writers and artists who work from the heart of those commonplace suburban streets, who recognise the weirdness of the ordinary, who record it before the version of it we have now is swept away. We want passion and intensity, and art that comes from places like Port Adelaide and Thebarton and Holden Hill; that stays unofficially wierd.

Barbara Hanrahan, from "Weird Adelaide", 1988

Danko is careful to link this view of the suburbs to his migrant father, who may after all have found in the suburbs precisely what he sought — peace and security. Besides, it would be impossible for any artist born in Adelaide, as Danko was, to take the alleged banality of the suburbs at face value, for, as artist and writer Barbara Hanrahan argues in "Weird Adelaide", the city of churches was notorious for its dark underbelly of sex crimes and serial killers. Danko's installation, which initially appears to be a straightforward condemnation of suburbia, turns out to be a highly ambiguous work, pointing to the intricacies concealed by cultural and artistic conventions alike, and commenting on art's relationship to the suburbs.

Since Danko is given to irony, he may have overstated the anti-suburban message in order to emphasise art's inability or unwillingness to find value in the suburbs. On other occasions, he contrasted the eccentricities of his studio practice with the normalcy of the suburban milieu in which they took place. Both tactics refer to artists' determination to register their difference from suburbia, to declare themselves the very opposite of suburban normality. For all their condemnation of the suburbs, Danko acknowledges, artists are parasitical on them. Artists need the suburbs in order to forge their own identity.

A NEW LANDSCAPE: VICTOR MAJZNER; KEN SEARLE

The suburban landscape, and the visual codes and conventions it adopts, provided evocative motifs for artists such as Arkley and Danko. Other artists sought to unite these features — in a critical way — with the strangeness or grandeur of earlier landscape traditions, which had provided such a pervasive iconography of Australian identity. Two distinctive marryings of suburban iconography and landscape conventions are provided by Victor Majzner and Ken Searle.

Majzner frequently contravenes the norms of landscape painting to raise questions about the versions of Australianness that are excluded from an imagery of national identity. His paintings bring together contradictory aspects of art and culture — footballers hover over outback landscapes, tourists mingle with Aboriginal rock paintings, decorative excess overwhelms the staid propriety of conventional landscape imagery. In *Creature Comforts* (1989) the suburbs, rather than being differentiated from the Australian landscape, are embedded in it, seeming to spring from its soil, with roof tops looming on the horizon like an outback mountain range.

Identity is a social invention. The individual's sense of identity is by its very nature fluid, compounded by understanding, emotion and a willingness to belong as much as by cultural or genetic make-up. The individual is a filtering device, continually re-assessing history, vigilant to social changes, sensitive to cultural developments, responsive to personal growth.

Victor Majzner, from *Towards Identity*, 1993

Following the influential historian Richard White, Majzner suggests that there is no real Australia, rather there are sets of ideas about 'Australianness' that are used to shape symbols of landscape and nationhood. Majzner's incongruous substitution of suburbs for outback allows him to make this point pictorially. When the suburbs appear in the wrong way — out of character, so to speak — the viewer is forced to reflect on the ways in which they usually appear, and the differences between the two options.

The surreal juxtaposition of imagery in *Creature Comforts* is accentuated by the bizarre chops that hover over the suburbs like a fleet of UFOs. The open-ended layerings triggered by the collage effect are emphasised by the multiple references of the title. 'Creature comforts' refers to the amenities of the suburban home — shelter and food in particular. But the creatures who provide that food — bred, butchered and sold — are presented in the raw, hinting at cruder human needs. The meat also suggests the pastoral industry, which itself transformed the Australian landscape, stripping it of vegetation, displacing its traditional owners and consolidating a vision of the land as something to be exploited. Majzner's painting, then, combines rural and urban, nature and industry, humanity and animality, the raw and the cooked.

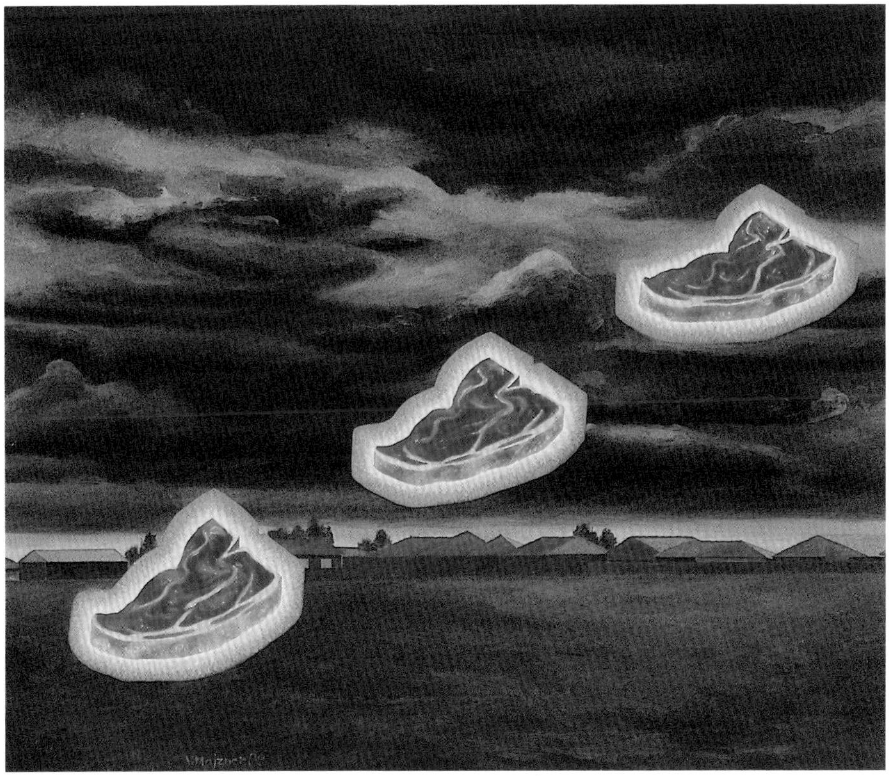

Victor Majzner,
Creature Comforts, 1989

Ken Searle also takes up the absences of Australian landscape conventions. His monumental series of paintings "West" (1991) [Plate 15] seems to grant substance to the suburbs on the basis of scale alone. More importantly, he takes issue with an entrenched class prejudice that belittled the working class suburbs of Sydney's west, holding them up as a model of bad taste and mediocrity, stereotyping their inhabitants —'Westies'— as ignorant, violent petty criminals and no-hopers.

Searle's canvases are a pictorial voyage tracing a train trip from the inner suburb of Newtown to Penrith in the west. While this journey maintains a sense of the distance between central city and outer suburb, the artist's compression of pictorial space and dense overlapping of buildings suggests an organic continuity in urban geography. By showing that a clear physical distinction between centre and periphery is impossible, Searle exposes the distinction as artificial, ideological. As Diane Powell suggests in her book *Out West*, the western suburbs are a kind of folk devil, whose difference from respectable society is never proven but instead is conjured up in the repetition of anecdotes and urban myths.

Searle's is a profoundly humanist vision of the western suburbs. Refusing to accept the clichés about Westies, he depicts an intricate suburban infrastructure, an elaborate set of spatial and social relations. Parks and factories, homes and shops, work and play: all fuse together. Significantly, the suburb is not discussed in terms of the old pairings of country and city, bushman and housewife — distinctions that Majzner unsettles through surreal juxtaposition. Searle points out that the polarities now used to distinguish acceptable from unacceptable Australianness centre on class and ethnicity.

HOMELANDS AND NEW HOMES:
SALVATORE ZOFREA; NICHOLAS NEDELKOPOULOS; CONSTANZE ZIKOS

The great waves of migration after World War 2 reshaped old suburbs and influenced the construction of new ones. Threaded through the postmodern suburb, their diverse histories and cultures confer different meanings on key motifs of suburbia — the home, the

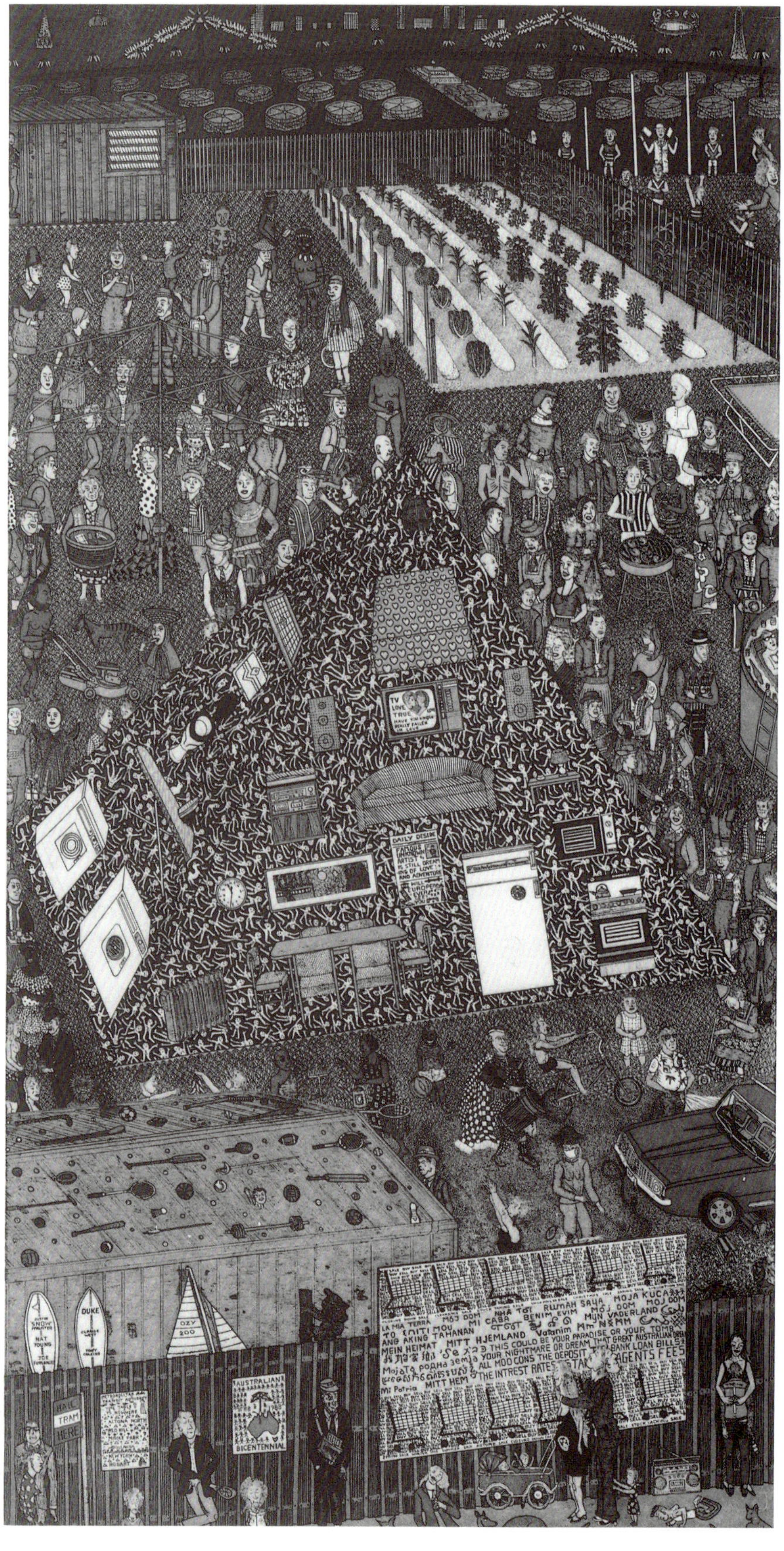

Nicholas Nedelkopoulos,
That Great Australian Dream, 1987

family, community and identity. Artists focusing on migrant experience and ethnic diversity in the suburb have followed three general strategies. Some, such as Salvatore Zofrea, have reflected on migrant culture in order to challenge the Anglo-Celtic bias in Australian culture; revealing different lifestyles, systems of belief, and patterns of behaviour. Others, including Nicholas Nedelkopoulos, have cast an ironic eye over Anglo-Australian culture, often gently mocking it. Finally, artists such as Constanze Zikos have explored the hybrid identities formed in the overlap of migrant and Anglo-Australian culture, often using clichés, stereotypes and prejudices to reveal the tensions within multicultural society.

In a series of woodblock prints made in 1989, Salvatore Zofrea constructed a narrative tracing the experience of a European migrant. A man arrives from Europe alone, working hard to earn the money to help his wife join him, eventually establishing a home for his family in the new country. The purchase of the home is a bitter-sweet event. It signifies putting down roots in the new country, but also a formal separation from the old. It carries with it the tensions of multiculturalism — the demand for assimilation and the desire to preserve links with another culture. Work, family and home are the foundation of the conventional Australian Dream, but Zofrea's series points to new resonances in the story, for the suburb also resonates with dislocation, isolation, alienation and even racism.

One way of resisting such resentment is to reverse its terms. Nicholas Nedelkopoulos melds his parents' home with signs of Anglo-Australian culture in a visual dramatising of the struggle of migration and assimilation. While the title of the work suggests aspiration to the Australian Dream, Anglo-Australian culture is depicted as a kind of ethnic enclave in its own right; barbecues, football matches, and gardening are depicted as quaint and eccentric rather than as the norm. In his *That Great Australian Dream* (1987), a bird's eye view of the streets and backyards of the suburbs, suburban activities, especially leisure and consumption, are depicted as the bizarre rituals of a peculiar tribal culture.

The relative value accorded to diverse cultural experiences is a problem that lies at the heart of attempts to proclaim contemporary Australia a 'multicultural' society. What might be a valued activity or lifestyle for a particular ethnic culture may be marginalised in favour of an official version of 'Australian' identity.

Such cultural hierarchies are often symbolised in debates over taste. The revival of old inner suburbs by successive waves of migration, and subsequent movement to more prosperous outer suburbs have produced new suburban forms. Often a thinly veiled resentment is evident in discussion of these changes, including derogatory references to the Mediterranean architecture of Southern European migrants, or condescending comments on the 'colourful' character of ethnic suburbs. In such comments, old fears are given new expression — where once the homogeneity of a suburb raised the spectre of conformity, now ethnically uniform suburbs are condemned as 'ghettos'.

Constanze Zikos invokes the idea of kitsch — a synthetic or mass-cultural style disdained by high culture — in order to highlight the hybrid qualities of migrant culture and the implicitly racist terms by which it is dismissed [Plate 16]. Studies of the migrant home have shown that it combines elements of Anglo culture (especially on the exterior) with a decor that seeks to maintain links with the migrant's country of origin. The home is both a sign of successful relocation and an attempt to compensate for detachment from the original homeland.

Zikos transfers this hybridity to the realm of abstract art. He uses the geometric abstract style that was the goal of many Anglo-Australian artists, which suggests his successful assimilation to the dominant culture. At the same time, he incorporates decorative motifs originating in classical Greece that have trickled down to the present, implying that his abstraction is made with a Greek accent. This accent is presented as something potentially threatening to the dominant aesthetic, since Zikos's lurid colours and Laminex grounds corrupt the purity of high art.

In part, Zikos's work is a meditation on the way abstract art can devolve into mere pattern-making. In this respect, his work might be linked to that of Rooney and Hickey, who had earlier used suburban elements to corrupt and parody abstraction. But more significant is the way that Zikos uses contrasting cultures of taste — suburban ethnic kitsch and the aristocratic elitism of abstract art — to echo the power struggle within debates on Australian identity. He points to patterns of denigration and exclusion that propel definitions of Australianness, exposing the way in which the complex identity politics of migrant culture are blithely dismissed as bad taste.

The North is where they put most of the wogs. Not in the beginning. In the beginning we clogged the inner city and the industrial suburbs of the west. But as wogs earned some money and decided to move further afield, into the bush-land-torn-down-to-become-housing-estates, more and more concrete and brick-veneer palaces began to be sprinkled across the Northern suburbs ... The North isn't Melbourne, it isn't Australia. It is a little village in the mountains of the Mediterranean transported to the bottom of the southern hemisphere.

Christos Tsiolkas, from *Loaded,* 1995

By insisting on the importance of such difference, Zikos argues for a disturbing disintegration of Australian identity. The postmodern suburb now appears as the very antithesis of the supposed homogeneity of suburbia. The threat of the suburb is no longer its uniformity but rather the impossibility of stability.

SUBURBAN AND ABORIGINAL: TREVOR NICKOLLS; LIN ONUS

The contemporary suburb appears increasingly as a place of hybrid or unfixed identities, in which 'Australian' identity seems to elude definition — or depiction — altogether. Artists can no longer concern themselves with the state of an abstract 'suburbia'. Nor are they able — or perhaps prepared — to try to resolve its complexities into an archetype.

Trevor Nickolls's vision of the suburbs is familiar in one respect — in works such as *Dreamtime to Machinetime* (1984) the regulated geometry of roads, yards and homes is evident. The regimented urban existence of 'Machinetime' is compared unfavourably to the spiritual values of Dreamtime. Nickolls's personal experience of both Aboriginal and Anglo-Australian culture introduces a rarely acknowledged version of Australian identity — urban aboriginality.

His fusion of supposedly separate cultures points to a tense and unstable Australianness, which is highly conscious of difference: different colour — in the meeting of black and white suburb-dwellers; different values — in the contrast of Machinetime and Dreamtime; and different politics — evident in Nickolls's juxtaposition of the Land Rights flag with suburban development. Nickolls's paintings emphatically avoid any suggestion of assimilation or reconciliation of black and white culture. Border conflicts and clashes of identity abound in his version of suburbia.

Lin Onus also plays with contrasting categories to emphasise the persistence of difference in spite of the political rhetoric of reconciliation. *Fruit Bats* (1990) [Plate 17] combines a found object — the Hill's Hoist — and sculpted forms; Western representational illusionism and the abstraction of an Aboriginal cross hatching technique; the technologies of manufacturing industry and the organic forms of the bats. Even the cleanliness associated with washing is contrasted with the bat droppings on the ground beneath the clothes lines. This contrast between nature and culture appears frequently in Onus's work, usually signifying a contrast between an Aboriginal engagement with nature and an Anglo-Celtic determination to control or exploit it.

The work is humorous — almost like an antipodean version of Alfred Hitchcock's film *The Birds* — and proves that there is still new life to be found in that most clichéd artistic symbol of suburbia, the Hill's Hoist. But there is an undercurrent of anger in the

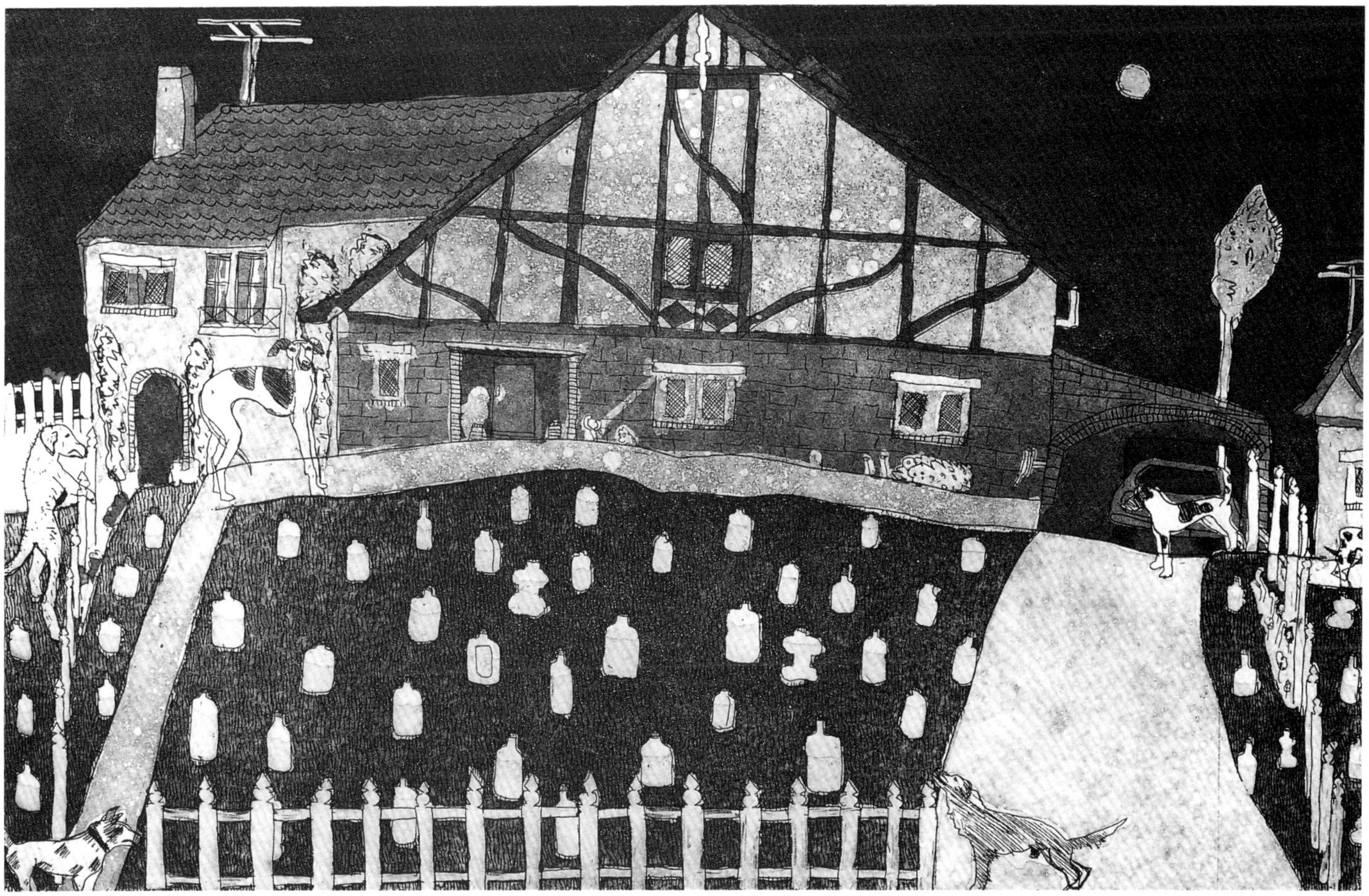

Ron McBurnie, *Dogs Bottles*, 1988

sculpture. It carefully avoids the easy platitudes of reconciliation, which attempt to sanitise difference and wish away its inherent conflicts.

RITES AND RITUALS: JON CAMPBELL; RON McBURNIE; RANDELLI

The legacy of Pop Art and the new discipline of Cultural Studies helped to popularise and legitimate a 'culturalist' attitude to the suburbs, which gave rise to an art unashamedly fascinated with local life, and combining the local and the international in one language. An image of the suburbs would acknowledge that Australia was part of a global consumer culture, and executing such an image in a received modernist style, be it Pop Art, Photorealism or expressionism, would reinforce the point. But for all that, it could still be argued that there was something peculiarly Australian about the suburb depicted, be it its architecture, its space, its inhabitants or their lifestyle.

In the mid-'80s many Australian artists turned to the suburbs with this culturalist attitude. It was as if Charles Baudelaire's nineteenth century call for an art that would capture the heroism of everyday life had been updated and transferred to the Australian suburbs.

Jon Campbell took that call almost literally when he based canvases depicting suburban youths lounging on cars or brawling in the streets on nineteenth century history paintings and the mural paintings of classical Rome. Like the sociologists of the Birmingham School, he charted the gestures, dress and often-violent rituals of youth subcultures. Like them, he also seemed to have a secret admiration for these street cultures, respectfully transcribing them and avoiding any moral judgements.

In deliberate contrast to Campbell's images of street culture were his images of

My relationship with suburbia is one of both love and hate. I hate the ugliness of our suburban estates and yet something draws me toward the variety that exists within a seemingly monotonous street. Dogs Bottles ... appeared in many yards in the late 80s and early 90s. I went on a number of searching sprees for these milky dog deterrents in Townsville, Brisbane and even Sydney. The house used for the etching was found in Milton, Brisbane. As I was making the image I thought of writing to the Brisbane city council and suggesting that they introduce a special 'Brisbane Dogs Bottle' day where the residents were invited to dress up their yard with bottles just as Australians are now beginning to do with Christmas lights during the festive season. Just after this etching was completed, the house appeared in *Vogue Living* magazine and, strangely enough, not one of the 29 dog's bottles was in the photograph of the front of the house. This I thought was a great shame.

Ron McBurnie, letter to the author, January 12th, 1996

his own family home in Altona, a semi-industrial western suburb of Melbourne. In *31 Myrtle Street* (1987) [Plate 18] the artist painted himself holding the suburban house in which he grew up, emphasising its significance to him and contrasting the securities of family life with the threats of street culture.

Like Arkley, Campbell uses the image of the suburb to reflect on its status within high cultural discourse; the image asserts bluntly that an artist could come from the suburbs, and the western suburbs at that. The artist seems to side with urban sociologist Hugh Stretton, who, in his classic text *Ideas for Australian Cities*, points out the ironic fact that most artists who condemn the suburbs seem quite happy to live in them. Campbell's work, and that of many of his peers, suggests that this hypocrisy is in decline. For Ron McBurnie, the reality of the suburbs is an accumulation of anecdotes, family memories, neighbourhood incidents and seasonal activities. Lost pets, raked leaves, mown lawns and abandoned drive-in movie theatres are the stuff of his art — the minor incidents that scatter colour throughout the apparent uniformity of the suburbs. These are all viewed with a combination of appreciation and bemusement, allowing the artist to demonstrate some sympathy for the suburbs while still pointing out its foibles.

Dogs Bottles (1988) draws together a number of subtly conflicting threads. Significantly, it does so through the motif of the garden which, as several sociological studies have argued, is one of the main areas of personal expression in the suburbs. Following a local folk wisdom, he shows water-filled bottles placed across the lawn, ostensibly to deter wandering dogs from 'fouling' the grass. Even in the contemporary suburb, it seems, vestiges of superstition remain. And for all its neatness and modernity, the suburb still retains elements of the wilds, as marauding dogs roam the streets in packs, ready to prey on undefended lawns — the moon is full and the wolves are out.

The irony, of course, is that the dog's bottles may not work, not to speak of the fact that the gardener has been forced to destroy the lawn in order to save it. It would be difficult to judge which would be less attractive, a lawn covered with plastic bottles or one with the occasional turd. The house-proud suburban obsession with cleanliness and appearances backfires.

All the same, McBurnie finds in the suburban garden a life that others have often denied. His many prints put the lie to claims by writers of fiction such as Elizabeth Jolley, who noted — in her essay for the collection *Inner Cities: Australian women's memory of place* — that suburban gardens are "most of the time, incredibly dull" and that suburb-dwellers "have no real feeling for their surroundings or for each other".

Fascinated as they are with the rites and rituals of suburban life, not all artists are generous or forgiving. Suburbia often triggers bitter humour as artists find a sinister conformism in its patterns of behaviour or suppressed conflict behind the veneer of neighbourliness. Robert Randall and Frank Bendinelli, working as Randelli, produced a suburban soap opera with a twist in their *Love Stories — Towards a Video Narrative* (1984).

Teenage social life, a central feature of television soap operas such as *Neighbours,* was presented as a set of narrative clichés. Plots were lifted from photo-romances in teen magazines, sets were radically simplified — often replaced by computer-generated diagrams — and actors embodied archetypes rather than individuals. Shallow language, cartoon-like graphics and synthetic music all exaggerated the formulaic mood of the video.

While culturalists found a degree of sophistication in suburbia, Randelli emphasised convention and repetition to the extent that suburbia appeared to be an abstraction rather than a real place where actual lives were lived. Their work indicates a point of fundamental conflict within contemporary artists' images of suburbia. The suburbia of flesh and blood is pitted against the suburbia of convention, human depth against ritual superficiality, the individual against the archetype.

CRACKS IN THE FACADE: VIVIENNE SHARK LEWITT; NICHOLAS MAU; ANDREW SIBLEY

Few contemporary artists condemn the suburbs outright, as their predecessors did, but neither do they see suburbia through rose-coloured glasses. The difference depends on the degree of their tolerance. By exploring the disparity between the image and reality — the 'cracks in the facade'— artists can engage in critique, while stopping short of a wholesale condemnation.

Vivienne Shark LeWitt's *MOR* (1991) has a stark, satirical style reminiscent of the work of John Brack, but she shows a greater familiarity with the languages and rituals of suburban life. 'MOR'— or 'middle of the road'— music describes an 'easy listening' pop music that, in its tasteful, unthreatening formulas, could almost be a metaphor for suburbia. But Shark LeWitt's painting humorously shows the effects of a normalcy so persistent that it becomes overwhelming.

Sick to death of their neighbours playing MOR records, her suburb-dwellers prepare to dynamite the house next door. "Everybody needs good neighbours", claims the theme song to *Neighbours*. The problem, according to Shark LeWitt, is that not everybody gets them. The suburbs are a double-edged sword — behind their neighbourly facades lie myriad petty disputes and irritations.

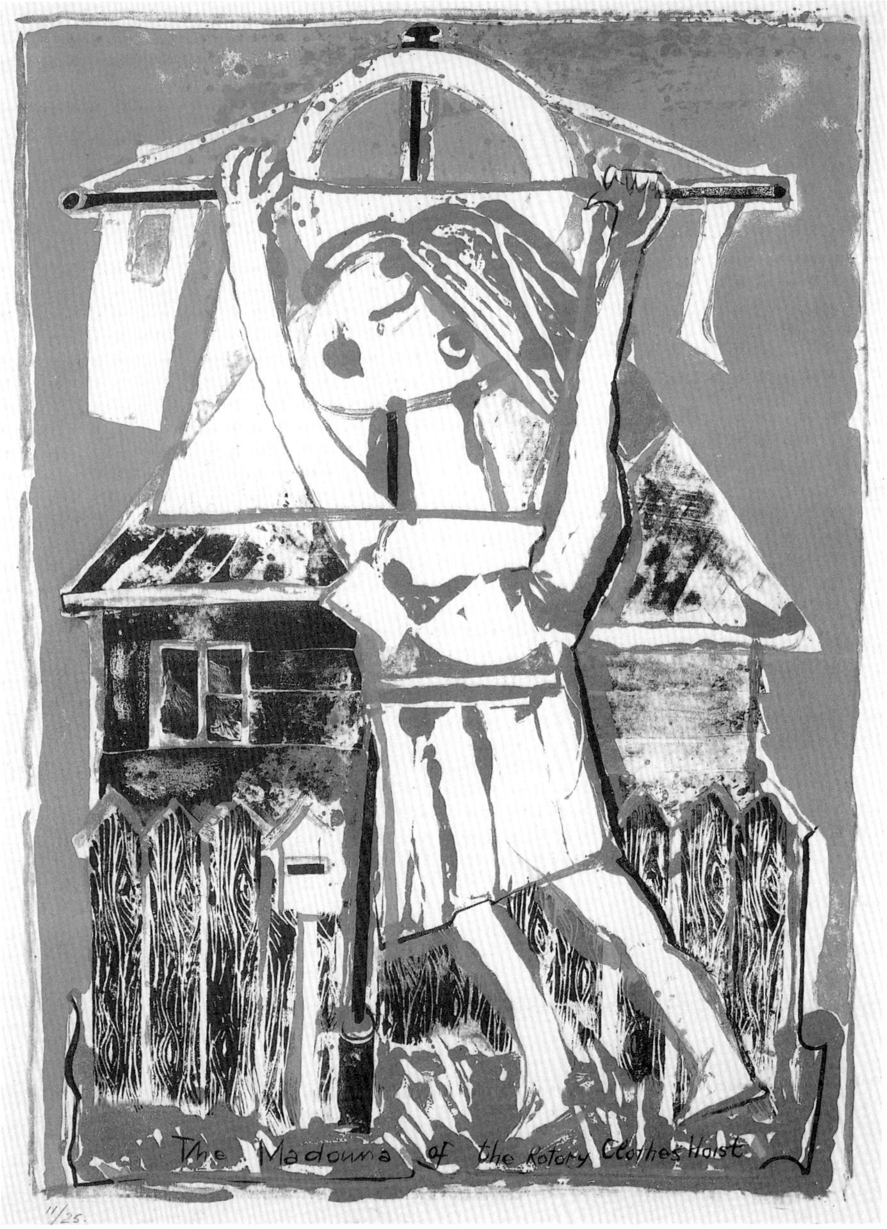

Andrew Sibley,
The Madonna of the Rotary Clothes Hoist, 1994

For Nicholas Mau of RedPlanet Graphics, the conventions of suburbia register the ways in which social identity is structured by gender roles and participation in consumer society. Seduced by the promises of advertising, egged on by banks and government policy, whole generations of Australians have locked themselves into a lifetime of labour and debt. The 'death' in his poster *Death of the Suburban Dream* (1993) [Plate 19] is the disillusionment that comes on realising that the dream home has become a prison.

He represents the Great Australian Dream of home ownership as a sinister ideology — the home, family and work required to sustain it are seen as institutions that construct and maintain rigidly defined systems of gender roles. The poster effectively diagrams the gender roles perpetuated in education, books and children's play: domestic chores are the role of the mother; the public face of the home — the garden — is the father's job; and the children follow their appointed models dutifully.

The pessimistic theme of suburbia's martyrdom of the housewife is also taken up by Andrew Sibley, in a series of paintings mourning the loss of spirituality in contemporary secular society. Sibley transposed motifs from religious narrative painting to the suburbs, using a hieratic style derived from Renaissance altarpieces. The image conveys a sense of pathos, for the artist's efforts to suggest a moral grandeur in the banality of domestic chores and trips to the shopping centre seem futile.

His *Madonna of the Rotary Clothes Hoist* (1994) is an inventive fusion of two powerful symbols, the clothes line — emblem of women's labour and suburban domesticity — and the crucifixion — emblem of self-sacrifice for the greater good of humanity. Sibley's condemnation of the secular banality of contemporary society is a common lament, and his long-suffering housewife a common enough heroine. However his transference of the traditionally masculine role of saviour to the woman — whose spreading arms echo the pose of a crucified Christ — is a novel touch that confers monumentality on domestic labour and shifts emphasis from the nurturing but passive Madonna to the more active and authoritative Christ.

FROM DREAMS TO NIGHTMARES: GORDON BENNETT

Artists' questioning of the merits of suburbia sometimes moves beyond humanist sympathy into outright anger. In Gordon Bennett's *Murder/Suicide*, from the 1993 series "Home Sweet Home", irony is abandoned. This is not an art of metaphor and reflection but of crude immediacy. In brutal imagery and seething texts, the artist vents his spleen against the evils of suburbia, the mass media that feeds off them, and an audience that seems indifferent or immune. For Bennett there is no suburban dream — or rather, such visions of domestic comfort conceal harsh reality. While suburbia might embody the Australian dream, the roles that this dream demands and the pressure to achieve them produce a nightmarish reversal.

The ideology of the family provides narrow roles, such as the husband as provider. When these roles are unrealistic or difficult to fulfil, no outlet is provided; the insecure provider, lord of his mortgaged manor, is driven ever deeper into the role, eventually reaching the conclusion that, if he cannot provide for his family, his role demands that he destroy it. For Bennett, the quarter-acre blocks of suburbia are literally and psychologically the killing fields of Australia. The series of watercolours from which this work is taken amounts to an encyclopedia of suburban neuroses. Bennett shows us domestic violence, drunkenness, child abuse, loutish youths and racism, embedded in the very culture of suburbia.

BEHIND CLOSED DOORS: JON CATTAPAN; SARAH CURTIS; TRACEY MOFFATT

The suburbs, as suggested throughout this book, are as much a state of mind as they are a physical space. This suburban mindset had frequently been characterised as one of conservative, small-minded conformity — in contrast with the free spirit of the artist. But when contemporary artists became interested in the fragmented, hybrid cultures of the postmodern suburb, they began to represent suburbia as a more intricate psychological state. The suburbs were mapped in terms of a 'psychogeography'— as a landscape whose monuments were not physical features but memories, emotions, fears and desires.

As a city planned from scratch to be an ideal urban space, Canberra and its suburbs might suggest the embodiment of reason and normalcy. But Jon Cattapan's *Woden Valley Insect No.3* (1994) [Plate 20] peels away the restrained facade of suburban streets and houses to reveal a passionate, even sexual landscape. The streets of Woden, seen in an aerial view, are likened to the labyrinthine tunnels of an ants nest.

An ant colony is an apt metaphor for suburban life, featuring as it does incessant labour, constant motion to and fro, and a rigidly defined social system. But Cattapan also has a surrealist's fascination with the sexual subtexts of insect life. The life of the ant colony revolves around the super-fertile queen, with all activity directed to laying,

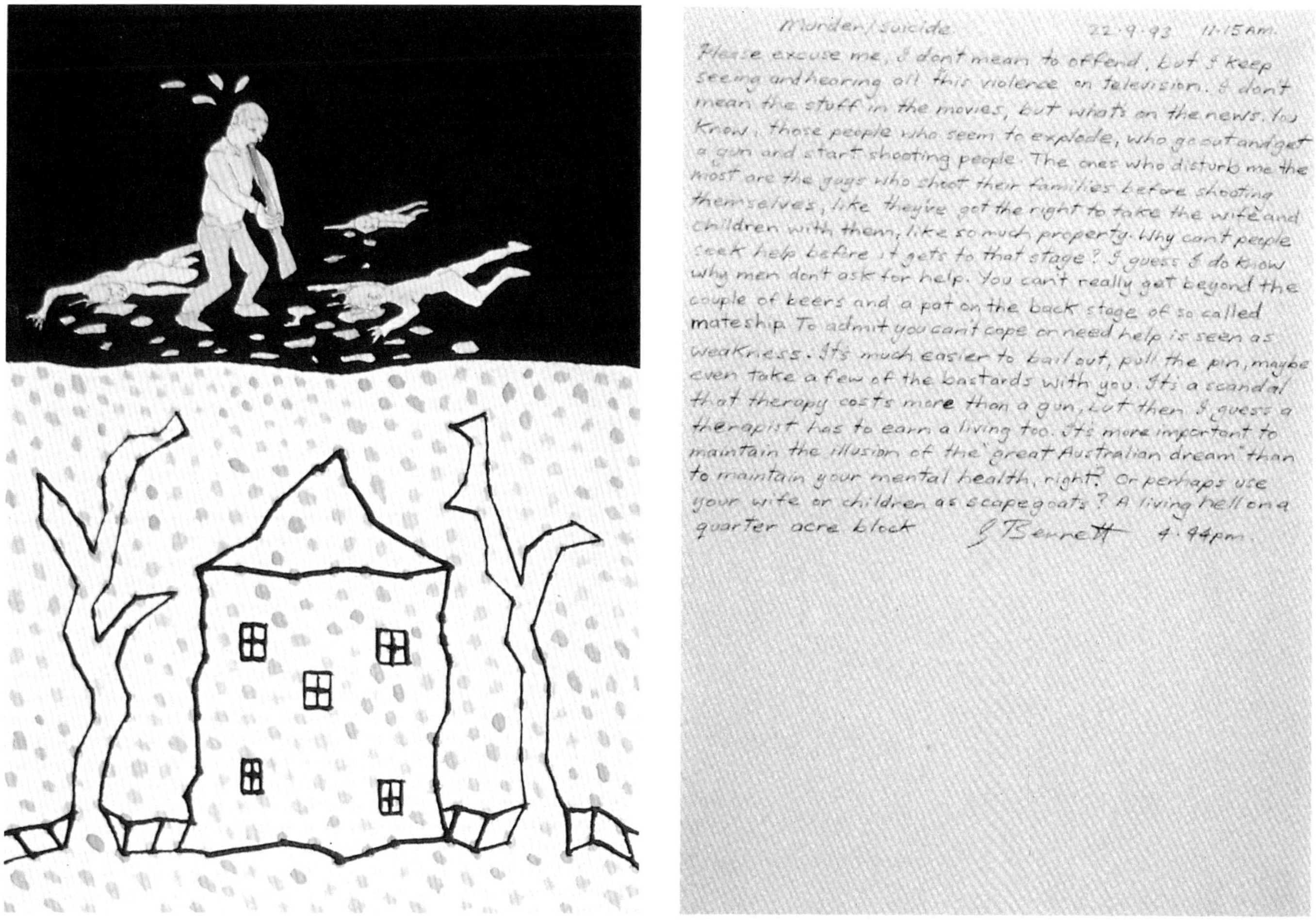

Gordon Bennett,
Murder/Suicide from the series
"Home Sweet Home", 1993

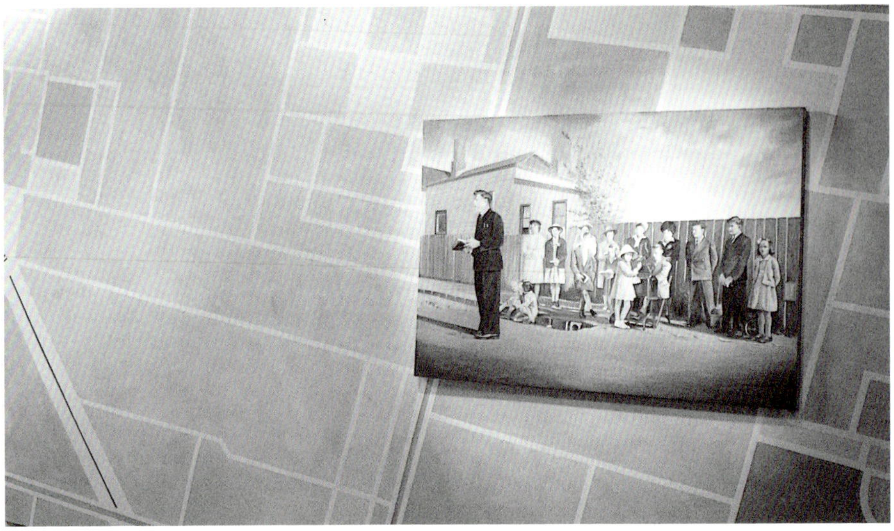

Sarah Curtis,
Neighbours Arcadia
(installation view, Temple Gallery, Melbourne), 1994

hatching and feeding. In the several works in the "Woden Valley Insect" series, Cattapan stresses the network of hotspots that litter the suburbs. Fragments of the suburb leap into focus like fetish objects, respectable houses glow with passion, and copulating couples writhe on front lawns.

In a similar vein, but approaching the theme from an opposite direction, is Sarah Curtis's *Neighbours Arcadia* (1994) [Plate 21]. This mural-scale installation traced a map of a Melbourne suburb, drawn from a street directory, onto the gallery wall. Superimposed on the map was an image of the artist's father preaching his evangelical Christian faith in the suburbs. The resonances of the image are both personal and conceptual. As an autobiographical painting, it reflects upon the artist's strict religious upbringing, which continued to affect her life long after she left it behind her. Like many artists, Curtis sees childhood as the formative period of an individual's personality, but she also suggests that childhood is fraught with traumas and conflicts that must be worked through in adult life.

On a more abstract level the work hints that the very conservatism of suburbia may exceed the bounds of propriety even as it strives to reinforce them. As the site of a religious crusade, Curtis's suburb has all the fervour of Cattapan's sexualised landscape. The high emotions of religious revivalism are shown to have a disruptive effect on the quiet suburban streets, spilling beyond its neat paths and gutters. Normalcy, it seems, is a good deal harder to achieve and maintain than we would think. Curtis, like Cattapan, uses the motif of the suburban map to indicate a desire for order, an effort to pin down meanings.

As artists explore the roots of the suburban psyche in memory and childhood, many reveal family life to be violent and cruel. While identity might be seen as increasingly mobile and fragmented, artists see the family and the home as institutions which still attempt to shape identity according to rigid, received patterns. Tracey Moffatt's 1994 series of photo-lithographs, "Scarred for Life" [Plate 22], is based on childhood memories passed on to the artist by colleagues. Moffatt's images emulate the look of the Time-Life coffee table books of the 1960s and '70s, as if the customs of the suburbs were being documented for the armchair traveller. The family home is a battleground: psychological warfare is its chief weapon.

Each print shows how children and teenagers are often brutally forced into line. Rules governing behaviour, gender roles and appearances are strictly enforced. Any deviation from the norm or exploration of 'inappropriate' activities is nipped in the bud, curtailed by a cruel remark or a physical blow. Insecurities are preyed upon.

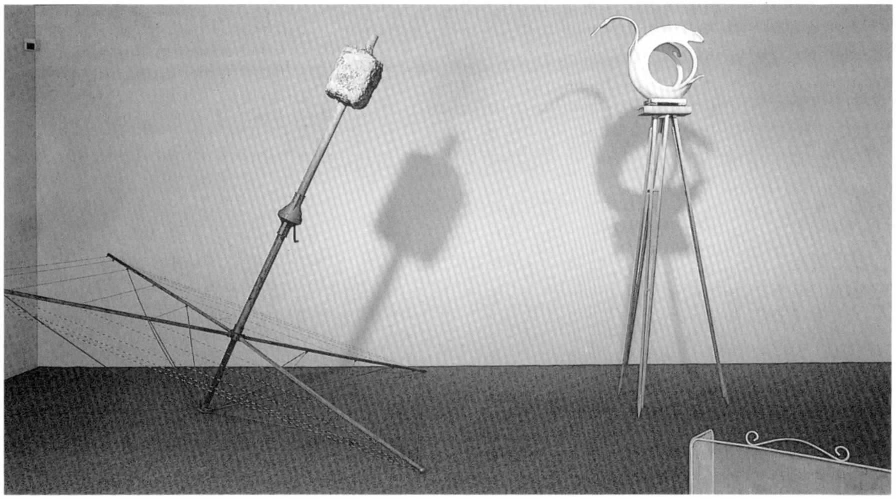

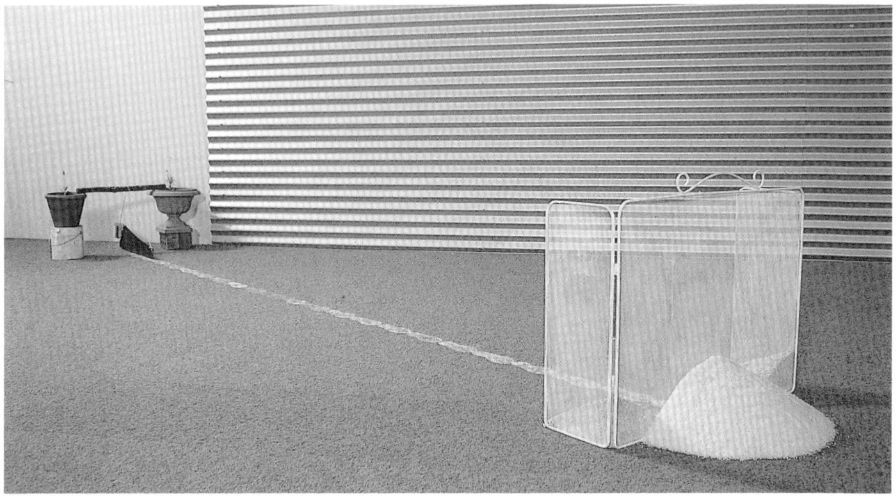

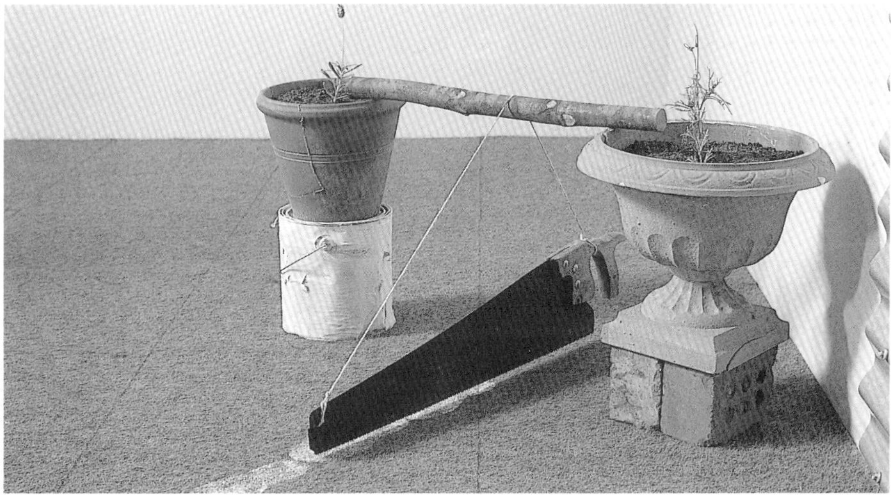

Glen D. Clarke,

Reductio ad Absurdum

(3 installation views, Plimsoll Gallery, Hobart, 1994)

Clumsiness, curiosity and lack of self-esteem — all part and parcel of teenage life — are singled out as things to be ashamed of. Moffatt demonstrates how the processes of socialisation train children to accept the conventions of society and repress any desire for difference.

WEIRD SCIENCE: GLEN D. CLARKE; REG MOMBASSA

Suggesting that the suburb is a complex web of psychic intensities reinforces the sense that it is beyond conventional measurement. The suburbs can no longer be explained purely in terms of empirical science such as geography or sociology, nor read through systems of morality and taste. In a 1994 installation, *Reductio ad Absurdum*, Tasmanian artist Glen D. Clarke used a typically postmodern strategy — parody — to attack modernist efforts at scientifically defining the suburbs. At the same time, his own highly eccentric system of measurement suggested a radically relative means of understanding the suburbs, deeply embedded in the peculiar logic of childhood.

Clarke placed familiar elements of the suburban backyard landscape — the Hill's Hoist, the barbecue, the carved-tyre swan planter — into an art gallery. By inverting or elevating these items, he converted them into totemic objects. Tracing mysterious connections between them with sand, Clarke suggested some strange ritual use.

Making the everyday seem unfamiliar is of course a common artistic tactic. In this case, it refers the ritual quality of backyard events such as barbecues, but also serves to parody the social sciences and their tendency to approach the suburbs as if they were an

Eric was a kid who believed that one of the first things that we are street wise with is our own back yard ... He knew that his memories were symbolic and significant but he was not exactly sure why. As a kid Eric discovered his space via three dimensional experiments in his back yard ... He would draw lines with his Mum's wool (12 ply Paton) connecting all the elements in the back yard. Plotting and navigating the space and distance between fences, garden beds, foot paths etc. "The distance between the grape vine trellis and the outhouse is the same as between the chook shed and the fly wire door" he once told me.

Glen D. Clarke, "Reductio Ad Absurdum (Non Essential Information Technology)", 1994

alien world. In a text that accompanied the installation, Clarke pursued this issue further, continuing his parody of empirical knowledge while arguing that suburban spaces might be mapped in more playful ways.

The weird science of this backyard geographer takes full advantage of the playful, parodic potential of art. It echoes the nonsense pataphysics of the Dadaist Marcel Duchamp. At the same time, Clarke points to the ways in which suburban experience is rooted in memory, play and psychology, all of which are focused on highly localised sites.

The 'alien' qualities of the suburbs had served a different purpose for earlier artists, who frequently used them, as a contrast, to reinforce an ideal vision of Australian culture that was sought, first, in the bush and, later, in a European cosmopolitan ideal. But in the 1980s and '90s, with difference being celebrated, it seemed the weirder the suburbs were, the better. Few could match Reg Mombassa on this score.

Working under the name of Chris O'Doherty in the mid-1970s, Mombassa had developed an iconography of suburban sterility. But in the 1990s his dry realism was transformed into a cartoon-like surrealism, with comic-book suburbs invaded by sombre aliens and motorcycle riding deities. The suburbs were now brimming over with life. Or rather, with works such as *Insectile Space-monsters Approach Sleeping Family* (1995) [Plate 23], Mombassa presented a hitherto invisible life of hallucinogenic vision and paranoid nightmares. Like Clarke, Mombassa used his eccentric vision both to parody earlier treatments of the suburbs as alien and to argue for psychic realities beyond the reach of rational knowledge.

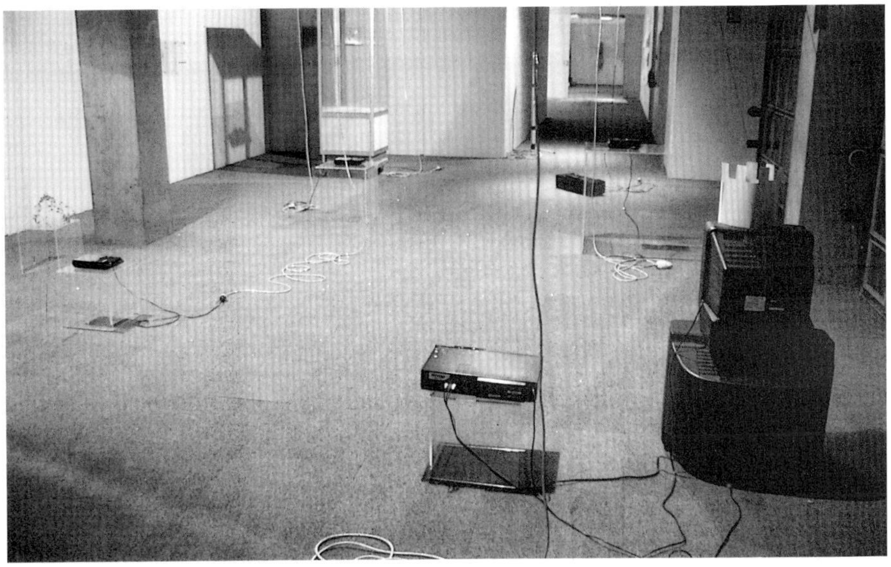

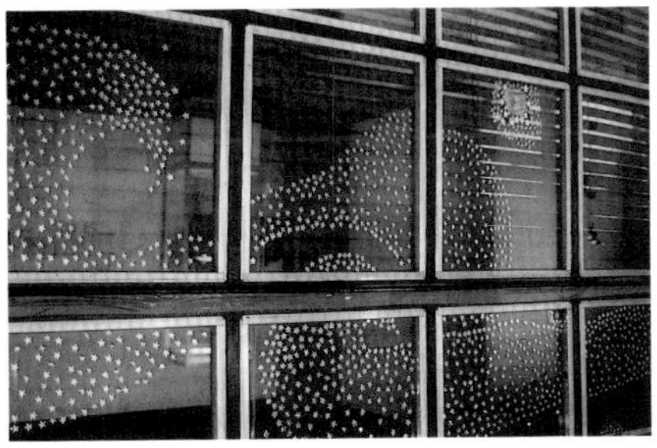

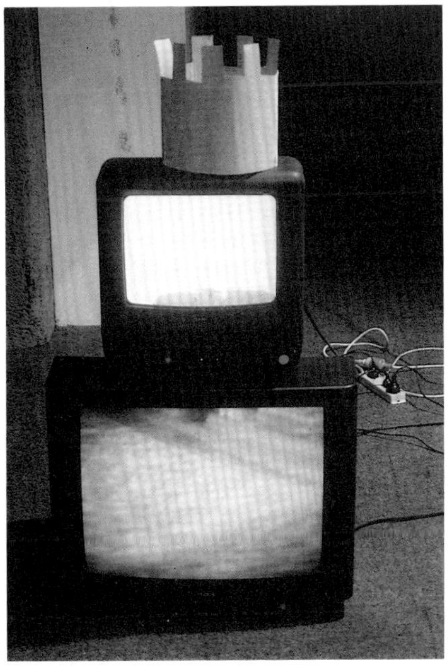

Mikala Dwyer,
Star (3 installation views, Plimsoll Gallery, Hobart, 1994)

FLUID IDENTITIES: MIKALA DWYER

Clearly artists of the 1980s and '90s no longer saw the suburb as a singular entity. Some negative responses to the suburbs were coloured by the politics of the 1970s. However, new understandings of the structures of social spaces, the politics of identity and the fluidity of meaning encouraged artists to treat suburbia as a site at which multiple discourses — including those of age, ethnicity, sexuality and gender — generated layered meanings. It no longer seems possible — if it ever was — to identify a generic suburb-dweller.

The task of the artists, then, is no longer to come up with an image of the generic 'suburbanite' but rather to explore the fluidity of identity in the suburbs and the forces that frame or shape it. Mikala Dwyer's *Star* (1994) exemplifies the new artistic strategies developed to engage with such mobile suburban identities.

Star combines multiple media — paint, video, sculpture, found objects, magazines, newsclippings, electrical appliances and stationery items — spread over the floor, walls and windows of the art gallery. The very nature of the work emulates those processes of interaction and overlay involved in the formation of identity. The artist has created a space or environment rather than a single object. Her uncontained installation suggests the ungraspable expansiveness of life itself. The distinction between art and life — which for so many years allowed artists to stand aloof from the suburbs — is left behind. The installation is not simply about everyday life but is built out of it. Dwyer begins with familiar symbols of suburban life. A VCR and monitor plays a tape of a woman vacuuming a house, evoking ideas of domestic labour but also of daytime television and the consumer culture that fills homes with appliances. In contrast with this feminised, private activity is the public, masculine role of the rock'n'roll singer — the cassette players blasts a repeating loop of Bon Scott singing AC/DC's "Whole Lotta Rosie". The juxtaposition of the two activities and the two appliances sets off a series of resonances and associations: the private and the public; the female and the male; the anonymous housewife and the superstar; labour and recreation; the mundane and the theatrical.

Significantly, these concepts are evoked or triggered, rather than being explicitly represented. Dwyer hopes to push viewers beyond their everyday conceptions of objects and activities towards a metaphorical reading of suburban roles. This associative reading can be carried further still. The star of the title might refer to Bon Scott, the rock star, but also to astrology, for the newsclippings pasted to the gallery wall features astrology columns predicting a rosy future, preying on the desire for a better life, pointing to the persistence of folk superstitions in the modern suburb. And on the window of the gallery, tiny pre-gummed gold stars are arranged in a swirling pattern derived form Vincent van Gogh's painting *Starry Night*. The macho superstar, the troubled artist, the bored housewife: all meet in a bizarre union of art, music and everyday life.

ConclusioN

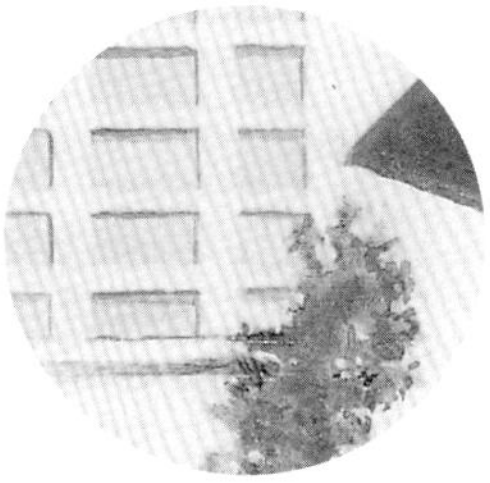

This book began by suggesting that the suburbs presented a problem to the nineteenth century Australian artist — the suburbs could not be depicted easily because they did not conform to the preferred model of national identity. In contemporary art, the suburbs remain a problem, though in a different way. It is still difficult to depict the suburb, but this is not because it has the wrong meaning. Rather, the suburb now seems to evade any *single* system of meaning. As identities and the forces shaping them multiply and become more fluid, the very possibility of proposing a homogeneous Australian identity, much less of symbolising this through a suburban archetype, fades away.

The suburb is now elusive, rather than absent — artists no longer ignore the suburb, but they accept the impossibility of naming or defining it in any conclusive way. The suburbs, contemporary art shows us, have become overwhelming and unassimilable. This effect becomes clear if we consider the work of four contemporary artists — Bill Henson, Bill Lane, Kate Daw and Darren Wardle — each of whom attempts to locate the suburbs in a different way.

The suburbs are not malevolent, any more than they are materialistic. They are now being recognized as the Australian communal form that possesses moral imperatives of its own ... The inhabitants of Doncaster and Templestowe are right; the issues of the soil are insurmountable. By turning their backs on the country, people in the suburbs have demonstrated good sense, and a fundamental capacity for survival.

Peter Corrigan, from "Learning from Suburbia", 1985

REVIVING MODERNIST METAPHORS: BILL HENSON

Attempts to express pessimistic attitudes to Australian culture through images of suburban banality or ugliness seem increasingly forced. Bill Henson is an acclaimed photographer, who exhibited in prestigious exhibitions throughout the '80s and '90s, and represented Australia at the 1995 Venice Biennale. However, his 1985–86 series of photographs of the suburbs returns to an earlier moment when the presumed banality of the suburbs was accepted as a given, and contrasted to the romantic transcendence of the visual arts. *Untitled 1985–86* (1985–86) [Plate 24] seems an almost direct illustration of Bruce Dawe's poem "The Sky Country", taken from his portentiously titled collection *Beyond the Subdivisions*:

Sometimes at evenings the winter clouds / above the Caltex signs and the leafless twigs / of TV antennae roll back soundlessly to reveal the vault of heaven / shining with undiminished splendour / in spite of everything ...

Both the poem and the photograph seek a pointed contrast between crass commercial culture and the romantic splendour of nature. They appeal to a distinction between nature and culture, the spiritual and the material, the sublime and the banal.

If anything, Henson pushes the metaphor even further than Dawe, for in his image the once-glorious Pegasus, the mythical winged horse of classical mythology, has been frozen in mid-flight, reduced to a petrol station's corporate logo. It is not just the pessimistic romanticism of the photograph that makes it seem so dated; it is the apparent belief that it is sufficient to say of the suburbs that they are materialistic, without reflecting on the ways in which their materialism and environment have changed so dramatically in recent years.

For Henson, the suburb forms one half of a familiar symbolic opposition between the earthly and the transcendent, the profane and the sublime. In making the suburb stand for something else — the 'human condition', the corrupted soul of Australian society — he is no different from many of the artists discussed earlier in this book.

For modernist artists, the appearance and behaviours of the suburbs were frequently a means to a larger metaphorical end — the depiction of the particulars of suburban life were a prelude to a general statement on the shortcomings of Australian culture. In this sense, modernist critiques of the suburb, such as Henson's, name the 'problem' but quickly transcend it, moving into the realm of poetic metaphor. This move simultaneously suppresses and maintains the uneasy presence of the suburb.

There is, however, a significant difference between Henson's symbolic suburb and the suburban imagery of a new generation of artists. Younger, postmodernist artists — such as Constanze Zikos, Mikala Dwyer and Jon Campbell — display a self-consciousness about the place of the suburb and suburbia within the symbolic vocabulary of national identity. Such artists recognise that the suburbs have a textual status (that their material condition is transformed into rhetoric, symbol and metaphor) but also that suburb-dwellers may themselves recognise and manipulate these textual elements. That is, suburb-dwellers shuttle readily back and forth between the material and the symbolic, rather than making a clear distinction between them.

Postmodern artists represent suburbia as a *site* formed within an intricate web of architecture, geography, ideology, memory, history and the mass media. Identifying the suburbs — their work suggests — means identifying both the voices that speak *about* the suburbs, and those that speak *from within* them. What contemporary artists attempt to do, then, is to chart the speaking positions that frame the suburbs — those who speak from without and within, from art and the mass media, from the present and the past. Of the many younger artists following this path, Bill Lane, Kate Daw and Darren Wardle perhaps best exemplify this reflection on the discursive status of the suburbs.

IRONIC EMPIRICISM: BILL LANE

Rather than Henson's symbolically loaded 'documentation' of the suburb, Bill Lane sets about his task empirically. His work takes the personal, affectionate, ironic or eccentric documenting of suburban streets and homes within recent Australian art — produced by artists such as Robert Rooney, Jenny Watson, Howard Arkley, Jon Campbell and Glen D. Clarke — and conscientiously pushes it to an ironic extreme.

In his 1994 project "Shades", Lane attempted to establish a measure of the suburbs by making a statistical survey. He chose — using here the description he gave on the cover of the exhibition's catalogue —"A photographic project documenting the 23 pattern variations in the canvas window awnings of one Corio housing estate". Each distinct awning pattern was photographed frontally. As well as documenting the pattern, the photography converted it into a 'stripe painting' of the kind beloved of formalist artists and critics. The resulting images were displayed along with an elaborate description of the mathematical formula determining their scale, and a pie chart documenting the relative frequency of each pattern.

The project is, of course, absurd, and Lane acknowledges this. He even gives his project the subtitle: "A Failed Attempt to Map Patterns of Convergence Between Suburbia, Greenbergian Aesthetics and Deleuzian Notions of Difference". We learn nothing about the suburbs or the people living behinds the shaded windows. Far from unearthing the secrets of the suburbs, Lane skims their surfaces. What might have begun as a survey of taste becomes a mute procession of stripes, flattened out by the photographic process and sterilised by Lane's mathematical formulas. Sociology, science, abstraction and Conceptual Art all come under attack in this parody of the search for knowledge.

The tools previously turned on the suburbs — empirical analysis, abstraction, deadpan documentation — are all parodied and collapsed. For all his effort, Lane has to admit that his is a project doomed to failure. The suburbs are ultimately unknowable. It is the *attempts* to know them that become the artist's subject matter.

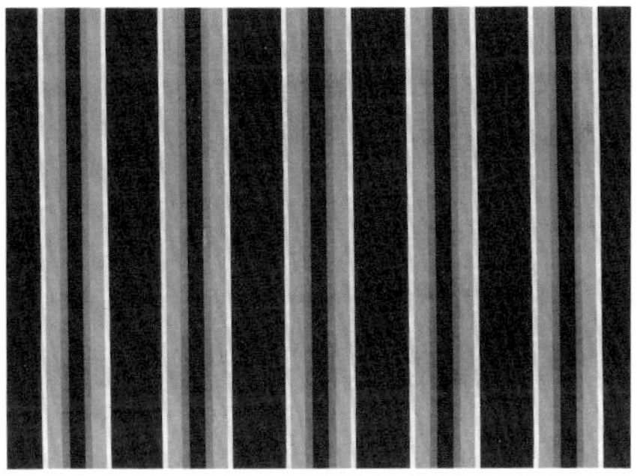

Bill Lane, *Shades Type 8A,* 1994–95

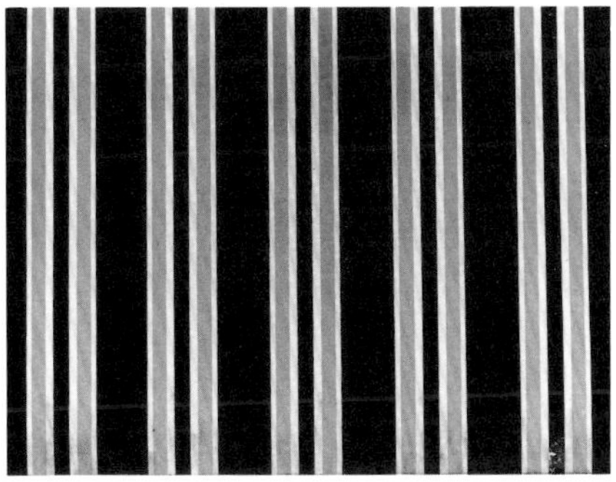

Bill Lane, *Shades Type 8B,* 1994–95

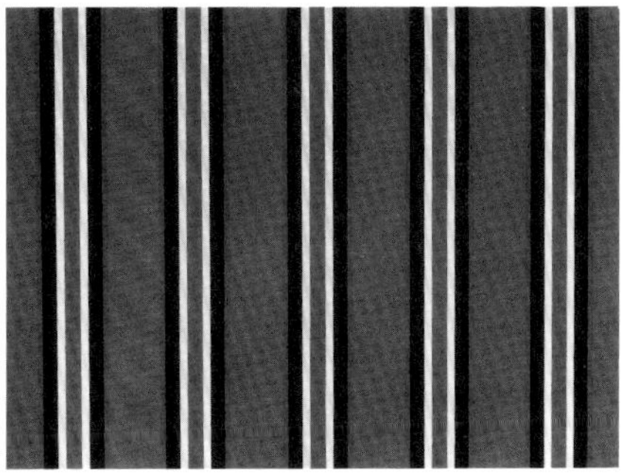

Bill Lane, *Shades Type 8C,* 1994–95

Popularity Breakdown (%)

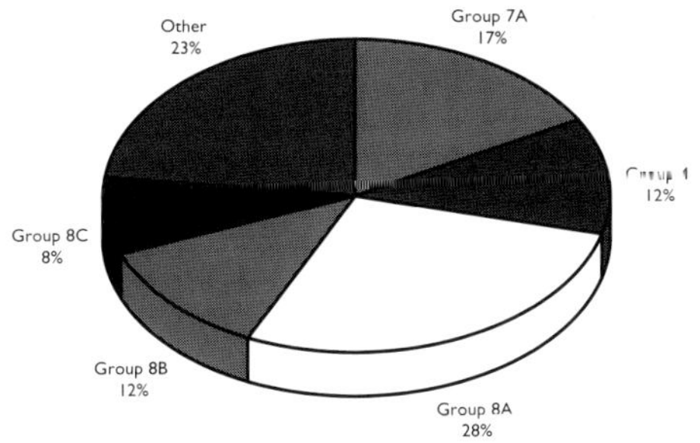

Percentage breakdown of "Other" samples is as follows

Group 1 ; 0.8%.
Group 2 ; A = 1.6%. B = 0.8%.
Group 3 ; A = 0.8%. B= 0.8%. C = 0.8%.
Group 5 ; A = 2.5%. B = 1.6%. C = 0.8%.
Group 6 ; 1.6%.
Group 7 ; B = 2.5%. C = 2.5%. D = 1.6%. E = 0.8%.
Group 9 ; 0.8%.
Group 10 ; A =).8%. B = 0.8%.
Group 11 ; 0.8%.

There were 120 houses in the sample area that had canvas awnings.

SUBURBAN VOICES: KATE DAW

Kate Daw's paintings continue what might be called the tradition — begun by artists such as Geoffrey Hogg and Peter Kennedy — of attending to the voices emanating from within the suburbs. Although a negative vision of the suburbs — as antithesis of art — weaves through Australian art history, another set of voices circulate around the inhabitants of the suburbs — those of aspiring suburb-dwellers and the markets, media and social mores that shape them. Daw tellingly combines these with the voices of the art world and its conventions, which speak of the suburbs as grey, faceless and abstracted.

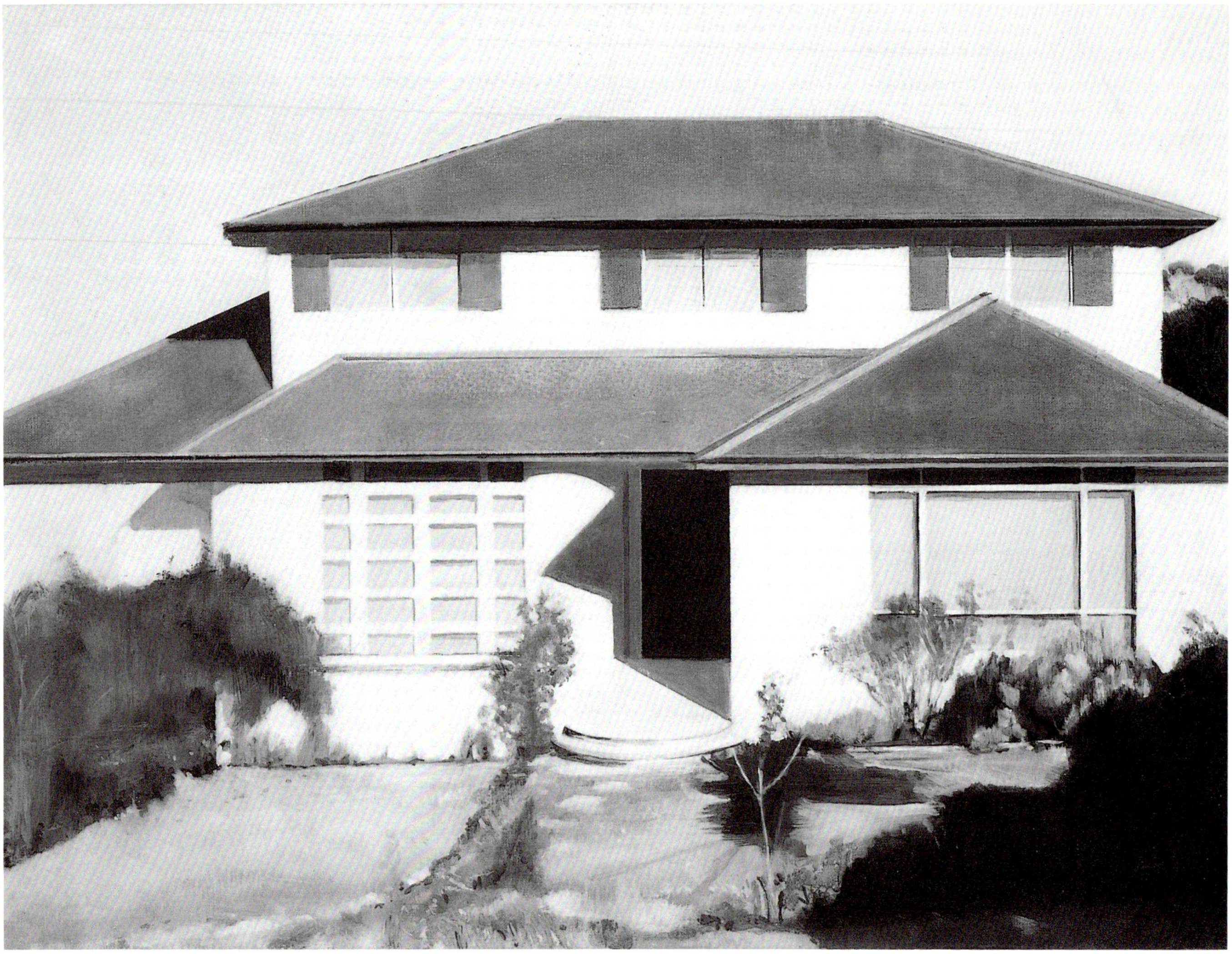

Kate Daw,

House, 1959, 1995

I am redecorating my daughter's bedroom for her twenty-first birthday present,and I hope you can give me some suggestions for making it look really charming and feminine. It is a small room, rather high ceilinged, and the outlook is dull. There are fitted cupboards and a divan bed, one chest of drawers and a small upholstered seat, but up to now she has not had a dressing-table. She likes delicate pastel colours. (E.W.,Cheltenham)

Chose a wallpaper with a fine gold trellis on white, and use a gold key-pattern border round the room at the cornice. Paint the ceiling palest grey-green, and have all the woodwork in white eggshell enamel. A deep celadon green fitted carpet would make the room more spacious.

The dressing-table fitted into the window alcove would be a perfect arrangement for your daughter's room. The venetian blind (pictured above) obscures the view without obscuring the light, and means that it is never necessary to draw the curtains. Choose a white blind, with a white-painted alcove and table, and have pale yellow silk taffeta curtains and drapes and a tailored ochre divan cover.

Kate Daw,

Voice, Homes & Gardens, 1959, 1995

In *Voice, Homes and Gardens, 1959* (1995), Daw cites a letter to a home-decorating advice column in a homemaker's magazine. The work points to the suburb-dweller's self-conscious construction of the suburbs, and the ways in which this consciousness is shaped by the media. If we can picture the identity of the person who will grow up in this decorated room, it is because we too have internalised the notions of femininity, of childhood, and of an ideal domestic space as articulated by the mass media.

But Daw does not presume that such discourses determine suburban culture in a simple, causal sense. Instead she suggests that suburb-dwellers participate knowingly and actively in their own definition. The suburbs, Daw helps us recognise, are a textual complex. They bring together history and memory, individual and society, gender and sexuality, interior and exterior, private and public, time and space, dreams and reality, difference and repetition.

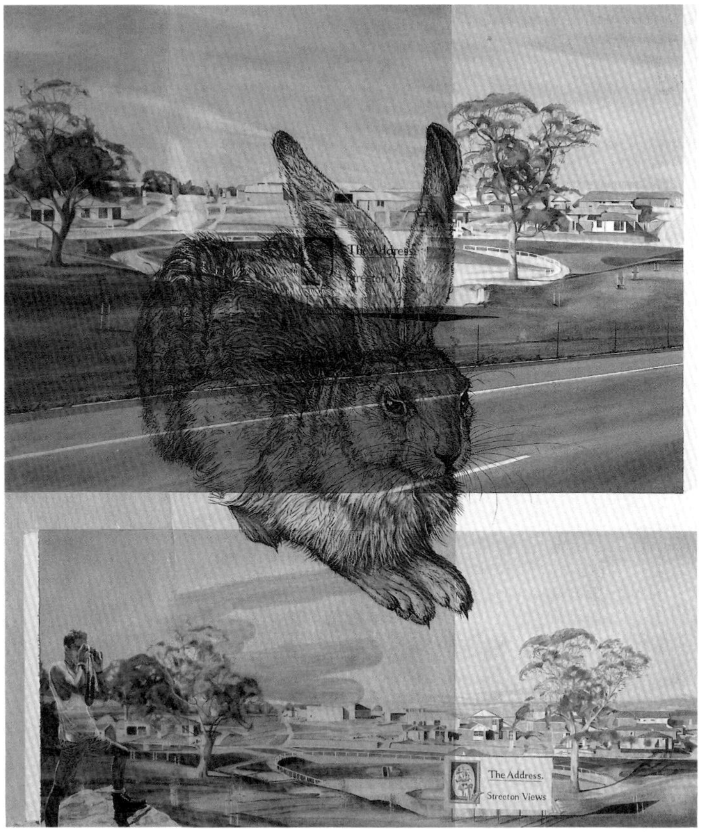

Darren Wardle,
Dust Control (Yallambie), 1995

FROM STREETON TO 'STREETON VIEWS': DARREN WARDLE

The appearance of the suburbs in art can now no longer be seen merely as a function of the artist's interest in them, be it positive or negative. The suburbs are now a site at which art's metaphors, the artist's gaze, and the material and symbolic economies of urban development are all brought into play.

Darren Wardle's *Dust Control (Yallambie)* (1995) builds on the artist's visits to a new housing estate near his suburban home. The painting captures something of the visible appearance of the suburb, but also acknowledges the image as the product of the artist's gaze — the artist/geographer is prominently placed in the foreground. Superimposed upon the suburb is a copy of Albrecht Dürer's famous image *The Young Hare*. If the allusion to the suburbs as a rabbit warren, or perhaps breeding ground, is heavy-handed, this is done deliberately, just as the clichéd character of the image may refer not only to suburban taste but also to artists' responses to it. Of equal interest to Wardle is the developer's deliberate affiliation of the suburb with art. Art, which for so long had been the sworn enemy of the suburb, is now its ally in a marketing campaign.

In 1890, when he painted *Near Heidelberg*, Arthur Streeton turned his back on the suburban development about him and clung fast to his belief in the essentially rural character of Australian identity. In retrospect, Streeton appears almost as an antipodean King Canute, vainly resisting the inexorable tide of the suburbs. Just over a century later, his defeat seems complete. It is not just that his name, along with those of other luminaries of the Heidelberg School, had long ago been given to streets in the suburbs, conferring an air of respectability on the newly desirable suburb. It was not just that his artistic heirs had given up on the task and surrendered to the pleasures and dangers of the suburbs. The defeat inflicted on Streeton was more cruel than this. In October 1993, a former army barracks in the Heidelberg area was subdivided for residential development. Following the environmentally sensitive principles of the 'Green Street' philosophy, the development incorporated large-scale planting of indigenous trees and sought to preserve what was termed the 'visual quality' of the landscape. In a moment of inspiration, the developers named their project 'Streeton Views'.

FURTHER READING

On art and artists

Arkley, Howard, "The Naked Suburb", *World Art*, vol.1, no.1, 1994.

Aspects of New Realism: 1981 travelling art exhibition [includes Ronald Hawke], National Gallery of Victoria, Melbourne, 1981.

Astbury, Leigh, "Victor Majzner", *Art and Australia*, vol. 20, no.3, 1983.

Astbury, Leigh, *City Bushmen: The Heidelberg School and the rural mythology*, Oxford University Press, Melbourne, 1985.

Australian Perspecta 1981: A biennial survey of contemporary Australian art [includes Geoffrey Hogg and Ann Newmarch], Art Gallery of New South Wales, Sydney, 1981.

Beier, Ulli, *Dream time–Machine time: The art of Trevor Nickolls*, Robert Brown & Associates in association with the Aboriginal Artists Agency, Bathurst NSW, 1985.

Binns, Vivienne (ed.), *Community and the Arts: History, theory and practice,* Pluto Press, Leichhardt NSW, 1991.

Brown, Richard, "Spraying the Suburban Dream" [Howard Arkley], *Tension*, no.18, October 1989.

Burn, Ian, "Beating About the Bush: The landscapes of the Heidelberg School", in his *Dialogue: Writings in art history*, Allen & Unwin, Sydney, 1991.

Burn, Ian, *Minimal-conceptual work 1965–1970*, Art Gallery of West Australia, Perth, 1992.

Butler, Roger, *Sydney by Design: Wood and linoblock prints by Sydney women artists between the wars* [includes Margaret Preston and Eveline Syme], National Gallery of Australia, Canberra, 1995.

Catalano, Gary, "Aleksander Danko", *Art and Australia*, vol.12, no. 1, 1974.

Claire, Stephanie & Anna Waldmann, *Salvatore Zofrea*, Hale & Iremonger, Sydney, 1983.

Clarke, Glen D., "Reductio Ad Absurdum (Non Essential Information Technology)", *Familiarity?: Re-examining Australian suburbia*, Plimsoll Gallery, Centre for the Arts, Hobart, 1994.

Dale Hickey: A retrospective exhibition, City of Ballarat Fine Art Gallery, Ballarat Vic.,1988.

De Groen, Geoffrey, *Conversations with Australian Artists* [includes Jenny Watson and Peter Kennedy], Quartet Books, Melbourne, 1978.

Dickerson, Jennifer, *Robert Dickerson: Against the tide*, Pandanus Press, Brisbane, 1994.

Downtown: Ruscha, Rooney, Arkley, Museum of Modern Art Heide: Melbourne, 1995.

Dunlop, Brian, "John D. Moore", *Art and Australia*, vol.11, no.4, 1974.

Exhibition 9: From the Bottom to the Top: Art process–options for response [includes Mandy Martin], Visual Arts Board, Sydney, 1980.

Fenner, Felicity, "Coming Up: The lowdown art of Mikala Dwyer", *Art and Australia*, vol.31, no.2, Summer 1993.

From the Homefront: Robert Rooney works 1953–1988, Monash University Gallery, Clayton Vic., 1990.

Gordon Bennett: Paintings 1987–1991, Epernay, 1992.

Graeme Sturgeon, *Michael Shannon: Painting and the poetry of daily life*, Craftsman House, Roseville NSW, 1990.

Green, Charles, *Peripheral Vision: Contemporary Australian art 1970–1994*, Craftsman House, Roseville NSW, 1995.

Grishin, Sasha, *Andrew Sibley: Art on the fringe of being*, G+B Arts International, Tortola BVI [distributed by Craftsman House], 1993.

Grishin, Sasha, *The Art of John Brack*, 2 vols, Oxford University Press, Melbourne, 1990.

HA: Howard Arkley, Monash University Gallery, Clayton Vic., 1991.

Harold Vike, 1906–1987: A retrospective, Kingstream Fine Art, Perth WA, 1990.

Hawkins, Gay, *From Nimbin to Mardi Gras: Constructing community arts*, Allen & Unwin, St Leonards NSW, 1993.

Herman, Sali, "The Artist's Integrity", *Daub: National Gallery School of Art magazine*, 1960–61.

Hickey, Dale, taped interview by Hazel de Berg, Oral History Section, National Library of Australia.

Hogg, Geoffrey, *Geoff Hogg: Public art – process and development*, Victorian College of the Arts Gallery, Melbourne, 1980.

Hollinrake, Rosalind, *Clarice Beckett: The artist and her circle*, Macmillan, Melbourne, 1979.

Holt, Stephanie, "Woman About Town: Urban images of the 1920s and 1930s", *Art and Australia*, vol.33, no.2, Summer 1995.

Hoorn, Jeanette, "Positioning the Post-colonial Subject: History and memory in the art of Gordon Bennett", *Art and Australia*, vol.31, no.2, Summer 1993.

Imants Tillers: 1978–1988, Institute of Contemporary Arts, London, 1988.

Johnston, Heather, *Roy de Maistre: The Australian years, 1894–1930*, Craftsman House, Roseville NSW, 1988.

Kennedy, Peter, "A Description of the Project", *Peter Kennedy/John Nixon: Two contemporary artists*, National Gallery of Victoria, Melbourne, 1976.

Lindsay, Robert, "Robert Rooney", *Art and Australia*, vol.14, no.1, July–September 1976.

Lindsay, Robert, *John Brack: A retrospective exhibition*, National Gallery of Victoria, Melbourne, 1987.

Living in the 70s: Photographs by Carol Jerrems, Art Exhibitions Committee, University of Tasmania, Hobart, 1990.

Lynn, Elwyn, "New Art and Old Sydney: Sali Herman talks to Elwyn Lynn", *Nation*, November 8th 1958.

Majzner: Towards identity, Monash University Gallery, Clayton Vic.,1993.

Mambo: Art irritates life [includes Chris O'Doherty/Reg Mombassa], Mambo Graphics, Surry Hills NSW, 1994.

Martin, Adrian, "The Go-Between" [Tracey Moffatt], *World Art*, no. 2, 1995.

McCaughey, Patrick, "Notes on the Centre: New York", *Quadrant*, July–August,1970.

McCaughey, Patrick, *Australian Abstract Art*, Oxford University Press, Melbourne, 1969.

Merewether, Charles, *Art and Social Commitment: An end to the city of dreams, 1931–1948*, Art Gallery of New South Wales, Sydney, 1984.

Mollison, James & Nicholas Bonham, *Albert Tucker*, Macmillan/Australian National Gallery, South Melbourne Vic., 1982.

Moore, Catriona, *Indecent Exposures: Twenty years of Australian feminist photography* [includes Micky Allan, Helen Grace and Carol Jerrems], Allen & Unwin, St Leonards NSW, 1994.

Moore, David, *David Moore Australian Photographer: Volume 1, black and white*, Chapter and Verse, McMahon's Point NSW, 1988.

Moore, Felicity St John, *Charles Blackman: Schoolgirls and angels – a retrospective*, National Gallery of Victoria, Melbourne, 1993.

Moore, Felicity St John, *Vassilieff and his Art*, Oxford University Press, Melbourne, 1982.

Moore, John, "Form", *Art in Australia*, March 1941.

More Suburban Etchings [Ron McBurnie], Perc Tucker Regional Gallery, Townsville Qld, 1990.

Newmarch, Ann, *Projects in Prospect: Artist-in-residence – Ann Newmarch, 1982–83*, Experimental Art Foundation, Adelaide, 1984.

Newton, Gael & Tracey Moffatt, *Tracey Moffatt: Fever pitch*, Piper Press, Annandale NSW, 1995.

North, Ian, *The Art of Margaret Preston*, Art Gallery Board of South Australia, Adelaide, 1980.

O'Ferrall, Michael, "Lin Onus", *Australian Perspecta 1991*, Art Gallery of New South Wales, Sydney, 1991.

Onus, Lin, "Languages and Lasers", *Art Monthly Australia Supplement: The land, the city – the emergence of urban Aboriginal art*, 1990.

Papasdergiadis, Nikos, "Constanze Zikos", in *Art + Text*, no. 48, May 1994.

Portraits in the Landscape: The house paintings of William Tibbits 1870–1906, Historic Houses Trust of New South Wales, Glebe NSW, 1984.

Preston, Margaret, "From Eggs to Electrolux" [1927], Ian North (ed.) *The Art of Margaret Preston*, Art Gallery Board of South Australia, Adelaide, 1980.

RedPlanet Graphics, *1994 RedPlanet Poster Catalogue*, Fitzroy, 1994.

Rooney, Robert, "Less than Five Hundred Words in Retrospect", *Survey 3: Robert Rooney* (education kit), National Gallery of Victoria, Melbourne, 1978.

Smith, Bernard, "The Antipodean Manifesto" [1959], *The Antipodean Manifesto: Essays in art history*, Oxford University Press, Melbourne, 1975.

Smith, Bernard, *Noel Counihan: Artist and revolutionary*, Oxford University Press, Melbourne, 1993.

Smith, Terry, "Provincialism in Art", *Quadrant*, March–April 1970.

Sowden, Tim, "The Suburbs of our Discontent: Art and suburbia in the post-war era", MA thesis, Department of Fine Arts, University of Melbourne, 1995.

Streeton, Arthur, "Some remarks on the History of Australian Art" [1916], Bernard Smith (ed.), *Documents in Art and Taste in Australia*, Oxford University Press, Melbourne, 1975.

Streeton, Arthur, *Letters from Smike: The letters of Arthur Streeton 1880–1943*, edited and compiled by Ann Galbally & Anne Gray, Oxford University Press, South Melbourne Vic., 1989.

Survey 13: Imants Tillers, National Gallery of Victoria, Melbourne, 1980.

Taylor, Paul, "Jenny Watson", *The Virgin Press*, no.10, February 1982.

The Object of Existence [includes Bill Lane], Australian Centre for Contemporary Art, South Yarra, 1995.

Tibbits, George, *William Tibbits 1837–1906: Cottage, house and garden artist,* Department of Architecture and Building, University of Melbourne, Parkville Vic., 1984.

Trioli, Virginia, "Spraying Suburbia" [Howard Arkley], *The Age* (EG section], November 22nd, 1991.

Walton, Leslie, *The Art of Roland Wakelin*, Craftsman House, Seaforth NSW, 1987.

West: Paintings by Ken Searle, The Lewers Bequest & Penrith Regional Art Gallery, Penrith NSW, 1991.

Whitelaw, Bridget, *The Art of Frederick McCubbin*, National Gallery of Victoria, Melbourne, 1991.

Willis, Anne-Marie, *Illusions of Identity: The art of nation*, Hale & Iremonger, Sydney, 1993.

Zen made in Australia [Aleks Danko], Museum of Art, University of Melbourne, Parkville Vic., 1994.

On cities, suburbs and architecture

Boyd, Robin, "Waking from the suburban dream: Australia's first substantial revolt against suburbia", *Architecture in Australia*, vol.59, no.1, February 1970.

Boyd, Robin, *Australia's Home*, Melbourne University Press, Parkville Vic., 1961 [1952].

Boyd, Robin, *The Australian Ugliness*, Cheshire, Melbourne, 1960.

Building Industry Congress of Victoria, "Modern homes for modern people", *Centenary Homes, 1934–35*, Melbourne, 1934.

Collins, Tony, *Living for the City: Urban Australia – crisis or challenge?*, ABC Books, Sydney, 1994.

Corrigan, Peter, "Learning from Suburbia", *Domus*, no. 663, July 1985.

Cuffley, Peter, *Australian Houses of the Forties and Fifties*, The Five Mile Press, Knoxfield Vic., 1993.

Daly, T. M., "The Australian City: Development in an open world", in R. L. Heathcote (ed.), *The Australian Experience*, International Geographical Congress, Longman Cheshire, Melbourne, 1988.

Davison, Graeme, *The Rise and Fall of Marvellous Melbourne*, Melbourne University Press, Carlton Vic., 1978.

Ferber, Sarah, Chris Healy & Chris McAuliffe (eds.), *The Beasts of Suburbia: Reinterpreting cultures of suburbia*, Melbourne University Press, Carlton Vic., 1994.

Garden, Donald S., *Builders to the Nation: The A. V. Jennings story*, Melbourne University Press, Carlton Vic., 1992.

Garden, Donald S., *Heidelberg: The land and its people*, Melbourne University Press, Carlton Vic., 1972.

Gibson, Katherine & Sophie Watson (eds.), *Metropolis Now: Planning and the urban in contemporary Australia*, Pluto Press, Leichhardt NSW, 1994.

Gilbert, Alan, "The Roots of Anti-suburbanism in Australia", in S. L. Goldberg & F. B. Smith (eds.), *Australian Cultural History*, Cambridge University Press, Melbourne, 1988.

Greenwood, Gordon, "Development in the '20s, 1919–1929", in his *Australia: A social and political history*, Angus & Robertson, Melbourne, 1955.

Greig, Alastair, *The Stuff Dreams are Made of: Housing provision in Australia 1940–1960*, Melbourne University Press, Carlton Vic., 1995.

Hanrahan, Barbara, "Weird Adelaide", *Adelaide Review*, no.49, March 1988.

Irving, Robert (ed.), *The History and Design of the Australian House*, Oxford University Press, Melbourne, 1985.

Johnson, Louise C. (ed.), *Suburban Dreaming*, Deakin University Press, Geelong Vic., 1994.

Kelly, Max (ed.), *Nineteenth Century Sydney: Essays in urban history*, Sydney University Press, Sydney, 1978.

Mayne, Alan, *Representing the Slum: Popular journalism in the late nineteenth century city*, History Department, University of Melbourne, Parkville Vic., 1991.

McWilliam, Gwen, *Hawthorn Peppercorns*, Brian Atkins, Melbourne, 1978.

Modjeska, Drusilla, *Inner Cities: Australia women's memory of place*, Penguin, Ringwood Vic., 1989.

Oliver, Paul, Ian Davis & Ian Bently, *Dunroamin': The suburban semi and its enemies*, Barrie & Jenkins, Melbourne, 1981.

Powell, Diane, *Out West: Perceptions of Sydney's western suburbs*, Allen & Unwin, St Leonards NSW, 1993.

Richards, Lyn, *Nobody's Home: Dreams and realities in a new suburb*, Oxford University Press, Melbourne, 1990.

Stretton, Hugh, *Ideas for Australian Cities*, Georgian House, Melbourne, 1971.

The Australian Dream: Design and the home of the 1950s, Powerhouse Museum, Sydney, 1992.

Venturi, Robert, Denise Scott-Brown & Steven Izenour, *Learning From Las Vegas*, MIT Press, Cambridge Mass., 1972.

Other reading

Adams, Francis, *The Australians: A social sketch*, T. Fisher Unwin, London, 1893.

Bean, C. E. W., *Making the Legend: The writings of C. E. W. Bean*, University of Queensland Press, St Lucia Qld, 1992.

Brett, Judith, *Robert Menzies' Forgotten People*, Macmillan, Chippendale NSW, 1992.

Carroll, John, *Intruders in the Bush: The Australian quest for identity*, Oxford University Press, Melbourne, 1982.

Esson, Louis, *The Time Is Not Yet Ripe* [1911], (edited by Philip Parsons), Currency (Sydney) and Eyre Methuen & Co. (London), 1973.

Hebdige, Dick, *Subculture, the Meaning of Style*, Methuen, London, 1979.

Hewett, Dorothy, *Wild Card*, McPhee Gribble, Ringwood Vic, 1990.

Horne, Donald, *The Lucky Country*, Penguin, Ringwood Vic., 1964.

Humphries, Barry, *A Nice Night's Entertainment*, Currency Press, Sydney, 1981.

Humphries, Barry, *Neglected Poems and Other Creatures*, Angus & Robertson, Pymble NSW, 1991.

Johnston, George, *My Brother Jack*, Fontana, Glasgow,1964.

Kostelanetz, Richard, (ed.), *John Cage: An anthology*, revised edition, Da Capo, New York, 1991.

Lawrence, D. H., *Kangaroo*, Heineman, London, 1923.

Lees, Stella & June Senyard, *The 1950s*, Hyland House, South Yarra Vic., 1987.

McGregor, Craig, *Profile of Australia*, Penguin, Ringwood Vic., 1966.

Tsiolkas, Christos, *Loaded*, Vintage, NSW, 1995.

Turner, Graeme, *National Fictions*, Allen & Unwin, Sydney, 1986.

Twopenny, Richard, *Town Life in Australia*, Penguin, Ringwood, 1973 [1883].

Vamplew, Wray (ed.), *Australians, Historical Statistics*, Fairfax, Syme & Weldon Associates, Broadway, 1987.

Walker, David, *Dream and Disillusion: A search for Australian cultural identity*, Australian National University Press, Canberra, 1976.

Ward, Russel, *The Australian Legend*, 2nd edition, Oxford University Press, Melbourne, 1966.

White, Richard, *Inventing Australia: Images and identity 1688–1980*, George Allen & Unwin, Sydney, 1981.

INDEX

The notes indicating illustrative material are:
illus = text illustration;
plate = colour plate;
map = subdivision or town plan;
plan = house plan.

AC/DC, 121
Adelaide, 108
see also Mile End; South Terrace; Thebarton
Allan, Micky, 98
"Live in Show", 98 (illus)
Altona (Melbourne), 34 (plate), 114
Antipodean Manifesto, 73
Arkley, Howard, 105–106, 125
Nubrick (1986), 29 (plate), 105
Secession (1979), 105 (illus)
Ultra Kleen (1992), 30 (plate), 105
Australian Panorama (Australian News and Information Bureau), 85
The Australian Ugliness (Robin Boyd), 70
Australian Womens Weekly, 70 (illus)
Australia's Home (Robin Boyd), 68, 70

"Balwyn Calling" (Skyhooks), 91
Beckett, Clarice, 51, 58
Bay Road, Foggy Morning (c.1926), 21 (plate), 58
Wet Day, Brighton (1921), 58 (illus)
Bell, George, 62
Bellbird, 91
Bendinelli, Frank
see Randelli
Bennett, Gordon, 116
Murder/Suicide (1993, "Home Sweet Home" series), 116, 117 (illus)
Bergner, Yosl, 54
Birmingham School, 104
Blackman, Charles, 65, 73, 75
Antipodean Manifesto, 73
The Shadow (1953), 74 (illus)
Bondi (Sydney), 52
Boyd, Robin, 105
The Australian Ugliness, 70
Australia's Home, 70
Brack, John, 65, 68–71, 75, 101
Antipodean Manifesto, 73
The Bar (1954), 71
The Car (1955), 71
Collins Street, 5pm (1955), 71
The New House (1953), 23 (plate), 70, 71
New Houses (1954), 70 (illus), 71
New Subdivision (1954), 71
The Unmade Road (1954), 69 (illus)
Brighton (Melbourne), 58 (illus)
Brisbane *see* Milton
Broadbeach (Gold Coast), 87 (illus)
Brunswick West (Melbourne), 17 (map)
Burke's Backyard, 14
Burn, Ian, 77, 79, 85, 87
Kangaroos (1968), 85
The Kitchen (1968), 85
The Suburbs (1968), 85, 86 (illus)
"Systematically Altered Photographs", 85
Burwood (Melbourne), 44

Cage, John, 84, 98, 104
Camberwell (Melbourne), 73 (illus)
Campbell, Jon, 103, 113–114, 124, 125
31 Myrtle Street (1987), 34 (plate), 114
Canberra *see* Curtin; Fisher; Queanbeyan; Woden Valley
Cant, James, 54
Canterbury (Melbourne), 79 (illus)
"Carlton" (Skyhooks), 91
Cattapan, Jon, 116
Woden Valley Insect No. 3 (1994), 36 (plate), 116, 118
Certain Women, 91
Chadstone Shopping Centre 78 (illus)
Cheltenham (Melbourne), 77
Clarke, Glen D, 125
Reductio ad Absurdum (1994), 119 (illus), 120
Clarke, Marcus, 71
Conder, Charles, 46
Corio (Geelong), 124
Corrigan, Peter, 124
Cossington Smith, Grace
see Smith, Grace Cossington
Counihan, Noel, 51, 54, 94
At the Corner of Nightingale Street (1944), 55 (illus), 56
Curtin (Canberra), 91 (illus)
Curtis, Sarah
Neighbours Arcadia (1994), 37 (plate), 118 (illus)

Daceyville (Sydney), 52
Danko, Aleks, 106, 108
Day in, Day Out (Second Version) (1991), 106 (illus), 107 (illus)
Davison, Graeme, 44
The Rise and Fall of Marvellous Melbourne, 44
Daw, Kate, 123, 125, 127
House, 1959 (1995), 126 (illus)
Voice, Homes & Gardens, 1959 (1995), 126 (illus), 127
Dawe, Bruce, 124
De Maistre, Roy, 58
Dickerson, Robert, 65, 73, 75
Antipodean Manifesto, 73
Wynyard Station (1959), 72 (illus), 73
Doncaster (Melbourne), 97 (illus), 124
The Doors of Perception (Aldous Huxley), 81
Drysdale, Russell, 14, 70
Duchamp, Marcel, 120
Durabestos, 53 (illus)
Dwyer, Mikala, 103, 121, 124
Star (1994), 121 (illus)

East Melbourne, 56
Emmins, Jim, 81 (illus)
Enmore (Sydney), 49
Esson, Louis, 53
'Everage, Edna', 71 (illus), 84 (illus)

Fisher (Canberra), 90 (illus)
Fitzroy (Melbourne), 20 (plate), 58
Foucault, Michel
The History of Sexuality, 11, 14

Geelong
see Corio
Glebe (Sydney), 49, 57
Glen Iris (Melbourne), 44
Gold Coast
see Broadbeach
Grace, Helen, 98
Time and Motion Study #1 "Women seem to adapt to repetitive-type tasks" (1980), 98
Greenberg, Clement, 79
Greig, Alastair, 67

Haddon, Robert J, 46 (plan)
Hanrahan, Barbara
Weird Adelaide (1988), 91, 108
Hawke, Ronald, 99
Hill's Hoist (1973), 99, 100 (illus), 101
Hawthorn (Melbourne), 18 (plate), 44, 48
Hebdige, Dick, 104
Heidelberg (Melbourne), 43, 46, 47 (illus), 48 (illus), 49 (illus), 52, 127
Heidelberg School, 43, 46, 49, 127
Henson, Bill, 123, 124
Untitled 1985–86 (1985–86), 40 (plate), 124
Herman, Sali, 51, 56
McElhone Stairs (1944), 56–57
Suburbia (1947), 57 (illus)

Hickey, Dale, 77, 79, 81–82, 84, 85, 87
Untitled (c.1968), 80 (illus), 81, 82
Untitled 67–68 (1967–68), 24 (plate), 81
The History of Sexuality (Michel Foucault), 11, 14
Hogg, Geoffrey, 92–93, 101, 125
Turana Mural, 92 (illus), 93 (illus)
Home and Away, 14
Horne, Donald
The Lucky Country, 78, 87
Housing Commission of Victoria, 66 (illus), 91 (illus)
see also Victorian State Housing Scheme
Humphries, Barry
see also 'Everage, Edna'
Wildlife in Suburbia, 70, 71 (illus)
Hurburgh, Tim, 104 (illus)
Huxley, Aldous
The Doors of Perception (1954), 81

Ideas for Australian Cities (Hugh Stretton), 114

Jenning, A V, Limited, 52
Jerrems, Carol, 89, 94–96
Sharpies (1976), 95 (illus)
Johnston, George
My Brother Jack, 70
Jolley, Elizabeth, 114

Kallista (Melbourne), 27 (plate)
Kangaroo (D. H. [David Herbert] Lawrence), 53, 54
Kennedy, Peter, 89, 94, 101, 125
Introductions (1974–76), 26 (plate), 94 (illus)
Kew (Melbourne), 48 (illus), 104 (illus)
Kings Cross (Sydney), 52

Lane, Bill, 123, 124–125
Shades (1994), 125 (illus)
Lawrence, D. H. [David Herbert]
Kangaroo, 53, 54
Learning From Las Vegas (Robert Venturi et al), 104–105
Leason, Percy
Getting on, 1927, 54 (illus)
Le Corbusier, 53
Lester, Kerrie, 99
Red Brick House (1981), 99 (illus)
LeWitt, Vivienne Shark
see Shark LeWitt, Vivienne
Love Stories – Towards a Video Narrative, 1984 (Randelli), 114
The Lucky Country (Donald Horne), 78, 87

McBurnie, Ron, 114
Dogs Bottles (1988), 113 (illus), 114
McCaughey, Patrick, 81
McCubbin, Frederick, 43, 46
The Pioneers (1905), 48
Winter Evening, Hawthorn (1886), 18 (plate),48–49
McGregor, Craig
Profile of Australia, 78–79
Majzner, Victor, 77, 84–85, 87, 108
Creature Comforts (1989), 108, 109 (illus)
Green Vent (1970), 84 (illus)
Martin, Mandy, 99
Picket Fences (1980), 28 (plate), 99
Mau, Nicolas, 115
Death of the Suburban Dream (1993), 35 (plate), 115
Melbourne
see Altona; Brighton, Brunswick West; Burwood; Camberwell; Canterbury; Cheltenham; Doncaster; East Melbourne; Fitzroy; Glen Iris; Hawthorn; Heidelberg; Kallista; Kew; Moonee Ponds; Moreland; Preston; St Kilda; South Yarra
Merchant Builders, 97 (illus)
Mile End (Adelaide), 91
Milton (Brisbane), 114
Moffatt, Tracey, 103
"Scarred for Life" series (1994), 38 (plate), 118, 120
Mombassa, Reg, 101, 120
Insectile Space-monsters Approach Sleeping Family (1995), 39 (plate), 120
Moonee Ponds (Melbourne), 84 (illus)
Moore, David
Surry Hills Street (1948), 56 (illus)
Moore, John D, 51, 53–54
Chaos (1923), 19 (plate), 53, 54
Moreland (Melbourne), 44, 45 (illus)
My Brother Jack (George Johnston), 70

National Gallery of Victoria, 77
Nedelkopoulos, Nicholas, 111
That Great Australian Dream (1987), 110 (illus), 111
Neighbours, 14, 114
Newmarch, Ann, 89, 98, 101
Backyard (1975), 98
The House that Peg Built (1981), 98
Newtown (Sydney), 49
Nickolls, Trevor, 112
Dreamtime to Machinetime (1984), 112
Nolan, Sidney, 14, 68, 70
Number 96, 91

O'Doherty, Chris
see Mombassa, Reg
Oldfield, Alan, 99
Onus, Lin, 103, 112–113
Fruit Bats (1990), 33 (plate), 112

Paddington (Sydney), 49, 82 (illus)
Parks, Ti, 77, 85, 87
St Kilda Street (1967), 85
Pinacotheca Gallery (St Kilda), 81 (illus), 82
Preston, Margaret, 51, 60
Implement Blue (1927), 61 (illus)
Preston (Melbourne), 52
Proctor, Thea, 61
Profile of Australia (Craig McGregor), 78–79

Queanbeyan (Canberra), 28 (plate), 99

Randall, Robert *see* Randelli
Randelli
Love Stories – Towards a Video Narrative (1984), 114
RedPlanet Graphics
see Mau, Nicholas
The Rise and Fall of Marvellous Melbourne (Graeme Davison), 44
Roberts, Tom, 46
Rooney, Robert, 77, 79, 82–84, 87, 125
AM–PM (1974), 84
Cereal Bird Beaks II (1969), 25 (plate), 82, 84
Garments: 3 December 1972–19 March 1973 (1973), 84
Holden Park 1 & 2, May 1970 (1970), 83 (illus), 84
Luna Park: St Kilda 8 January 1975 (1975), 84
War Savings Streets (1970), 84

St Kilda (Melbourne), 52, 55 (illus), 56, 85
Searle, Ken, 103, 108
West #6 (1990), 31 (plate), 109
Shannon, Michael, 75, 96
Abandoned Footy Ground (1971), 96
The Corner Shop (1965), 96
Suburban Landscape, Melbourne (1978), 96 (illus)
Shark LeWitt, Vivienne
MOR (1991), 115
Sibley, Andrew, 115–116
The Madonna of the Rotary Clothes Hoist (1994), 115 (illus), 116
Skyhooks, 91

Smith, Grace Cossington, 61
South Australian Housing Trust, 67 (illus)
Stow Court development, 68 (map)
South Terrace, Adelaide, 67 (illus)
South Yarra (Melbourne), 52
Southland Shopping Centre (Cheltenham, Victoria), 77
Stella, Frank, 82
Stow Court development, 68 (map)
Strachan, David
The Gossips (c.1937), 61–62, 63 (illus)
Streeton, Arthur, 43, 46–48, 127
Near Heidelberg (1890), 46, 47 (illus), 127
Stretton, Hugh
Ideas for Australian Cities, 114
Strizic, Mark
The City from Prospect Hill Road, Canterbury (1967), 79 (illus)
Riversdale Road, Camberwell (c.1960), 73 (illus)
Surry Hills (Sydney), 56 (illus)
Sydney
see Bondi; Daceyville; Enmore; Glebe; Kings Cross; Newtown; Paddington; Surry Hills; Western Suburbs; Woolloomooloo
Syme, Eveline
Sydney Tram Line (1936), 59 (plate), 60

Thebarton (Adelaide), 91
Tibbits, William, 43, 44–46, 49
Why Pay High Rents? Inspect the pretty villas and family mansions of Moreland Park (c.1886), 45 (illus)
Tillers, Imants, 105–106
Tucker, Albert, 51, 56, 68
"Images of Modern Evil", 56, 94
Turana Youth Training Centre, 92 (illus), 93 (illus)

Van Gogh, Vincent, 70–71, 121
Vassilieff, Danila, 51, 56, 57–58
Children Playing, Fitzroy (c.1937), 20 (plate), 58
Venturi, Robert
Learning From Las Vegas, 104–105
Victorian State Housing Scheme, 52
Vike, Harald
Untitled (The Saint) (1947), 22 (plate), 62

Wakelin, Roland, 58
Wardle, Darren, 123
Dust Control (Yallambie) (1995), 127
Warner, Dave, 91
Watson, Jenny, 89, 97–98, 101, 125
House Painting, Kallista (1976), 27 (plate)
Weird Adelaide (Barbara Hanrahan), 91, 108
West Brunswick (Melbourne), 17 (map)
Western suburbs (Sydney), 31 (plate), 109
White, Richard, 108
Whiteley, Brett, 14
"Whole Lotta Rosie" (AC/DC), 121
Wild Life in Suburbia (Barry Humphries), 70, 71 (illus)
Woden Valley (Canberra), 36 (plate), 116, 118
Woolloomooloo (Sydney), 56, 57, 59 (illus), 60
Wunderlich, 53 (illus)

Zikos, Constanze, 111–112, 124
Death Double (1992), 32 (plate), 111
Zofrea, Salvatore, 111

£28-00